Two Reformers

Two Reformers
*Martin Luther and Mary Daly
as Political Theologians*

CARYN D. RISWOLD

Cascade Books
A division of *Wipf & Stock Publishers*
199 West 8th Avenue, Suite 3 • Eugene OR 97401

TWO REFORMERS
Martin Luther and Mary Daly as Political Theologians

Copyright © 2007 Caryn D. Riswold. All rights reserved. Except for brief quotations in critical publications or reviews, no part of this book may be reproduced in any manner without prior written permission from the publisher. Write: Permissions, Wipf and Stock Publishers, 199 W. 8th Ave., Eugene, OR 97401.

ISBN 13: 978-1-59752-826-9

Catalogue-in-Publication Data:

Riswold, Caryn D.
Two reformers : Martin Luther and Mary Daly as political theologians / Caryn D. Riswold.

x + 206 p. ; 23 cm.

Includes bibliographic references.

ISBN 13: 978-1-59752-826-9

1. Luther, Martin, 1483–1546. 2. Daly, Mary, 1928–. 3. Political theology. 4. Christianity and politics. I. Title.

BT764.2 R57 2007

"Virgin" illustration copyright © 1985 by Sudie Rakusin. Used with permission.

Contents

List of Illustrations vi
List of Abbreviations vii
Acknowledgments ix

Introduction: An Unlikely Pair 1

PART ONE
Disaffected Catholic Youth

1 · Martin Luther: Eisleben to Wittenberg and Back Again 11
2 · Mary Daly: Schenectady to Rome, Boston, and Beyond 25
3 · Martin and Mary: Parallels, Differences, and Inversions 39

PART TWO
Substantive Connections

4 · Theological Anthropology: Freedom in Captivity and for Community 57
5 · Institutional Authority: Corruption and Confusion 85
6 · Snools and Snot: Reforming Rhetoric and Wicked Words 113

PART THREE
Interpretation and Analysis

7 · Legacies and Limitations 149
8 · Two Reformers as Political Theologians 179
9 · Conclusion: Was It All Worth It? 197

Bibliography 203

Illustrations

Page 125 "*Ortus et Origo Papae*—Origin and Birth of the Papacy" by Lucas Cranach, 1545

Page 130 "Virgin" by Sudie Rakusin. Copyright © 1985 by Sudie Rakusin. Used with permission.

Abbreviations

BCPT   *The Blackwell Companion to Political Theology.* Edited by William T. Cavanaugh and Peter Scott. Oxford: Blackwell, 2004
B.E.   Biophilic Era
LW   Luther, Martin. *Luther's Works, American Edition.* 55 vols. Edited by Jaroslav Pelikan and Helmut T. Lehmann. Philadelphia: Fortress [Muhlenberg]; St. Louis: Concordia, 1955–1986
WA   *D. Martin Luthers Werke.* Kristische Gesamtausgabe. 58 vols. Weimar: Böhlau, 1883–1928 [Weimarer Ausgabe]

Acknowledgments

The seeds for this book were planted in southern California, sprouted in New Orleans, nurtured in Chicago's Hyde Park, and finally bloomed in central Illinois; so I owe my sincerest gratitude to people and places along the way. My earliest attempts to articulate this analysis of such different figures as Luther and Daly took place in the thesis I wrote for my master's degree at the Claremont School of Theology, and Marjorie Suchocki and Garth Baker-Fletcher were invaluable guides and examiners as I began seriously exploring the connections I first noticed while waiting in line and reading Luther at the In-n-Out Burger in Upland, California.

I first presented a version of this analysis at the gathering of Lutheran Women in Theological Studies prior to the American Academy of Religion meeting in New Orleans in 1996. Through the intervening years, that group has continued to nurture my professional spirit through its collegiality and commitment to enhancing theological scholarship by Lutheran women. Elaine was there from the beginning as we shared hotel rooms, looked for jobs, and navigated the academy together. While a doctoral student at the Lutheran School of Theology at Chicago, I pieced together further analysis of Luther and Daly with Kurt Hendel and Vitor Westhelle as my trustworthy Luther scholars and conversation partners. Other aspects of my analysis were presented over the years at meetings of the Midwest American Academy of Religion and the Illinois College Faculty Symposium.

The final pieces of this puzzle fell into place while I was a professor at Illinois College. The opportunity to participate in the Lutheran Academy of Scholars at Harvard University in the summer of 2005 provided the resources and the environment necessary to put it all together. DeAne, Kit, and Jacquie in particular asked the right questions and pointed me in the best directions that summer and in the following year as this book began to take its final form. My colleagues here at Illinois College have been eager readers and priceless friends throughout the writing and revising process. Kelly, Beth, Lisa, Jenny, Almut, Margaret, and Jan all read drafts of my chapters, continually sharing their collective and diverse wisdom with me. My husband Mark Schelske has been a scholar's best friend with his energetic editing, brilliant suggestions, and patient listening throughout all the years of our life together.

I am finally grateful to K. C. Hanson and the staff at Wipf and Stock Publishers for their commitment to excellence in theological scholarship and for giving this little book its final missing piece: a home. All of the people and places I mention here, along with many others, have contributed something extraordinarily valuable to this book, and whatever flaws and limitations exist herein are entirely mine.

Introduction

An Unlikely Pair

By them we have been carried away out of our own land, as into a Babylonian captivity, and despoiled of all our precious possessions.
—Martin Luther, 1520[1]

Their goal is our deracination, which is "detachment from one's background (as from homeland, customs, traditions)." Thus women and other Elemental creatures on this planet are rendered homeless, cut off from knowledge of our Race's customs and traditions.
—Mary Daly, 1984[2]

What is this land, this world of which these two theologians are speaking? Why do the two statements above sound similar in the author's longing for a true home, for our own land? And who is this "them" who carries us away and cuts us off? Could it be possible that Martin Luther and Mary Daly, different in almost every way, are saying something similar? Why do these key figures in the Christian theological tradition, who come from different times, places, and politics, engage in such a parallel task? How is this possible?

These are some of the first questions that raced through my mind when reading Martin Luther's reformation treatise on the Babylonian captivity of the church while waiting in the drive-through at In-n-Out Burger in Upland, California, in the mid 1990s. A strange location for a theological insight, perhaps, but one where the seeds of this project first sprouted. It might have been that I was reading Luther for one graduate class, while reading Mary Daly for another; it might have been the constantly whirling mind of a graduate student; it might have been mere hunger for a good

---

1. Luther, "The Babylonian Captivity of the Church" (1520), in *LW* 36:47.
2. Daly, *Pure Lust*, 6.

burger and milkshake that opened a space for such questions and observations. Or, it might in fact be that similar substantive and structural things are in fact going on in the work of Luther and the work of Daly. That possibility will form the core argument of this book.

As reformers, Luther and Daly were catalysts for movements that grew far beyond their own work and their own lives. The movements eventually went in ways they did not intend, but their reforming work has left an indelible mark on the tradition from which they emerged. One cannot study the Christian tradition without learning something about Protestantism and Martin Luther's pivotal role in completely altering the landscape of a major world religion. One cannot examine Christianity today without knowing something about feminism and its impact on the study and practice of the religion, and scholars regularly consider the challenge of Mary Daly insisting that "if God is male then the male is God."[3] In isolating and examining these two figures, we learn much about the historical ebb and flow of Christianity as it exists in context, and as it claims to offer good news to people. We also learn how the political dimension of the context affects what the religion can and cannot offer.

Political circumstances defined the lives and work of Martin Luther and Mary Daly from beginning to end. Even before each became a controversial scholar of religion, each lived in a time and place ripe for social transformation. Circumstances both within and beyond their control placed Luther and Daly at the forefront of social, political, and theological movements that altered the tradition of Christianity as well as the societies in which they lived. Because their work grew out of concrete political issues about the allocation of power and authority in human communities, and because it had far reaching political ramifications beyond even that which they actively sought, both Luther and Daly can be seen as political theologians.[4]

Examining Luther and Daly as "political theologians" has not really been done by other scholars, and a comparison of the two has not been done by other scholars at all. Aspects of Luther's political thought and some of the political strategies of Daly's work have been studied, and will be briefly mentioned later. For purposes of this book, the comparison of the two and the label of political theologian work together to explain the

3. Daly, *Beyond God the Father*, 19.

4. I offer initial reflections on Luther and Daly as political theologians in the article, "Two Reformers."

parallels, differences, and inversions in Luther's and Daly's work that will be noted throughout. The ultimate expression of their political theologies, found in their exclusive utopian visions, invites sustained attention at the end of this discussion.

Before moving into the substance of this book, I will outline some of the basic characteristics of political theology as found in the work of widely recognized political theologians. By identifying three major characteristics of political theologians at the outset, the analysis of Luther and Daly that follows will pay attention to the ways that they integrate theology and politics in their lives and work, the way that they pay explicit attention to the political realities of their day, and the degree to which their theologies have political content and consequence.

Characteristics of Political Theology

The term "political theologian" is applied to certain figures familiar to those who study Christian theology: Johann Baptist Metz, Jürgen Moltmann, Dietrich Bonhoeffer, and Dorothee Soelle are widely considered to be political theologians in the modern sense. Looking at why this is provides some justification for eventually including Luther and Daly in this group.

Integration of theology and politics is the first characteristic that distinguishes political theology. Descriptions of major political theologians show this: For Moltmann, "political theology is not a separate topic, but a dimension and a language which permeates everything."[5] For Metz, "theology should address believers at those points at which their identity as persons is most threatened by the social and political catastrophes of history."[6] Bonhoeffer's life and work is widely understood to be the most integrated theological commitment in the modern era: "at once theological and political."[7] Scholars examining these three major figures in Christian theology point to this integration of theology and politics in their lives as a significant characteristic of political theology.

Dorothee Soelle provides extended clarification of what political theology is in her own words:

---

5. Adams, "Jürgen Moltmann," 227.
6. Ashley, "Johann Baptist Metz," 247.
7. Hauerwas, "Dietrich Bonhoeffer," 139.

> Further, political theology is not an attempt to develop a concrete political program from faith. . . . Political theology is rather a theological hermeneutic, which . . . holds open an horizon of interpretation in which politics is understood as the comprehensive and decisive sphere in which Christian truth should become praxis.[8]

Political theology is not a segregated area or topic in theology, separate from others. It is a method of doing theology that affects everything the theologian says. For Soelle, politics is the place where theology is enacted. Like Metz, Moltmann, and Bonhoeffer, Soelle understands theology and politics as thoroughly integrated, where one is the location for enacting the other. We will see how this characteristic appears in the lives and work of Luther and Daly in the chapters to follow.

Another difference that marks a political theology is the second characteristic to identify here: the extent to which it takes explicit account of the relationship between God (*theo*, the Greek word for God) and the human organization of life (*politia*, the Latin word for politics; *polis* – Greek for city or state). Wrestling with the need to distinguish the phrase and the idea of political theology from theology more generally speaking, John Shelley states in his introduction to Dorothee Soelle's text *Political Theology* that "there is no pure ecclesiastical neutrality, just as there is no apolitical theology; there are only those who are conscious of their political assumptions and consequences and those who are not."[9] Theology may inherently be political, he suggests here, but the consciousness or the explicitness of the attention to the *polis* is the second key characteristic distinguishing theology and *political* theology.

Theologians who directly respond to and directly affect the variety of human institutions set up to regulate the life of the community are political theologians. These human institutions may include such things as secular government, religious hierarchies, educational systems, families, and cultural ideologies.

While I do not pretend to offer here a comprehensive review and analysis of the history of political theology, a few things can be noted about the history of the label to clarify this second characteristic and how it is being used. For the ancient Stoics, "political theology was the expres-

---

8. Soelle, *Political Theology*, 58–59.
9. Ibid., xiv.

sion of those religious practices which served the needs of the state."[10] In early Christianity, St. Augustine argued against this view using his binary cosmology, suggesting that the city of God was a realm distinct from the city of this world, and that theology and religion were activities that were primarily for the service and worship of God. Augustine's vision of the relationship between religion and the state, and the heavenly and earthly cities, was much more nuanced than that of the Stoics. He described in the first chapter of book eleven of *The City of God*, "the two cities that in this world lie confusedly together, by the assistance of the same God,"[11] suggesting the complexity of discussing them. He did not see that religion served the state or the state served religion, rather, as Jean Bethke Elshtain notes, "Augustine creates barriers to the absolutizing and sacralizing of any political arrangement."[12] His reasons for doing this include the concern to distinguish the unique claim that the city of God makes upon Christians and the world. That claim includes God's work of salvation which cannot be granted by the state. Augustine was therefore a theologian who paid explicit attention to the *polis* in order to clarify its proper role and claims upon the human soul. That both Luther and Daly inherit aspects of this Augustinian tradition in their own ways, via the monastery and via St. Thomas Aquinas respectively, is a point worth noting here.

The phrase political theology was largely ignored until the early twentieth century. It returned when Carl Schmitt used the phrase in 1922 to argue the Stoic position anew, that political theology was theology for the purpose of justifying and supporting political systems. Subsequent discussions in Germany about the interplay between theology and politics were fraught with difficulty as responses to Schmitt emerged during and after Hitler's rise to power and decimation of the European population. Schmitt and the ancient Stoics shared an assumption that political theology was theology that existed to support the political system. This view was challenged almost completely when Johann Baptist Metz reintroduced the label in 1965, and ushered in a new era of political theology, wherein the phrase indicates clearly this second characteristic: Explicit attention to the *polis* inevitably leads to theological criticism and challenge to political realities. Luther and Daly are both theologians who in their work pay

10. Cobb, Jr., *Process Theology as Political Theology*, 1. I rely here on the brief history of political theology as described by Cobb.

11. Augustine, *The City of God*, 312.

12. Elshtain, "Augustine," 42.

sustained attention to the allocation of power and resources in human institutions.

Each of the figures identified thus far is primarily a theologian, but all of their work has had political consequence and content at every step. This is the third characteristic of political theology. Bonhoeffer's participation in a plot to assassinate Hitler was a decidedly political act that brought the end of his life in a Nazi prison, and his theological work was a key motivator for his actions. Metz had a "relentless focus on theodicy, on the memory of suffering" that began and ended with the "dangerous memory" of Auschwitz.[13] Christian theology, for him, had to place this tragic experience at the center rather than at the periphery of all consideration in order for the idea of hope to have any authenticity. Moltmann in the early 1970s wrote on deeply complex political topics: "poverty, institutionalized violence, racism, the environment, and people's increasing sense of their life's meaninglessness."[14] He constructed a theology that helped people make sense of life in these concrete moments of human existence, articulating the significance of the crucifixion and resurrection. Soelle was intensely involved in peace activism throughout her life. Among other things, she was instrumental in organizing the Political Evensong at the University of Cologne in Germany in 1968 when many people found the linkage of Christianity and politics to be scandalous.[15] Of the work and worship in this group, she noted later, "Every statement has to be at the same time a political one."[16] The political content of each of these theologies has had significant and direct consequences, as has the work of Martin Luther and Mary Daly.

Two Reformers

The three characteristics thus identified from this brief history and review of political theology will be applied to Martin Luther and Mary Daly after a detailed analysis of elements of their lives and work. The book will begin with comparisons of the biographic details of the lives of Luther and Daly that further my proposal of a connection between their approaches and their work. The differences between them are obvious, but the paral-

---

13. Ashley, "Johann Baptist Metz," 253.
14. Adams, "Jurgen Moltmann," 233.
15. Soelle, *Against the Wind*, 37–41.
16. Ibid., 38.

lels even in their personal stories are striking and lead to some interesting inverse situations. Each comes from a modest working family, each is educated and employed at Catholic institutions, and each is immersed in religious and academic controversies that affect their professional and personal lives for the duration.

The theological content of their work which produced these controversies will be examined around two main focal points in the middle section of the book: anthropology and authority. I focus first on what each theologian says about what it means to be human in relationship to God. Both focus on freedom, and both understand that the human being is presently being held captive and longing for community. But the barrier between the self and the true home remains, so I then focus on their criticisms of institutional authority. Luther's critique of the papacy and Daly's critique of patriarchy zone in on the deception, threats, and falsely constructed worlds perpetrated by each.

Their critiques rely heavily on creative and cantankerous language that I also consider at length in the middle section of the book. Walter Altmann describes Luther as "an irascible human being,"[17] and Daly becomes the epitome of what Altmann calls "lexical creativity" by the time she writes her *Wickedary* in 1987. A shared rhetorical style again indicates that the two reformers are engaged in a similarly impassioned struggle against tyranny and for freedom.

In the final section of the book, I will consider legacies and limitations of the work of these two reformers before returning to my proposal that Luther and Daly be named among the company of political theologians. Why did Luther fail, according to some, to produce an effective social ethic, and what is the legacy of this seen throughout history? Why did Daly leave the church and theology altogether, and what is the legacy of that for feminism and Christianity today? Is Luther truly anti-Semitic, and is Daly truly anti-male? Examining all of these issues and the people who authored them supports the proposal that they are both engaged in the work of political theology. Considering their exclusive utopian visions for a new world supports the proposal that such visions are themselves a final characteristic of political theologians.

---

17. Altmann, *Luther and Liberation*, 2.

PART ONE

Disaffected Catholic Youth

Even though Martin Luther and Mary Daly were both disaffected Catholic youth, the differences are obvious:

1. Martin Luther was no feminist.
2. Mary Daly no longer considers herself a theologian.
3. Daly would dismiss any connection between her work and that of Martin Luther.
4. Luther would not consider Daly a Christian.
5. Germany in the sixteenth century differs wildly from the United States in the twentieth century.

There are some powerful commonalities, however, between the two reformers that begin with their personal lives. Martin Luther and Mary Daly are both theologians raised, educated, and employed in the Roman Catholic tradition. Each came to a crisis point in his or her respective theological and academic work that disallowed him or her to ever view "the church" in a favorable light again.

And in one pivotal moment in each life, these two reformers found themselves in Rome, utterly dismayed at what they saw there:

> He [Martin Luther] mentioned the city of Rome and observed: "Since our Lord God has put me into this disagreeable and horrible business [of writing against the pope], I wouldn't take a hundred thousand gulden in exchange for what I saw and heard in Rome, for otherwise I'd always be afraid that I was doing him an injustice. I speak of what I've seen. . . . 'If you wish to live a holy life, depart from Rome; everything is permitted there except to be a virtuous man.'"[1]

> The women sat docilely, listening to the senile, cracking whines of the men in red droning on in Latin, which the readers as well as the listeners barely comprehended. . . . That moment of revelation in Rome continues to work subliminally, inspiring my humor and stoking the Fires of my Fury not merely against the catholic church and all the other religions and institutions that are the tentacles of patriarchy but against everything that dulls and diminishes women.[2]

In order to appreciate these two moments, we must look at the lives that came before and the work that came after. This shows how a priest's and a scholar's visit to Rome became a pivot point in the life and career of each reformer. In the three chapters that follow, I turn briefly to some biographical details of the personal and professional lives of Martin Luther and Mary Daly. Chapter 1 is a biographical sketch of the life and work of Luther, and chapter 2 focuses on Daly. Chapter 3 proposes some broad themes that identify parallels, differences, and inversions noticed when comparing the lives and work of the two reformers. By examining these very different lives with the same outline, a broad path is traced for subsequent detailed theological and political analysis.

---

1. Luther, "Rome Had a Reputation for Wickedness," Table Talk No. 3478, in *LW* 54:208.
2. Daly, "Sin Big," 80.

I

Martin Luther
Eisleben to Wittenberg and Back Again

> *I think that from the days of my childhood Satan must have foreseen something in me which is the cause of his present suffering. He has therefore raged against me with incredible plans to destroy or hinder me....*[1]

German Catholic Youth

Martin Luther was born in Eisleben, Germany, on November 10, 1483. Luther's family was among the peasant class and his parents were strict disciplinarians, like many parents of the time.[2] Luther's father worked in copper mines and his family is described by many biographers as rugged and devout. Devotion to the saints characterized their life with regular prayer at home and school. Bernhard Lohse describes the era of Luther's youth as the most pious period in the history of Germany, as well as one in the midst of political transition. Both of these things affect Luther's sense of the world. The young man Luther certainly had little sense of the political situation in which he was to become enmeshed.

As a young student, Luther was by most accounts proficient and diligent. He attended cathedral schools in Magdeburg and Eisenach, where he learned Latin as the language of the Church and the law, and sought to please his teachers whenever possible. As a boy, he loved music, was a proficient lute player, and admired the German countryside that surrounded him. For the young Luther, home and school reinforced each other in a

---

1. Luther, "Letter to Hans Luther" (1521), in *LW* 48:332.
2. Biographical details summarized here come from Bainton, *Here I Stand*, and Lohse, *Martin Luther*.

religiously ordered and structured world, providing him with a childhood quite common for a peasant boy of his time.

The political context of Luther's early life was that of a country and continent in transition. Three German emperors reigned during his lifetime, and humanism was a growing intellectual movement throughout Europe. These and other factors affected the culture and the politics around him dramatically. Lohse thoroughly describes this situation and details the expanding power of the princes, shifting economic reality and sporadic challenges to the church. These were significant factors in the world that shaped Luther.[3] German humanism was emerging at the time, and had a profound effect on Luther's life and work. Lewis Spitz suggests that Luther believed "humanism made the Reformation possible" because of elements like "knowledge of the languages, the critical handling of the sources, [and] the attack on abuses."[4] Intellectual culture grew during Luther's time, as universities took hold and really shaped life in Germany while the previous scholastic era was coming to an end. Spitz further notes that Luther preferred humanism over scholasticism, and Lohse recognizes that at this time, the humanist return to ancient languages and sources suggested "a devaluation of the Middle Ages."[5] As a figure on the cusp of this intellectual shift, Luther was positioned both for conflict and for participation in significant cultural and intellectual transformation.

These are some of the reasons that the Reformation era in which Luther was to play a major role is the subject of much scrutiny as an era, as to whether it is the end of the medieval or the beginning of the modern. It occupies a space between the two that, depending on one's interests, can be seen to reflect both. In any case, "Luther occupies the most permanent place in this manifold process of transition between the Middle Ages and the modern age."[6] Whether he is seen as a conservative defender of the faith, a progressive activist for change, or an annoying agitator of Rome, all images which will emerge in this book, it is clear that a web of shifting cultural and political influences defined Luther's life and work.

---

3. Lohse, *Martin Luther*, 1–18.
4. Spitz, *Luther and German Humanism*, 20.
5. Lohse, *Martin Luther*, 15.
6. Ibid., 18.

Catholic Education, Shifting Vocation

When Luther went to study at the university in Erfurt in 1501, his Catholic education and training continued. At the age of eighteen he intended to become a lawyer, in part to satisfy his father's wishes, and he pursued a course of study accordingly. Luther's sustained immersion in this rigorous Catholic education irrevocably shaped him. Eric Gritsch describes his early study at the Latin Grammar School in Mansfield that prepared him for the University, since by the time he was twelve, "he could read and speak Latin, appreciate the rhetoric of Roman prose and poetry, and he knew elementary musical theory, especially hymnody and liturgy."[7] At Erfurt, Luther earned his baccalaureate degree and a master's degree. Gritsch suggests that this education taught Luther "severe academic discipline" and "strict rules of moral behavior."[8]

One factor in Luther's life that emerges in his youth and has been the subject of much study is his mood. Roland Bainton describes Luther's early years as marked by an oscillation of moods—from being exuberant to being depressed.[9] Luther himself writes frequently about his depressions, and this becomes the subject of much later scholarly speculation when psychohistory emerges as a new field of study in the twentieth century. Many Luther biographers take note of the reformer's mood swings along with his physical illnesses and weigh their influence on his work in varying ways. Gritsch, for example, chronicles Luther's documented ailments alongside his written work, noting for example that in 1521 he was "sick with constipation for seven months" while he produced "70 sermons, 100 letters, 30 tracts," worked on his translation of the New Testament, took his fateful trip to Worms, and was in exile at the Wartburg.[10] In 1958, psychoanalyst Erik Erikson examined evidence in the texts and suggested that Luther suffered throughout his life from what are now identified as manic-depressive episodes. He linked the later obscenity of Luther's writing to this illness, "which has to maintain a state of unrelenting paranoid repudiation of an appointed enemy."[11] Since then, Luther scholars and others have critiqued this "diagnosis" based on methodology and theo-

---

7. Gritsch, *Martin—God's Court Jester*, 3.
8. Ibid., 5.
9. Bainton, *Here I Stand*, 20.
10. Gritsch, *Martin—God's Court Jester*, 155. See extensive list on 155–58.
11. Erikson, *Young Man Luther*, 246.

logical understanding.[12] Nevertheless, it remains an interesting suggestion borne out in part by Luther's own words.

One question for readers is not whether Luther had a variety of neuroses and illnesses, since that is fairly evident from reading his texts, but rather what was the cause or the effect of those things. Was he vexed by religious anxiety already as a youth? Was he, as Erikson also suggests, terrified of his father so much so that it translated into terror of God and fixation on the pope? Was he abused as a child? Was his father a violent alcoholic? Even discussions of Luther's youth make mention of his noticeable mood swings, because they seem to be the only indicator of his later temperament and prolific work.

Despite the often dramatic mood swings, Luther had a relatively ordinary life and successful education. His career track toward becoming a lawyer was interrupted with the now-famous thunderstorm incident described here by Lohse:

> This plan for his career changed radically on July 2, 1505, when Luther was caught in a fierce thunderstorm near Stotternheim, close to Erfurt. In his fear he called on St. Anna, the patron saint of the miners, and swore, "I will become a monk." . . . On July 17, 1505, Luther entered the Black Cloister of the Augustinian Hermits in Erfurt.[13]

Gritsch points out that we cannot know with complete accuracy what events preceded Luther's entrance into the monastery. There may have been other specific events that led up to this momentous decision. He mentions Luther's account of an incident when he cut his leg while traveling back to Erfurt, probably in 1503, and felt he was on the verge of death. A colleague recorded Luther's account of this injury in a Table Talk:

> When he set out for home and was on the way, he accidentally struck his shin on his short sword and cut an artery in his leg. At the time he was alone in the open field except for one companion, and he was as far from Erfurt. . . . That is, a half mile. The blood gushed from the wound and could not be stopped. . . . Then he was in danger of death and cried out, "Mary, help!" "I would have died," he now added, "with my trust in Mary." . . . He almost bled to death and again prayed to Mary.[14]

12. See the collection of essays in Johnson, *Psychohistory and Religion*.
13. Lohse, *Martin Luther*, 23.
14. Luther, Table Talk No. 119, in *LW* 54:14.

The experience clearly affected him deeply, given this retelling in 1531, and it is similar to the thunderstorm story in the way that grave physical danger forces him to call out in fear to God and the saints for help. Regardless of the precise circumstance, it is clear from Luther's writings that some traumatic event preceded his entering the Black Cloister, and that deciding to become a monk changed everything.

Luther's immersion into the Augustinian traditions and teachings heavily influenced his education and habits early in life, and even though he later renounced his vows to the order, his formation in this tradition indelibly marked him. In another Table Talk recorded in 1539, for example, Luther discussed his high regard for Augustine, even though he suggests that the other church fathers are not to be valued much when reading scripture: "Except only for Augustine, there was great blindness among the fathers."[15] He even goes on here to rank Augustine as second to the Bible in authority: "After the Holy Scriptures, Augustine should especially be read, for he had keen judgment."[16] He refuses, however, to use any of the other early church fathers as resource for biblical interpretation. Throughout all of Luther's written work, Augustine is referred to numerous times in the context of interpreting biblical texts. In his lectures on the Psalms, for example, he refers to Augustine dozens of times, and says that "he was truly a blessed man, who did not walk in the counsel of the ungodly."[17] He also mentions in a letter to a colleague that "our theology and St. Augustine" are "progressing well."[18] Despite shifts away from official association with the Augustinian order, Luther continues to hold the work of St. Augustine in high regard, even as an aid for interpreting scripture.

It is further clear from Luther's writings that his father Hans was not happy with his son's change in direction. This disapproval upset the young Luther who seemed to seek his father's approval. Of his entry into the monastery, Luther later wrote to his father that he had not become a monk because he wanted to, but rather because he was compelled to by the "terrors from heaven."[19] Fear is fairly obviously a major motivating factor early in Luther's understanding of his vocation. As a monk in the

---

15. Luther, Table Talk No. 4567, in *LW* 54:352.
16. Ibid.
17. Luther, "First Psalm Lectures," (1513), in *LW* 10:27.
18. Luther, "To John Lang" (1517), in *LW* 48:41.
19. Luther, "Letter to Hans Luther" (1521), in *LW* 48:331.

Augustinian order at Erfurt, Luther had intensified the strictly disciplined life begun in his childhood. Bainton describes the life as one of prayers, song, "meditation, and quiet companionship, in disciplined and moderate austerity."[20] This was the lifestyle through which he attempted to calm those terrors and soothe his anxious soul.

The 2003 feature film *Luther* dramatically and effectively depicts some of these moments of Luther's internal life while in the monastery, including depressive struggles against this terror of God while he thrashes around his dark room in the middle of the night. He argues with an invisible Satan, prays feverishly to God, and lies prone on the floor spreading his arms in cruciform surrender. In the scene depicting his first celebration of mass, Joseph Fiennes plays Martin Luther who, with trembling hands, elevates the cup of wine transfigured into the blood of Christ, spilling several bright red drops of it on the crisp white altar linens. In a subsequent scene, following this public shame in front of his Augustinian brothers, Luther is chastised by his father Hans who rides off in disgust and in a cloud of dust. One of the strengths of this moderately successful major studio film is that such moments are based on Luther's own descriptions of his life and his struggles. Of that first mass, Luther said "I was so frightened that I would have fled (from the altar) if I hadn't been admonished by the prior."[21] In addition, Luther described his monastic life as pressured and sometimes tormented because of his piety and devotion. After missing required prayers because of his work lecturing and writing, he says

> then I would take a Saturday off, or shut myself in for as long as three days without food and drink, until I had said the prescribed prayers. This made my head split, and as a consequence I couldn't close my eyes for five nights, lay sick unto death, and went out of my senses. Even after I had quickly recovered and I tried again to read, my head went 'round and 'round. Thus our Lord God drew me, as if by force, from that torment of prayers.[22]

He uses this sort of experience to begin later mounting criticism of mandated prayers that brought him such anxiety. His description, though, of a splitting head, and going out of his senses speaks to some of the physical and mental pain that appears to have affected his health. The terrors that

---

20. Bainton, *Here I Stand*, 29.
21. Luther, Table Talk No. 3556A, with insert from No. 3556B, in *LW* 54:234.
22. Luther, Table Talk No. 495, in *LW* 54:85.

compelled Luther into the monastery seemed to stay with him for some time.

In addition, Luther wrote occasionally about the tension between him and his father. A letter to his father in 1521 is one fragment that reveals some of this tension. In it, he discusses "taking the vow without your knowledge and against your will"[23] and notes his father's wishes to see his son married out of fear for his future. Luther explains that it was not his own wish to become a monk, rather he was compelled to follow the will of God. Luther refers to a conversation that he and his father had after they had begun speaking again after some time of estrangement. This tells us much of the conflict between them. In that conversation, according to Luther, his father said about the necessity of his son's vow, "Let us hope that it was not an illusion and a deception." Luther responds that these words "penetrated to the depths of my soul and stayed there."[24] Nevertheless, the tension and conflict between them did not erase the son's desire for his father's approval and support.

This relationship is one with which scholars have specifically wrestled. Psychoanalyst Erikson goes so far as to suggest that Hans' likely harsh discipline of Martin as a child led to fixations on the pope as the devil, and that it led to Luther's extensive use of anal imagery in later polemics as well as his constipation struggles later in life. This is because "a transference had taken place from a parent figure to universal personages, and that a central theme in this transference was anal defiance."[25] Bainton recognizes that Erikson's study of Luther may have some insights, but that it ends in much conjecture that may or may not be fully based in fact.[26] Regardless of the psychological diagnosis of its effect, it is safe to say from Luther's own reflections that Hans and Martin had a close and tempestuous relationship. As Luther's education progressed, his vocation shifted from being a lawyer to a monk and a priest. This shift finally positioned him to make a dramatic impact on the life of the church and the culture of Germany.

---

23. Luther, "Letter to Hans Luther" (1521), in *LW* 48:331.
24. Ibid., 332.
25. Erikson, *Young Man Luther*, 247.
26. Bainton, "Psychiatry and History," 19–56.

Priest in Rome

In 1510, Luther was asked to represent the order of Erfurt on a journey to Rome. While there, Luther traveled the well-worn route of devoted pilgrims, visiting relics and shrines and seeking the forgiveness and grace of God. At the time he was desperately trying to be as faithful as he possibly could, and some years later describes his frantic activities this way:

> When I made my pilgrimage to Rome, I was such a fanatical saint that I dashed through all the churches and crypts, believing all the stinking forgeries of those places. I ran through about a dozen Masses in Rome and was almost prostrated by the thought that my mother and father were still alive, because I should gladly have redeemed them from purgatory with my Masses and other excellent works and prayers. . . . We did not know any better, and the Holy See did not punish such gross lies.[27]

Most biographers of Luther agree that even though at the time of the trip he did not write extensively on it, or immediately understand its implications, what he saw and experienced there informed much of his later polemics against corruption in Rome. He became disillusioned at the gritty reality of the holy city, which was more city than holy, and filled with more vice than seemed appropriate. He certainly heard the stories of clergy engaged in immoral acts, and seems to have been shocked by the cavalier attitude of those celebrating mass and hearing confession.

Luther described the hypocrisy of those who were supposed to be church leaders, and the problem that came from their control of the political leaders:

> In Rome I myself saw some cardinals who were esteemed highly as saints because they were content to associate with women. Hence unspeakable infamies are committed there, not in secret or in privacy but openly, because of the example and the influence of the leading men and of the entire city.[28]

The "unspeakable infamies" were out in the open in Rome, horrifying the young faithful Luther. While he was there, he participated in the ritual of climbing the *Scala Sancta*, the holy stairs supposed to have been climbed by Christ on his way to face Pilate. As was the ritual for devoted pilgrims,

---

27. Luther, "Preface to Psalm 117," in *LW* 14:6.
28. Luther, "Preface to Genesis 19," in *LW* 3:6.

Luther paid his indulgence, recited the *Pater Noster* (prayer to Our Father), and kissed each of the 28 steps on his way up in order to release his grandfather's soul from purgatory. Again, the 2003 feature film dramatizes this key moment with the young Luther atop the stairs, bewildered and watching the poor wretched folk around him crawling up the stairs en masse seeking mercy from a God not seen. What Luther said when he reached the top is believed to be: "Who knows whether it is so?"[29] Whether or not he indeed uttered these words, scholars do agree that his doubt was increasing at this time: He was less certain of the integrity of the church than he had ever been before and his trust in the Roman authorities was faltering. This trip to Rome arguably is the pivotal experience that irrevocably shifted Luther's view of the church and took a lifetime to understand.

An Early Public Controversy in the Church

Over the next several years, Luther was transferred from Erfurt to Wittenberg where he undertook an extensive in-depth study of the scriptures. In the decade between 1509 and 1519 he made his "discovery" of the righteousness of God,[30] as the theological breakthrough answer to his vexing question perhaps first uttered in Rome: How can one know whether one has done enough to merit salvation? Have I climbed enough steps? Have I said enough prayers? Have I paid enough indulgences? In his detailed examination of Luther's breakthrough, Alister McGrath describes the dilemma this way: "if man cannot know whether he has fulfilled the condition laid down for his justification, he cannot know whether God will justify or condemn him."[31] We can see how this is easily the root theological reason for many of Luther's terrors and anxieties: He was afraid of God; he was afraid that he was not good enough.

Out of these questions and struggles, he produced his lectures on the Psalms and Romans, ultimately focusing on Paul's writings on justification. This is where he was struck with Paul's declaration of how a Christian is made right in the eyes of God: "since all have sinned and fall short of the glory of God; they are now justified by his grace as a gift, through the redemption that is in Christ Jesus." (Romans 3:23–24). Luther found this

---

29. Bainton, *Here I Stand*, 38.

30. An extended analysis of this period is found in McGrath, *Luther's Theology of the Cross*.

31. Ibid., 110.

insight not only in scripture but also "confirmed in the writings of the great church father Augustine."[32] Eventually, Luther's theological breakthroughs led to an early moment of public conflict that further defined the course of his work. Intense focus on scripture actually brought clarity to his feelings about the hypocrisy and corruption in the church. His theology quickly became political. On October 31, 1517, Luther posted his "Ninety-Five Theses" for debate and discussion. Though the exact date and nature of "posting" is now the subject of some debate and disagreement, and the actual posting did not bring the sustained academic discussion that Luther sought, subsequent translation and wide dissemination of Luther's statements on indulgences, papal power, purgatory, and other matters crystallized his conflict with Rome.

The Roman church saw his work as a growing threat to its teachings and practices, and Luther was summoned on charges of heresy that led to much negotiation and eventually to his trial at the Diet of Worms where he was excommunicated in 1521. The many tracts, sermons, and writings that Luther composed in the intervening years were brought out at the trial as evidence of his heresy. He was asked a series of questions about his work, asked if he was the author, and asked if he would publicly recant what he had written. His carefully structured speech defending each of the categories of his writings ended with words that have since become famous:

> Unless I am convinced by the testimony of the Scriptures or by clear reason (for I do not trust either in the pope or in councils alone, since it is well known that they have often erred and contradicted themselves), I am bound by the Scriptures I have quoted and my conscience is captive to the Word of God. I cannot and I will not retract anything, since it is neither safe nor right to go against conscience. I cannot do otherwise, here I stand, may God help me, Amen.[33]

The final sentence appears in varying forms in translations, as the Weimar edition of Luther's work has it in German at the end of a Latin text, indicating that it was perhaps a later addition. The American edition translation of this passage notes that Luther may have only said at the end "may God help me!" Discrepancies in accounts of this speech are relatively

---

32. Gritsch, *Martin—God's Court Jester*, 8.
33. Luther, "Luther at the Diet of Worms" (1521), in *LW* 32:112–13.

minor, however, and the main point of these closing remarks is that Luther saw himself as bound to the Word of God and to the words of scripture. The words of popes and councils are declared meaningless in this way, thus sealing Luther's fate as a heretic in the eyes of the Roman church, an excommunicated priest and former monk.

Career Publications and the Reformation

Despite loss of status in the Roman church, Martin Luther went on to produce an extensive collection of essays, letters, and treatises expanding on his basic theological realization that the Christian is justified by grace through faith in Christ, reclaiming the Pauline insight that he believed was lost to the corrupt greedy church of his day. Luther's own categorization of his work at the Diet of Worms is an interesting place to start appreciating the scope of his writing. In 1521, he described the body of his work at the time in three categories: First, "there are some in which I have discussed religious faith and morals simply and evangelically." Second, "another group of my books attacks the papacy and the affairs of the papists." Finally, he spoke of "a third sort of book against some private and (as they say) distinguished individuals—those, namely, who strive to preserve the Roman tyranny."[34] Though he would go on to write for twenty-four more years, this division of his work holds up to this day as fairly accurate and descriptive of the types of things he wrote. The first type of work reflects Luther who was a devoted student of scripture primarily concerned with understanding and spreading the gospel. The second type emerges as the consequence of the first. His deep theological reflection and exegesis of scripture led him into direct conflict with the institution of the papacy. The third type of writing follows as a product of that institutional conflict, when he writes against particular individuals in public disputes. Examples from each of these categories will be discussed throughout this book.

Categorizing Luther's monumental body of work over the entire course of his life has been done in a variety of other ways. The collection *Martin Luther's Basic Theological Writings*, edited by Timothy Lull, is a widely used primer on Luther's work. It divides thirty-seven representative writings by topic, beginning with Luther's writing about himself as a person. The reader then moves into a selection of writings on the task of theology itself. This is followed by a section of writing on the word of

34. Ibid., 109–11.

God, and one on the righteousness of God in Christ. Practical matters are the focus of the next two sections, on the sacraments and on the church. The topic of the final section of this collection is Luther's writing on living and dying as a Christian.[35] Lull's categorization gives a good sense of the scope of topics, format, and content over 28 years of Luther's work: It is personal, theological, political, and practical.

The authoritative English language collection of Luther's Works, the American Edition, in print a collected fifty-five volumes and also available on CD-ROM, categorizes his writings in a more precise way. Exegesis and commentary on biblical texts describes nearly half of the volumes in this collection. Then, the titled categories of the volumes include "career of the reformer," "word and sacrament," "church and ministry," "devotional writings," "the Christian in society," "letters," "sermons," and "liturgy and hymns." The final volume prior to the index volume contains "table talks" recorded by several of Luther's colleagues throughout his later years. Again, this categorization shows the wide range of writings that the theologian engaged in over the course of his life. It also provides a narrative consistent with his own three-fold typology of writings given at the Diet of Worms. This shows the man Luther who began with intense immersion in the scriptures that led him to reforming theological insights. These theological insights focused on word and sacrament, which are the foundation of the church and its ministry. As the pastoral leader of a growing community he wrote devotional pieces, catechisms, sermons, and worship resources like liturgy and hymns. As a political figure, he was in regular communication with followers and supporters.

Adhering to Luther's own categorization of his works makes the most sense, even though he made it before the full body of his work was completed. The further details added by later scholars describing his work are helpful, but do not add anything new to what Luther already understood about his own work as both theological and political. He was by 1521 already a widely respected though highly controversial theologian whose insight about the gospel was at the same time radically simple in its return to the texts of Paul, and radically dangerous in its inevitable criticism of the institutional church. The first and second categories of Luther's works of which he speaks at Worms are indisputably connected—the theological insight and the political criticism of the institution are bound up together.

---

35. See Lull and Russell, *Martin Luther's Basic Theological Writings*.

The third type of writings, those against persons, are a consequence of the culture of dispute and polemic in which Luther wrote. Those too are a consequence of his theological insight and political conflict with the papacy.

Segregating Luther's works by topic is difficult because scripture, theology, history, and politics are interwoven in almost all of his writings. The examples of ways scholars can organize his work given here provide a sense of what was important in his life. It also shows how he attempted to put his thought into practice over several decades of writing, and how everything he advocated was influenced by his emphasis on the Word of God as the way for individual Christians to come to know the grace of God.

Because of his career publications, Luther was a catalyst for the Reformation that had perhaps been attempted in smaller more isolated ways in earlier centuries. Lohse discusses the movement of John Huss and the Hussites in the fourteenth and fifteenth centuries as earlier indication of dissatisfaction of Christians with the Roman Church. Luther's work and life catapulted such critique to the status of a major social, political, and theological movement that forever altered the Christian tradition and the societies in which it took root. Further, the Reformation for which Luther was a leader quickly moved beyond him and his personal concerns: "if we are to understand the Reformation movement, we must recognize that it was from its very beginning a pluralistic movement."[36] Lohse notes a variety of issues that divided reformers including the extent to which the Old Testament law was binding on Christians, and the role of the Spirit in interpreting it. Debate about the extent of necessary church reform also grew during and after the life of Luther.

Major opponents and critics of Luther's thought on various issues also emerged during and after his life. Several of them will be discussed at length in later analysis, though a few merit mention here. With Thomas Muntzer, who was influenced by a German mysticism and who participated in the Peasant's War, Luther disagreed vehemently on issues of order and the distinction between law and gospel. With Erasmus, another intellectual foe, Luther disagreed vehemently about the status of the human will as free or bound. Luther's emphasis on the sacraments brought a debate with Swiss reformer Ulrich Zwingli. No less than the reality of the presence of Christ himself was at stake in this exchange, and other theologians were inevi-

---

36. Lohse, *Martin Luther*, 50.

tably drawn into this public controversy. As advocates for various issues and positions emerged throughout the decades of Luther's life, he found himself writing to and about many of them at great length to defend his own position and criticize those that he did not support.

As Luther's life continued, his writings became more intensely polemical and his conflict with the church more divisive. His physical and mental health continued to be a factor; Gritsch notes that in 1545, the final full year of his life, Luther was "sick for ten months with stones, exhaustion and old age" but still produced "35 sermons, lectures, 80 letters, [and] 15 tracts."[37] This year saw some of the most violent of Luther's writing against the papacy, as we will see at length in later chapters. He died after a heart attack while on a trip to his birth place of Eisleben on February 18, 1546.

Lohse suggests that Luther's reform of the church in Germany had far reaching impact, influencing the basic structure of Protestantism there until 1918. The multifaceted movement that came to be known as the Reformation had a lasting impact on the Christian tradition, leaving the indelible imprint of the peasant son of a miner on the practice of the religion for all who were to follow. Richard Marius has a far less charitable reading of the impact of Luther's life and work, saying that "whatever good Luther did is not matched by the calamities that came because of him."[38] These calamities include the centuries of conflict and violence that followed the Reformation. Marius is critical of much in the reformer's life and work, including and especially Luther's claims to certainty and his unacknowledged skepticism.

Scholarly analysis of and insight into Luther's life abounds, and only a brief introduction to it is provided here. I have deliberately highlighted the things that have particular bearing on this study of his life and work in conversation with another disaffected Catholic who will come several generations later. Specifically, the social and political context of Luther's life as a transitional time between major eras of world history cannot be ignored. His connection to his family and his Catholic education come to mean a great deal throughout the course of his life. In addition, the interplay between his theology and his politics becomes a key factor heretofore under appreciated. These things taken together provide fresh insight into the complex life of one reformer.

37. Gritsch, *Martin—God's Court Jester*, 157.
38. Marius, *Martin Luther*, xii.

2

Mary Daly
Schenectady to Rome, Boston, and Beyond

As a student in a small, working-class catholic high school in Schenectady, New York, I was a voice crying in the wilderness when I declared that I wanted to study philosophy.[1]

Irish American Catholic Youth

Mary Daly was born in Schenectady, New York, in 1928, and grew up in a working-class Irish Catholic community that she speaks of both fondly and honestly. She recounts her childhood with remarks like "Let me assure the reader that I have always, that is spasmodically, made abortive efforts to conform."[2] She describes herself as a child who loved books, was a willing scholar, and who had an early sense that "it would be intolerable to give up my own name and become 'Mrs.' something or other."[3] Understanding Daly's early life is uniquely affected by the fact that she has written rather extensively on her own story. The benefit of her own narrative of her life also becomes the burden of sorting out the influence of later opinions and ideas and discerning what has not been included. Regardless, Daly's autobiographical sketch is an invaluable source toward understanding her as a reformer.

The women's movement was all but nonexistent during Daly's youth. This was the period of time in the United States between the first wave of feminism, which had culminated with women's suffrage and the 19th amendment in 1920, and the second wave of feminism, in which Daly was

---

1. Daly, *Outercourse,* 22. The source for all biographical details that follow is this text, 22–76.
2. Ibid., 24.
3. Ibid., 27.

to play a leading role beginning in the 1960s. Nevertheless, her memories of childhood contains many "intuitions" like those already mentioned that she later recognizes as feminist. Describing her parents and her family connection to Ireland, Daly emphasizes the women and their strength; she suggests that this is what enabled them to survive the potato famine, migrate to America, and hold large families together through difficult circumstances. Growing up during the Depression of the 1930s and the world war of the 1940s contributed to Daly's understanding of social inequality and conflict. This was a time of political and economic transition for the United States and a time of cultural and ideological transition throughout the world. The modern era can be seen as beginning with the end of the Reformation and flowering with the influence of the Enlightenment in the eighteenth century. Some argue that modernity ends or begins to end with the colossal destruction and fragmentation of the twentieth century. This fragmentation leads to discussions and theorizing about a new postmodern era that is currently debated and discussed.[4] Whether or not that major demarcation of eras can clearly be made and whether Daly was part of it is yet to be determined. It is certain that the middle and late twentieth century was a remarkable time of change in the United States and around the world.

In this transitional era, Daly's life and work began amidst ordinary circumstances in what were to become extraordinary times. Her mother worked for the telephone company and her father worked as a traveling salesman selling ice cream freezers. He also wrote advertising slogans and authored a book about selling ice cream equipment. Daly describes finding copies of his book when she was young, and says that this sparked an early idea that she herself might write a book some day. Her social life in high school included being "president" of her group of friends, "The Polka Dots." These bits and pieces of evidence about her youth show a life that was relatively common for a girl coming of age in the 1930s and 1940s. While discussing her mother, however, Daly notes that the tragedy of Anna's life had been when she was "yanked out of school when still a sophomore in high school to go work as a telephone operator."[5] Daly interprets this experience as an example of the oppression her mother faced as a girl that Anna refused to inflict upon her own daughter.

4. See for example Bertens, *The Idea of the Postmodern*.
5. Daly, *Outercourse*, 28.

Daly's later account of her early years is filled with interpretation of what these things come to mean in her life. She narrates sneaking suspicions ("my growing Sense of Direction as Subliminal Sea Sailor"[6]) and interpretations of experiences understandably colored by later insight and analysis. What is not present is what many critics and suspicious minds expect to find in the childhood and youth of a lesbian and future radical feminist: trauma. Whether based on stereotype, fear, or paranoia, the notion that radical feminists are just angry because of some terrible experience with a man or some traumatic incident in their childhood has no merit in all that we know about the life of Mary Daly. She was a girl who basically liked her parents, (in fact she dedicated four of her eight books to both Anna and Frank, and two of them to Anna along with other women), a girl who chose her father's name for her confirmation middle name (Frances), who was a leader (Mary and the Polka Dots), a bit of a nonconformist ("I deliberately became a sort of slob as the years of high school went on."[7]), an inquiring child, and an independent thinking girl ("I became known as 'the brain,' but I did not dislike this appellation"[8]) who worried about things that most of her peers did. As a young Catholic girl, she describes being truly fearful of becoming unexplainably pregnant, since she was convinced by the way others spoke about it that it was simply a condition that fell upon some girls. Of course, she notes, sex education and birth control were not topics for much discussion in a working class Irish Catholic neighborhood in the 1940s.

Catholic Education, Shifting Vocation

As a young adult, Daly intended to study Catholic philosophy at the College of Saint Rose which was nearby in Albany, but received her degree in English instead in 1950 because they did not offer a major in philosophy to students at the women's college. She did study philosophy as part of a minor course of study, and says that she devoured all the textbooks in the discipline. Her experience at Saint Rose, however, gave her a first taste of something wrong with the world: In what ought to have been an empowering community of all women—women teachers and women learners—Daly experienced an unexplainable dullness. She later called it

6. Ibid., 40.
7. Ibid., 38.
8. Ibid.

"an enforced narrowness of horizons"[9] which stunted the growth of all of the women in the community.

This experience is one which Daly's own later analysis names as definitive for her understanding of the world constructed by patriarchy. "The whole setup was an illusion" she says, because women's colleges ought to be places where women learn about themselves and about "our own history, literature, science, philosophy. Women's colleges have been—and still are—dim foreground simulations of such Places of Study."[10] Since Saint Rose was an institution fully controlled by and situated within patriarchy and the Roman Catholic Church, the "dream of a Feminist University" she later names was to remain only a dream. Daly recognizes that in the narrow confines of patriarchy, even communities that are entirely female are fully subsumed into and defined by patriarchal myths, values, and practices. Daly later attempts to create female-only space to correct this and to bring that feminist dream to life.

After receiving her college degree, Daly moved on to do graduate work at the Catholic University of America in Washington, D.C. She studied English there also because the full tuition scholarship depended on her studying the subject that had been her undergraduate major. She notes in her autobiography that this detail about why she continued to study English is important to mention as it was yet one more obstacle to her desire to study philosophy. She took philosophy courses on the side again, describing a continual push toward it, until it began to emerge repeatedly in dreams. One key dream that she recounts as "the dream of green" stayed with her for decades: "I dreamt of Green—Elemental Green. When I woke up, the message was clear—clear as Be-Dazzling Green. It was: 'Study philosophy!'"[11] Sometime later, she began having dreams of teaching theology, which she describes as unexpected, but those dreams led her to answer an ad for a school offering a Ph.D. in religion.

Daly moved to Notre Dame, Indiana, to study religion in the doctoral program and teach English to undergraduates, both at St. Mary's College. She was introduced to the philosophical theology of Thomas Aquinas at this point in her journey, and recalls being enthralled and "carried away" with things like the doctrine of the Blessed Trinity. This immersion in

9. Ibid., 43.
10. Ibid., 44.
11. Ibid., 49.

the work of Aquinas comes to define the nature of her work long after she abandons the Christian tradition. She describes it as "a philosophical habitus—a habit of thinking philosophically in a rigorously logical manner."[12] She received her first Ph.D. in religion in 1953 at the age of 25, but still felt pulled to study philosophy. In the same year, she applied to the doctoral program in philosophy at the University of Notre Dame, but was rejected because she was a woman. Founded in 1842, the University did not admit women until 1972.[13] This is a further indicator of the cultural and political realities which shaped Daly's life: She was a woman seeking higher education in a society where women were simply not permitted to enroll in major universities. This obstacle was not insurmountable, however, for Daly and for other pioneering women.

Daly describes surviving the rest of the 1950s teaching classes at Cardinal Cushing College in Brookline, Massachusetts, and auditing lectures by theologian Paul Tillich at Harvard Divinity School. She notes how important it became later that she had heard and seen Tillich in person, and did not just know him by his books. Her later critical engagement with his work was made possible by these encounters. By the end of the 1950s, Daly moved to Europe to live and study in Fribourg, Switzerland, where she found an intellectual and cultural freedom that she hadn't found yet in the United States. She completed her second doctoral degree at the University of Fribourg, this one in sacred theology, in 1963. She describes her second dissertation as a passionate defense of the life of the mind, and a fight for intellectual independence.

It was through this work that she continued to rigorously engage in the scholarly analysis that characterizes her work for the duration of her career. It remains important enough that in her 1992 autobiography she continues to capitalize "Thomist" and "Thomistic," referring to the work and methodology of medieval theologian and saint Thomas Aquinas, long after she moved into strategic capitalization practices that refuse to capitalize words that indicate persons and practices associated with patriarchy. She explains this in a note:

> I capitalize the words Thomist and Thomistic whenever they occur in this book because of my regard for the intellectual training and treasures which I acquired in my study of that tradition. This

12. Ibid., 51.
13. "About Notre Dame" http://newsinfo.nd.edu/content.cfm?topicid=56.

study strengthened and sharpened my intellectual powers—both rational and intuitive—preparing the way for the creative work that was to come.[14]

The influence of Thomism on Daly's scholarship and methodology provides excellent reason for my continuing referring to her as a theologian even though she refers to herself as a philosopher. She notes that "medieval theology, especially that of Aquinas, was philosophy carried into an Other dimension."[15] In the same way, I believe that her work is theological, that is, it is philosophy in an Other dimension.

Not yet satisfied as a philosopher, with two doctoral degrees, one in religion and one in sacred theology, Daly enrolled in a doctoral program in philosophy at Fribourg and wrote her third dissertation on Maritain's intuition of being. Finally, she had her doctoral degree in philosophy in 1965, at the age of 37. She describes this lengthy "journey by degrees" and the three dissertations all as preparation for writing her later books. Indeed this work as a Thomist theologian and philosopher continued to define her method and style, as much as she in other ways tried to distance herself from the Christian theological tradition. She says, "my training as a Thomist theologian and philosophy became my Labrys, enabling me to cut through man-made delusions to the core of problems and to Dis-close the deceptive deadly devices that are used by academics, media men, and culture controllers of patriarchy."[16] Calling her a theologian not only points out how she, like Aquinas, concocts "philosophy in an Other dimension," but it also takes account of the fact that her work irrevocably affects the Christian theological tradition. It is that effect with which this book will be mainly concerned. The fact that Daly is in fact one of the most highly trained scholars of religion in the twentieth century is not something to be taken lightly.

Scholar in Rome

While living in Europe in the 1960s, Daly traveled to Rome to visit sessions of the Second Vatican Council. Her description of sessions she witnessed appears in the 1975 Feminist Postchristian Introduction to *The Church and the Second Sex*. Her words are vivid and reveal how this became a

14. Daly, *Outercourse*, 60n.
15. Ibid., 51.
16. Ibid., 75.

pivotal moment for her thought and work. Since she had no official status at the Council, Daly borrowed a journalist's pass to attend a session in St. Peter's Basilica. Her description of the scene is worth quoting at length:

> Sitting in the section reserved for the press, I saw in the distance a multitude of cardinals and bishops—old men in crimson dresses. In another section of the basilica were the "auditors": a group which included a few Catholic women, mostly nuns in long black dressed with heads veiled. The contrast between the arrogant bearing and colorful attire of the "princes of the church" and the humble, self-deprecating manner and somber clothing of the very few women was appalling. Watching the veiled nuns shuffle to the altar rail to receive Holy Communion from the hands of a priest was like observing a string of lowly ants at some bizarre picnic. . . . Although I did not grasp the full meaning of the scene all at once, its multi-leveled message burned its way deep into my consciousness.[17]

In her description of Vatican II here and later in her 1992 autobiography *Outercourse*, Daly also mentions a sense of hope which was palpable at that time among Catholic feminists and activists at the Council. The stimulating conversations that they had allowed them to believe that real change in the church was in fact on its way. But a sense of the strangeness of the scene was also evident—the dichotomy between the "princes" in crimson robes and the "lowly ants" in black shuffling around the basilica is the paradigmatic power dynamic of patriarchy. She called it a "moment of revelation in Rome [that] continues to work subliminally, inspiring my humor and stoking the Fires of my Fury. . . ."[18] Though she did not put words to the experience at the time, it clearly was etched in her mind as she moved into the public phase of her scholarly journey. It arguably was a pivotal experience that irrevocably shifted her view of the church in Rome and took a lifetime to understand.

This is a key example of Daly's life as enmeshed in shifting cultural realities. The Second Vatican Council is one of the most important events for the Christian tradition in the twentieth century, if not since the Reformation. Catholic church history is now routinely marked as "pre-Vatican II" and "post-Vatican II." Catholic theologian Robert Schreiter also points out that Vatican II, "coming to fruition as it did in the 1960s, . . . intersected with powerful social and cultural influences that magnified

17. Daly, *The Church and the Second Sex*, 10.
18. Daly, "Sin Big," 81.

its effects in many parts of the world."[19] Not only was Daly an advanced scholar at a Catholic university at the time, she was there, in Rome, observing the sessions that were to have a remarkable effect on the global Roman Catholic church.

An Early Public Controversy in Academia

Mary Daly began teaching at Boston College as an assistant professor with a two-year contract in 1966. Her first published book followed shortly after she began teaching at the Jesuit university. *The Church and the Second Sex* came out in 1968 and was written around the time of Daly's visit to the Second Vatican Council. She says that she began writing it before she went, and finished it after the journey. She describes the book in the 1975 introduction as incarnating the anger that emerged from the scene of crimson and black. The book contains some of her most basic insight into the problems of inequality in the church. For example, she states that "the Catholic Church appears to many as the last stronghold of anachronism and prejudice, refusing to adapt its structures to the condition of modern women."[20] After establishing "the case against the church" in the first chapter, she goes on throughout the book to expose the contradictions in the history of Christianity regarding the status and treatment of women. She also indicates who needs to begin the work for change:

> The people of God have responsibility for the future of the man-woman relationship on all levels. The primary responsibility of the Church in this regard is the reform of its own doctrine and practices.[21]

The book is a harsh criticism of the past and present state of the Church as well as a constructive call for renewal, embodying what Daly had described as that optimistic spirit present at the Second Vatican Council. She writes extensively about how to change the Church, and does insist here that it will come through men and women working together.

However, the book is a thorough critique of the history and practices of the Church, exposing its sexist past and calling for reform in its doctrines about and its treatment of women. And, Daly was at the time it was

---

19. Schreiter, "The Impact of Vatican II," 158.
20. Daly, *The Church and the Second Sex*, 54.
21. Ibid., 213.

published employed as a professor by Boston College, a Jesuit institution. She was subsequently given a terminal contract, which amounted to being fired from teaching. Since it was the 1960s in Boston, there was great public outcry at this development, and thousands of students rallied and protested and signed petitions. She was at the center of the era's fight for academic freedom. Her description of this moment in the 1975 introduction to the book is quite dramatic:

> I recognized that it was—and was more than—a war between "it" and me, and I willed to go all the way in this death battle. . . . The practical/personal/political issue was simple. Under the insidious guise of "confidentiality" my teaching career was being destroyed. The university officials had refused to give any reasons publicly or to me privately for my firing but the well-known phenomenon of grapevine innuendo would destroy my college teaching career.[22]

Daly was eventually reinstated and continued to teach at Boston College until her forced retirement in 1999, amidst another battle with university officials—this time not over her publications but over her work in the classroom. That battle will be examined in a later chapter as paradigmatic of the legacy and limitation of her work.

Career Publications and the Women's Movement

Despite the ongoing threat of losing her job and academic status, Mary Daly went on to produce several key texts in feminist theology and philosophy. *Beyond God the Father: Toward a Philosophy of Women's Liberation* emerged as her second book five years after her first. Published in 1973, it represents just what its title suggests—a move beyond God. In fact, this book would be the last time she really considered God as a substantive topic. Though it is a move beyond, the book in fact represents Daly's systematic theology, considering as it does the major loci of theology: god, sin, christology, ethics, church, and eschatology. The influence of the Catholic philosophical and theological tradition from her youth, education and three dissertations did not leave Mary Daly even as she left it.

In addition to being a complex systematic theology, *Beyond God the Father* is infused with political and cultural commentary engaging the society in which Daly lived. She comments extensively on the politics of abortion, for example, writing as she was in the years leading up to the

22. Ibid., 12.

momentous Roe vs. Wade Supreme Court decision federally legalizing the procedure. The book and the decision, in fact, came out in the same year. This context has direct bearing on her theological reflection about women's independence, agency, and the tendency of the Christian tradition to scapegoat and control them. Political fallout from the Vietnam War also infuses her theological reflection on ethics and values. These are just two specific examples of the many ways that politics and theology are intertwined throughout this work.

In *Gyn/Ecology: The Metaethics of Radical Feminism,* published five years later in 1978, Daly spins and spirals around the globe and throughout patriarchal history to investigate the many ways by which men have systematically sought to maim, shatter, and destroy women: These practices include footbinding in China, genital mutilation in Africa, gynecology in America, and burning women as witches in medieval Europe. This book showcases fully the move that Daly made to go beyond focusing primarily on religious and theological issues toward focus extensively on what she calls the religion of patriarchy. Her first two books focused on the history and the theology of patriarchy, and *Gyn/Ecology* focused on the rituals and sacred practices that are used to reinforce it. Cultural critique is embedded throughout the book, but theological rhetoric and inference are never far away. She closes the book with these words familiar to Christians and intended for feminists: "In the beginning was not the word. In the beginning is the hearing. Spinsters spin deeper into the listening deep. . . . Spinsters Spin all ways, always. Gyn/Ecology is Un-Creation; Gyn/Ecology is Creation."[23] Daly begins to fully communicate her Otherworldly ideology in this text, and it represents a new stage in her development as a philosopher and theologian.

Daly describes various stages or "galaxies" in her autobiographical reflection. The first spiral galaxy of her life is from the beginning through 1970, including *The Church and the Second Sex.* The second spiral galaxy she describes as "moments of breakthrough and Re-Calling" from 1971–1974. This brought about *Beyond God the Father.* She describes 1975 as "The Watershed Year, the year my world split open, in the most Positively Revolting ways imaginable."[24] Following this is the third spiral galaxy, "moments of spinning" which lasts from 1975 until 1987. During this

23. Daly, *Gyn/Ecology*, 424.
24. Daly, *Outercourse*, 200.

period of time, Daly "spins" and creates work that is of a wholly new nature, including *Gyn/Ecology*. Six years later, *Pure Lust: Elemental Feminist Philosophy* is published. Appearing in 1984 it is a dense philosophical treatise that moves deeper into her lexigraphical creativity and fleshes out with greater depth a binary cosmology including the patriarchal necrophilic foreground and woman-centered Biophilic Background. In order to encapsulate her growing vocabulary and to specify even further the structure of this Otherworld, Daly works "in cahoots" with Jane Caputi to produce *Websters' First New Intergalactic Wickedary of the English Language*, published in 1987. This complicated text will be itself a focus of a later chapter focusing on the creative application of language that Daly perfects at this stage of her work.

After this period of time, Daly moved into what she calls the fourth spiral galaxy, "moments of momentous re-membering." This era is not categorized by years, but rather is "off the calendar, off the clock."[25] Her final three books to date emerge out of this new time. She shared her autobiographical reflections in *Outercourse: The Be-Dazzling Voyage* in 1992, and moved toward a re-engagement with past resources, future visions, and present issues in both *Quintessence: Realizing the Archaic Future* (1998) and *Amazon Grace: Re-Calling the Courage to Sin Big* (2006). In *Quintessence* she relies more and more on imagined conversations with futuristic creatures. For example, she is in contact with Annie, who inhabits the year 2048 BE (biophilic era) in order to reflect on the present (1998) and the future. In the text, she confronts scientific issues like cloning and chastises it as another attempt at male motherhood. *Amazon Grace* shows her in regular conversation not only with inhabitants of the future but also with inhabitants of the past, like Matilda Joslyn Gage, nineteenth-century proto-feminist philosopher. In this 2006 text, Daly again engages political issue surrounding her. She provides her caustic reading of the twenty-first century's "war on terrorism." She insists that "the expression . . . is nonsensical. War IS terrorism."[26] This is one example of how she continues throughout all of these texts to engage issues of the present day, and to use her labrys of scholarly insight to cut through the deceptions she sees being promoted by patriarchy.

---

25. Ibid., 331.
26. Daly, *Amazon Grace*, 40.

These eight major books along with numerous articles to date have informed the theological and philosophical underpinnings of much North American feminist theology, and defined the edge of what many consider radical feminism in the United States. While Daly's work in the two decades between *The Church and the Second Sex* and the *Wickedary* is theologically the most substantive, the direction of her later works is philosophically compelling. However, the later work from her "fourth spiral galaxy" represents a further break with any established scholarly circles. Though still marked methodologically by her Thomistic analysis and theological insights, *Quintessence* and *Amazon Grace* do not neatly fit into theological categories, serving primarily as cultural commentary and radical feminist philosophy. It is worth pointing out, though, that the subtitle for her 2006 book is "Re-Calling the Courage to Sin Big"—an intentional echo of theologian Paul Tillich's idea of the "courage to be" which she had earlier debunked, and Martin Luther's exhortation in a letter to Philip Melanchthon in 1521: "Be a sinner and sin boldly, but believe and rejoice in Christ even more boldly. . . ."[27] Daly's camp used her version of it, "sin big" on bumper stickers sold to support The Mary Daly Defense Fund in 1999. The stickers also feature the image of a labrys.

Throughout her career, Daly embodies one trajectory of the second wave of feminism in the United States: radical feminism. Her theories and practices are paradigmatic of that form of feminism which is woman-identified and woman-centered. Another description of this type of gynocentric feminism is this:

> It is the primacy of women relating to women, of women creating a new consciousness of and with each other, which is at the heart of women's liberation, and the basis for the cultural revolution.[28]

As one voice in the chorus of theories in second wave feminism, radical feminism is for Daly the only authentic way to Be: to be feminist, to be woman, to be human. Throughout her work she operates with an idealized image of that which could be called a peaceable kingdom, a community of women and animals relating in peace and harmony. The *Wickedary* is filled with artwork depicting free-spirited women cavorting with each other

---

27. Luther, "To Philip Melanchthon," (1521) in *LW* 48:282. The phrase "sin boldly" has since been critiqued and even retranslated, but now appears on everything from t-shirts to mugs and other items from the kitschy marketing company Old Lutheran.

28. Radicalesbians, "The Woman Identified Woman," 157.

and with their "Familiars: a Super Natural Spirited Background Animal, the Graceful Friend of a Witch."[29] The purity of her vision is a defining strength of her work. The problems of patriarchy are clear. This idealized Otherworld informs survival in this world.

The limits of radical feminism are also apparent, and contribute to the limits of her work that will be considered later in this book. How does a world without males re-produce itself? How does radical feminism actually enable women to live, survive and thrive in the world which remains patriarchal? Can a movement of "only" women actually effect change? And the big question of course, what about the men? Many feminists and social scientists argue that men suffer under the narrow strictures of patriarchy, albeit in different ways than women. But insofar as patriarchy is a narrow hierarchical way of defining what it means to be human, male or female, it limits all who inhabit it. Popular second wave feminist Gloria Steinem acknowledges that gender is a prison for both men and women, but notes of course that for men it is a prison with wall-to-wall carpeting and someone to bring you coffee.[30]

Whatever the limits of radical feminism, as a part of the chorus of feminist theories in the second wave it has provided invaluable criticism of patriarchy and constructive options for women and men. The political character of the movement is central, and Mary Daly is a key figure in it because of her philosophical and theological work. Her insights into women's humanity and their deep connection to another reality that she calls the Background, as well as her caustic critiques of Christianity and patriarchy, are intertwined throughout a body of work that is simultaneously political and theological.

Thorough and comprehensive scholarly analysis of Mary Daly's life and work is sporadic and continues to emerge in part because she is still alive and working at the time of this writing. I have highlighted aspects of her biography here that have particular bearing on this study and bring her into conversation with a very unlikely partner in Martin Luther. Specifically, the social and political context of her life meant that her theology developed during decades that brought monumental change to the lives of women in the United States and around the world. Her connection to family and to the Catholic tradition means much throughout

---

29. Daly, *Wickedary*, 123.
30. Referenced in Shaw and Lee, *Women's Voices, Feminist Visions*, 120.

her life, even as she decisively rejects the religion out of which she comes. The insight that this provides will perhaps encourage further sustained analysis of this reformer's monumental achievements, only begun here in the pages of this book.

3

Martin and Mary

Parallels, Differences, and Inversions

> *If someone in the twentieth century espoused these views with the vehemence and conviction that Luther did in the sixteenth century, one might justifiably doubt the individual's touch with reality.*[1]

The early lives of Mary Daly and Martin Luther give suggestions but no obvious indications of the reforming work to come. Examining them together provides a glimpse into interesting parallels between their lives and work. General observations lead to several themes around which this comparative analysis will be based. Both come from working class families and both are devoted to their parents throughout their lives. The influence of the Roman Catholic church on both of their childhoods and their education is evident. Despite the obvious fact that each takes a critical turn away from this tradition later in their lives, they both remain marked by it throughout their work, whether it be in method, content, or both. The rigor with which they engage in their later criticism and constructive proposals is ironically a consequence of this education and upbringing in a tradition that encouraged them to engage in the life of the mind. The indelible imprint of Thomism marks Daly as a philosopher and theologian from her earliest to her latest writings, while the influence of the Augustinian order and discipline on Luther is seen in his piety as well as in the content of his theological construction.

That both of these reformers were notably marked by an early journey to Rome is compelling. While each had a sense of their own dissatisfactions with the church prior to the visits of 1510 and 1965, being physically present in the midst of it made the issues real beyond immediate articula-

---

1. Edwards, *Luther's Last Battles*, 17.

tion. Both are more aware of the impact of this visit in their later writings. Arguably, all of the criticism and theological construction after these visits grows from seeds planted there. Daly's stunned observation of the string of black-veiled nuns seeking the sacrament at the hands of the crimson robed princes of the church is later described as typical for a world of reversals, where women are "grateful to the paternal predators for their priestly ministrations . . . little suspecting that what these fathers, sons, and holy ghosts bestow upon their faithful followers . . . is a bag of illusions."[2] Luther's concern for the angst of the Christian seeking righteousness through paying coins for indulgences and crawling up the *Scala Sancta* is answered by his liberating message of justification by grace through faith in Christ. Both reformers understand at a deeper level that something is wrong in Rome, and both know that they must do something about it.

By the standards of the eras in which they lived and worked, Daly and Luther were both prolific and proficient scholars as well as activists. Daly is clearly a political activist in the era of second wave feminism as she speaks and writes not only about her academic disciplines of philosophy and theology, but as she engages with social issues like abortion, presidential corruption, and war. Her writings appear in journals as diverse as *The Thomist*, *The Notre Dame Journal of Education*, *Ms.*, and *The New Yorker*. Like Luther's, her work was immediately accessible to ordinary people through mass distribution, as well as taken seriously by scholars. In addition to being an academic, Daly was an activist in the church early in her career as she leads a mass exodus out of Harvard Memorial Church in 1971, after being the first woman to preach the Sunday sermon there. She closed the sermon with these words and this charge:

> Sisters—and brothers, if there are any here: Our time has come. We will take our own place in the sun. We will leave behind the centuries of silence and darkness. Let us affirm our faith in ourselves and our will to transcendence by rising and walking out together.[3]

They did walk out, and this enacted the strategic separation that characterized much early feminist community organizing. Theology was put into practice in this and other ways throughout Daly's career.

---

2. Daly, *The Church and the Second Sex*, xiv.
3. Daly, "The Women's Movement," 332–33.

Luther was also an activist of the church insofar as he suggested and implemented practical reforms in worship life, in catechetical instruction, and in the celebration of the sacraments. He wrote numerous hymns and composed new liturgies to provide resources for the reform of the church. In addition, his treatises and essays were widely distributed because of the newly invented printing press. The public was involved in his theological disputes from early in his career. Access to texts in local languages is a key element of Luther's entire system of thought, and his work is built upon this access. His theology was put into action not only through wider access to biblical texts, but by dissemination of Christian educational materials for families to use in their homes. To the present day, young Lutherans are educated about their faith with the words of Martin Luther's Small Catechism.[4]

The vast amount of writing that the two reformers produced is only introduced in these chapters. Several major theological issues however, are identified easily and early: The human soul is in a state of bondage. It has a keen sense that there is another dimension of reality to which it belongs, but an earthly power structure continually seeks to impose its order on that soul. This basic problem is key to understanding Daly's and Luther's views on all other topics. Why do these two figures share this criticism and this ideal? How can such parallels exist between two very different figures? Their biographies make clear that each was raised during an era of transformation between major eras in western history. The different contexts for both were unique transitional historical periods: For Daly, the shift from poverty to prosperity in the U.S. following the Great Depression and the second world war, movements for liberation among African-Americans and women, anti-war activism opposing the U.S. intervention in Vietnam, and the transformation of the church effected by the Second Vatican Council influenced the ways in which her work and her insights could impact the world. Luther lived in the period of time when the medieval became the pre-modern, while Daly lived in the shift from the modern era into what some identify as the postmodern. For Luther, the situation of increasing power in the hands of the German princes, the peak of scholasticism, and a flourishing church influenced the landscape in which he emerged and had such a dramatic impact.

---

4. See Borgstadt, "Celebrating the Small Catechism."

In complex but similar ways, Daly and Luther were both products and producers of the unique social and political scenes around them. Both were Catholic, working class, angry, personally driven, and highly educated. Both seem devoted to their parents, were avid readers and thorough scholars, and became early leaders of major social and theological movements. Their work and their lives share an abiding concern for reform, and most importantly both have core theological issues that define all that emerges from their creative minds. As their lives continued and careers progressed, each focused less on the church and more on constructing their own system of thought and practice. Daly understood that Christianity was only part of the problem encompassed by patriarchy, so her writing becomes less reform-minded and more focused on another reality as she increasingly focuses on gender. Luther eventually understood that the Roman Catholic church was not going to reform in the ways he identified, so his writing about them became less reform-minded and more polemical as the years went by.

Five broad themes can be lifted out after this introduction to the lives and work of Daly and Luther as the heart of the comparative analysis between them. The first theme grows out of their personal histories, the next three are examined in depth in the chapters that follow, and the final theme guides the analysis of the third section of this book. Here, the ideas that bring them together are briefly introduced to show basic parallels, differences, and inversions between them.

First, an element in the personal lives of both emerges as a political statement: Both Daly and Luther reject the imposed model of appropriate sex and marriage for persons in their positions. Second, the importance of a community of believers can be seen in both reformers: for Daly there is an ideal community of women and be-ing, and for Luther the ideal community is the priesthood of all believers. The importance of this community undergirds a rejection of church and hierarchy that is the third broad theme that brings their work together. As part of rejecting of hierarchy, both employ criticism of institutionalized authority and the use of sacrament and ritual. The fourth theme which their work shares is an intense focus on texts and language as not only a dangerous tool of the dominant class, but also as a weapon that each reformer wields in both critical and constructive ways. Finally, the political context and consequence of their lives and work form a fifth theme where connection is found. Bringing the two reformers together through this analysis highlights the ways that their very different lives shared parallel political and theological impulses.

Rejection: Sex and Marriage

Daly and Luther both reject the Catholic church's official teachings on sexuality and marriage. For both reformers, this is an ideological shift enacted in their personal lives that has political consequences. Daly, the twentieth century woman who should marry a man, is a lesbian. Luther, the priest who should be celibate, marries Katharina von Bora in 1525.

Remarkably, in doing the same thing, rejecting the sexual teachings of the church, they end up with inverse situations. Daly was raised in an era that assumed the centrality of marriage and family in women's lives. Prior to the women's movement of the 1960s, women were unquestioningly expected to marry and spend their lives primarily as wives and mothers. Because of this, they could not legally control their own reproductive capabilities. Daly lived through a groundbreaking change in the social and legal acceptance of birth control and reproductive freedom, when women gained specific legal rights: The 1965 Griswold vs. Connecticut Supreme Court decision made it legal for married couples to use birth control, and the 1973 Roe vs. Wade Supreme Court decision made it legal for women to have an abortion to terminate a pregnancy. The social and cultural impact of these decisions made during Daly's early scholarly years is still being felt and even challenged generations later.

Daly wrote passionately in her books and articles in defense of a woman's right to control her own body through safe and legal access to abortion, and through choosing whether or not to become pregnant at all. In response to the broader cultural pressures and realities, she took issue with a *Time* magazine cover story from February 22, 1982, which focused on the emerging trend of women having children later in life. Daly lambasted the article, titled "The New Baby Bloom," saying that it "emphatically enforced the trend of embedding pseudopassions."[5] She argued that the magazine's coverage of prominently pregnant celebrities functioned entirely as propaganda to promote the archetype of the woman-as-baby-machine. In this context, though women had the legal rights to choose not to be wives and mothers, Daly took aim at the powerful ideology of

---

5. Daly, *Pure Lust*, 209–10.

patriarchal culture, where women were celebrated *only* for choosing those paths.

Daly was also raised in an era when she was expected to marry a man. She had an early sense that this was not for her, and she discusses this occasionally. While she was a graduate student in the 1950s working on her master's degree, she says:

> I was going on occasional dates with my friend Charlie. . . . I enjoyed his company and that was all. But to him this was a serious matter. He wanted marriage, and described his idea of this state: the wife would definitely work only at home. I was horrified. All of my escape reflexes sprang into action.[6]

She rejects marriage, and what she later calls "potted love," that is, relationships between men and women that are falsely imposed on everyone in the foreground. Her personal identification as a lesbian seems marked by an experience in 1972 when she first read a woman's reflection on loving another woman. Daly notes that after reading this, she and a friend "sprang into action" and after that "nothing was ever the same again."[7] That relationship ended a few years later, but "the transformation was permanent. . . . Now I could live and create more boldly."[8] She describes this as having "broken the Taboo sexually and Realized how very Natural/Elemental this was."[9] This is the most that can be discerned about Daly's own "coming out" or conscious recognition of her sexual identity. Marriage between man and woman is no longer accepted as what is natural for everyone, and she rejects it personally and ideologically through her vision of the peaceable gynocentric communion of women and their Familiars.

Luther was indoctrinated to believe that a priest must be celibate and not engage in sexual relations with women. The legacy of early and medieval Christian asceticism remained strong in the Catholic church in his time. The dominant view with which Luther was indoctrinated devalued the body and all things physical, including and especially sex, while the soul and all things spiritual were highly valued. He rejected this Catholic dogma on a personal level with his marriage to Katharina, often referred to as Katie, a former nun.

6. Daly, *Outercourse*, 50.
7. Ibid., 144.
8. Ibid.
9. Ibid.

This personal decision reflected what he discussed on ideological level in his treatises on the value of marriage. Though he disagreed with the sacramental status of marriage, which some interpreted as a devaluing of it, he insisted instead that it is a gift from God that was universal in scope: "O what a truly noble, important, and blessed condition the estate of marriage is if it is properly regarded!"[10] This comment from a sermon preached and published in 1519 reveals that he viewed marriage favorably as a gift from God even before his own marriage in 1525.

In Luther's theological system, marriage was not a sacrament because it was not formally instituted with a sign by Christ in scripture, nor was it a means of grace. He takes this position by 1520 in "The Babylonian Captivity of the Church." In this way, he rejects the church's imposed model of marriage. He is congruent with his cultural context in arguing that a main purpose of marriage producing offspring, but he adds to this that the proper rearing of children is equally important. In a sermon, he speaks disapprovingly of "people [who] seek only heirs in their children" and he rejects this notion. Instead, he goes on, people can "do no better work and do nothing more valuable either for God, for Christendom, for all the world, for themselves, and for their children than to bring up their children well."[11] Marriage and raising children are activities whose purpose is serving God. This focus is consistent with the rest of his theological reform, to return God to the center of Christian faith, and to de-center the hierarchy of the church. To make this clear, Luther writes on marriage several times throughout his career.[12]

As for Luther's personal life, fragments of remarks from letters reveal some things about his own marriage. The reasons given at the time for his marriage reveal practical as well as theological concerns:

> Indeed the rumor is true that I was suddenly married to Catherine; [I did this] to silence the evil mouths which are so used to complaining about me. For I still hope to live for a little while. In addition, I also did not want to reject this unique [opportunity to obey] my father's wish for progeny, which he so often expressed

---

10. Luther, "A Sermon on the Estate of Marriage" (1519), in *LW* 44:13.
11. Ibid., 12.
12. Including "The Estate of Marriage" (1522); "That Parents Should Neither Compel or Hinder the Marriage of their Children" (1524); and "On Marriage Matters" (1530).

.... God has willed and brought about this step. For I feel neither passionate love nor burning for my spouse, but I cherish her.[13]

In this letter along with others, Luther invites colleagues to the wedding banquet in order to celebrate the union. He manages in these lines to convey that he (still) wishes to please his father, that he believes that God willed the path of his life, and that even though he might not have burning passion, he truly "cherishes" his wife.

Many biographers of Luther and scholars of the era have put forth theories about the Luther's marriage, whether it was happy or not and what role his wife played in his work. In the many letters to her that have been collected, he occasionally refers to her with phrases like "Dear Sir Katie," indicating that she "had become for Luther a person of extreme importance, not only as mistress of his house, or as mother of his beloved children, but, and this above all, as spiritual companion. . . . [S]he was both preacher and teacher to Luther, their children, and their friends."[14] His own thoughts are recorded in various places, giving evidence for this line of analysis. He says in 1531 that

> I wouldn't give up my Katy for France or for Venice—first because God gave her to me and gave me to her; second, because I have often observed that other women have more shortcomings than my Katy; and third, because she keeps faith in marriage, that is, fidelity and respect.[15]

His marriage was one example of his public and politically charged theology becoming personal. Family became for Luther a central way in which he served God and encouraged others to do the same.

This is one of the remarkable inversions in the lives of Mary Daly and Martin Luther: Both have the same impulse to reject the imposed models of marriage and love, but carrying out that rejection takes two completely opposite forms: the lesbian feminist and the married priest. Several other significant inversions in their lives and work will be noted throughout the following chapters.

---

13. Luther, "To Nicholas von Amsdorf" (1525), in *LW* 49:116. Katie's name is spelled in a variety of ways throughout Luther's writing, as seen in the comments included in this section.

14. Luther, "To Mrs. Martin Luther" (1529), in *LW* 49:235 n10.

15. Luther, Table Talk No. 49, in *LW* 54:7–8.

Community: Priesthood of Believers / Womanhood of Be-ing

The communities which Daly and Luther envision are important indicators of what they value, and showcase a significant parallel in their work. Because Daly values women and their personal connection to Be-ing through their intuition, her communal vision embodies just that: "be-ing: actual participation in the Ultimate/Intimate Reality—Be-ing, the Verb."[16] Because Luther values Christians with their internal connection to God through the word, his communal vision embodies just that: "all Christians are truly of the spiritual estate, and there is no difference among them except that of office."[17] Daly writes of a gynocentric community of women and their Familiars, rejecting the sexual caste system imposed by patriarchy that values men over women. Luther writes of a priesthood of all believers where all Christians are of equal spiritual value, rejecting the spiritual caste system which the Church imposed by giving a bishop more power than a peasant.

In both cases, the power of this ideal vision of the human community is remarkable. Both Daly and Luther express a political position through their proposal of how the world "really" is or how it ought to be. In doing so, they immediately critique reality insofar as it does not live up to this ideal. There is in fact great injustice among men and women in Daly's world, where men are more valuable than women, and one gender is seen to be more like God than the other. There is also great injustice among Christians in Luther's world, where the priests are more valuable than the peasants, and one class of people is seen to be closer to God than another.

Radical feminists like Daly are often criticized for envisioning a woman-only utopia. The criticism is something like this: It could never really work, it couldn't sustain itself, and it rejects men. This criticism is worth exploring further as a possible limitation to her work. Such an exclusionary vision also surprisingly emerges as a potential limitation to the legacy of Luther. Daly's gynocentric community obviously does not really exist in the material world because there are actual men in it. Likewise, Luther's priesthood of all believers is itself a utopia, an imaginative construct. It doesn't really exist because Christians live in the world

---

16. Daly, *Wickedary*, 64.
17. Luther, "To the Christian Nobility of the German Nation" (1520), in *LW* 44:127.

with actual non-Christians. It is exclusive because it rejects nonbelievers. Both reformers have ideologically exclusive utopias that work based on the internal logic of their worlds, but finally exclude entire classes of people. For both reformers, this community is not and will not be a complete physical concrete reality. It exists wholly in the understanding, and therein lies its power. Its potential liability is real, however, and will be examined further in later chapters. What does Daly think is the role of non-women? What does Luther think is the role of non-Christians? These questions will be considered as this parallel construction of an ideal community is examined further.

Rejection: Church and Hierarchy, Sacraments, and Ritual

What clearly marks Daly and Luther as reformers is the specific rejection of the church hierarchy that is made explicit through their work. It is the rejection that was compelled by their respective visits to Rome. Daly rejects the church altogether because it is a central part of patriarchy. Luther attempts to reject only the corruption of papal authority seen primarily in the abuse of indulgences, but he ends up rejecting the Roman Catholic Church altogether. We can imagine each young reformer standing in Rome unconsciously recognizing this: "If this is what the church is, then I will have none of it." A notable parallel in their approaches to the problem of institutional authority and the Roman Catholic Church appears as they work out its implications.

Daly's crucial observation in Rome was of a specific rite of the church, the sacrament of communion. However, the dynamics of the relationship between black-veiled nuns and crimson-robed princes of the church was paradigmatic of the patriarchal power structure that she decried. This is why it remains a vivid example of her breakthrough. Luther's observation in Rome was of another ritual of devoted Christians, climbing the *Scala Sancta* in penitence for one's own or another's soul. However, the dynamics of the relationship between God and the human being that it illustrated was deeply troubling for Luther. In fact, both Daly and Luther reject the power-as-control model that manifests itself in those moments: Daly insists that men shall not have control over women; Luther insists that God shall not be a tyrant over the soul of Christians.

Daly obviously abandons the church out of which she comes, and in fact has basically nothing to do with it in her work after her self-described watershed year of 1975. However, feminist theologians within Christianity continue to claim her as a source and insight for reforming the church. Luther less obviously abandons the church out of which he comes. He does abandon the church as he sees it presently structured, and he does abandon its idea of a tyrannical God and fearful Christian. However, it abandons him first with the excommunication of 1521. But, Luther allows a redefinition of church that ushers in the age of Protestantism, where there emerges a different understanding of the gracious god and humble Christian.

Both Daly and Luther examine in depth the function that rituals have played in maintaining the power of the church hierarchy. They do away with those rituals that reflect mere self-justification, and claim those rituals that serve their larger ideals. Each refuses the orderedness of ritual life that the church imposes. Daly rejects that order altogether, while Luther retains a truncated version of it.

As part of her rejection of the church altogether, Daly particularly rejects the rituals that the church practices. In an essay in *The New Yorker* in 1996, she relates her memory of being a ten year old girl, told mockingly by a boy classmate that she could never serve Mass because she was only a girl, and describes a "repulsive revelation of the sexual caste system" that "burned its way" into her consciousness.[18] She later associates rituals of the church with the tools by which the patriarchal powers attempt to remind women of their place, their role, and their limits. It does this by attempting to order the chaos that is feminist consciousness. Daly uses sociologist Peter Berger's language to describe the social ordering process that continually responds to the terror of chaos leaking into the cosmos. She notes that Berger was "quite unaware that he is describing precisely the spiritual dimension of feminist consciousness" when he observes that "to be in a 'right' relationship with the sacred cosmos is to be protected against the nightmare threats of chaos.'"[19] Daly understands that to be in right relationship in patriarchy is to be protected against the threat of chaos found in women. She suggests that women should fully inhabit that which patriarchy sees as chaos, and they should refuse the orderedness that it imposes.

---

18. Daly, "Sin Big," 76.
19. Daly, *Beyond God the Father*, 141. She is quoting Berger, *The Sacred Canopy*, 26.

Luther's reform of the Roman church ultimately focuses on the sacramental system. The practical legacy of his criticism is a reduction in the number of sacraments for Protestants from seven to two. In lengthy treatises he argues against the scope of the sacramental system as another abuse of power, another way by which the papacy misinterprets scripture, misuses power, and misinstructs the Christian faithful. He describes the sacraments as being actually captive to the Roman tyranny. Throughout his argument, Luther insists that where there is no physical sign and spiritual promise instituted by Christ, there is no sacrament. Any insistence to the contrary is a papal power play. In addition, he offers powerful reinterpretation of the two sacraments of communion and baptism based on his core theological reclamation of the grace of God.

While Daly and Luther mount parallel critiques of the Church, important differences exist in the substance of their criticism. Luther was basically unconcerned with gender equality and liberation, for example, while that can be seen as the sum whole of Daly's concerns. Daly was completely unconcerned with the truth of the Christian gospel, while that can be seen as the central issue for Luther. These and other differences remain as key distinguishers of their often parallel theological work.

Texts: Deceptive Language of the Dominant

As Daly and Luther developed their theologies, they revamped the use of language. For both, language was a methodological tool of liberation because it could be used to translate concepts and texts out of the language of the dominant power structure into the vernacular, the language of the people. The tool of liberation was first a tool of domination that each reformer reclaimed and reenergized. Daly and Luther focused extensively on the rhetoric used by the hierarchy which they criticized. In order to effectively disarm the hierarchy, the reformers used the tools that were being used against them, and recalibrated them for use in new theological expression.

Daly liberates language from patriarchy by reclaiming root meanings, transforming spelling patterns, and play-fully punctuating, Capitalizing, and hyphenating. She understands that language is one of the means by which patriarchy deadens sensibility to Reality, denying Women their intuition of Be-ing. By refusing to play by the imposed rules of punctuation and capitalization, she visually communicates the difference between such concepts as being and Be-ing. Her monumental achievement in this regard is writing the *Wickedary* which she also calls a Metadictionary. It is a combination of new definitions for old words, newly crafted words, and dis-covered ancient meanings for ordinary words that shed new and liberating light on them. Because of this eclectic method and style, she says it is at the same time "entirely New" and Ancient/Archaic. It brings re-newed insight to Elemental ideas.

Luther's monumental achievement of translating both the Old and New Testaments into German, the language of his people, embodied his theological point that the Christian must have access to the word of God for himself or herself. Knowing Latin for reading scholarly texts or studying the scriptures in Greek and Hebrew was not possible for the peasant folk of Germany who wanted to grasp the word for themselves. Luther saw that the priests were the ones who had set themselves up as sole conduits of the word. Because he determined that the clerical caste was no longer to be trusted in practical matters of management and finances, they were absolutely not to be trusted to translate and transmit the word of God appropriately. Luther saw the word as a powerful liberating force; It had freed him from tutelage and tyranny, and therefore he sought to bring that liberating potential to all Christians.

Daly and Luther construct as well as de-construct in their use of language. As will be examined in greater detail later, both reformers wrote crass and often nasty criticism of the people, ideas, and institutions that they targeted. Whether it be Daly's reference to the holy trinity as a divine drag queen in *Gyn/Ecology*, or Luther's reference to the pope of sodomists in a particularly polemic piece, language is vividly employed in the service of extensive political and theological critique.

Both Daly and Luther see the language of the dominant as a tool by which they mask themselves and dominate the masses. Both substantively overthrow this language in their own work. Luther's linguistic shift has had far wider repercussions throughout the course of the Christian tradition than Daly's has thus far, because it was so very basic and fundamental to give people access to texts in their own native language. Daly's linguistic shift has perhaps been more marginal and risky, because it moves beyond Luther's shift toward basic access to texts to enacting Real freedom to create, name, and construct. In a later chapter, sustained discussion of their parallel use of language reveals another inversion in their use of accompanying images.

Political Context and Consequence

A final broad theme that brings the work of Mary Daly into the same book as the work of Martin Luther is the influence of political contexts on their work, and the political consequences that each confronted because of their work. The biographical sketches of the two reformers already make clear how both were living and writing in times and places undergoing massive political and cultural shift. From the beginning of their lives to their final years, their home countries are almost completely different. The United States in 1928 and the United States in 2006 are almost light years apart in their cultural realities. Germany in 1483 is nearly unrecognizable in comparison to Germany in 1546. When the focus is even more precisely on the role of women in the U.S., and the church in Germany in these years, the differences are even more stark.

The changed situation for women in the United States between 1928 and 2006 is remarkable. In 1928, the year of Daly's birth, women had received the right to vote only eight years prior. The country was relatively prosperous, but on the cusp of economic depression. It was the end of the era when "Victorian" ideas about womanhood still dominated, and women were idealized as docile mothers and wives. The stereotype specifically described an ideal of womanhood that was upper-class, white, and submissive to men. The years between 1928 and 2006 contain a traumatic economic crash, an explosive second world war that included genocide of epic proportion, a baby boom that accompanied the emergence of the U.S. as a dominant world power, social and political upheaval with civil rights and women's rights movements, along with an anti-war student culture, and a revolution in the power and accessibility of technology. Women and the women's movement in 2006 are more educated, more diverse, and more independent than in any previous generation.

Daly's life and work was at the same time a product and producer of this massive cultural swing. The consequence of her work was such that almost any discussion of Christian feminist theology now has to consider her widely quoted truism: "if God is male, then the male is God."[20] Even beyond theology, Daly's influence on feminism and the women's movement has been such that she and her work embody the radical gynocentric version of it which is either embraced or rejected or merely avoided by many other feminisms. The consequences of this are broadly cultural

---

20. Daly, *Beyond God the Father*, 19.

as well as personal. Daly's early intense criticism of the church and her practice of teaching feminist ethics to men and women separately are two examples of events where her decisions threaten her employment status. She nearly loses her job in 1968, and is forced into retirement in 1999. Her work had indisputable political consequences.

Bernard Lohse's notes on Luther's world show some of the shifts in political and cultural tides in these years. In 1483, the year of Luther's birth, German emperor Frederick III was in the final decade of his "incompetent" reign. His son, Maximilian I, married Mary of Burgundy, which had the effect of laying groundwork "for the meteoric rise of the Hapsburgs." Ensuing conflict between the Hapsburgs and France "dominated political and ecclesiastical history during the first decades of the sixteenth century."[21] By 1546, the year of Luther's death, the German emperor, Charles V, had to deal with conflict between "Catholics" and "Protestants" that simply had not existed in Germany some 50 years prior. Lohse describes Charles' attempts to secure Protestant support for many of his political goals. In this way, a religious movement that was all but nonexistent in previous generations became a major force to be reckoned with. Lohse also suggests that at the beginning of the sixteenth century, "the Western church was basically unchallenged."[22] By the end of Luther's life in the middle of the same century, "challenged" is perhaps a mild descriptor for the condition of the Western church.

The shifts seen in this context are partly a consequence of Luther's own work. His reformation movement established even more diverse expressions of Christian faith, and irreversibly affected the cultural and political situation not only of Germany but eventually of the entire world. In addition, his reformation writings brought particular consequences for his own life and employment status. He was stripped of official status by the Roman Catholic Church, spent years in hiding, had to depend on others for safe travel, and saw his works venomously attacked as well as actually burned by those who disagreed with him.

To consider both of these reformers as political theologians, a sustained look into key elements of their theologies is required. The broad themes identified here serve as signposts indicating those things that are most significant and worthy of analysis. The method of considering each

---

21. Characterization of these emperors is from Lohse, *Martin Luther*, 1.
22. Ibid., 8.

reformer on her or his own terms, and then bringing them together by analyzing parallels, differences, and inversions will define the following chapters. In order to fully understand why and how such apparently different people emerge from what are very different contexts as such parallel reformers with inescapable consequences for the Christian tradition, we now dive deeper into their work.

PART TWO

Substantive Connections

To deepen the analysis of the theological systems of Martin Luther and Mary Daly, I will focus on three major themes identified in the previous section of this book. As noted, both reformers construct an understanding of the human person in relationship with God and a deeper authentic reality. In order to compare their theological anthropologies in chapter 4, I will focus on their ideas about human freedom, spiritual and physical captivity and the ideal human community for which they both long.

Then, in chapter 5 I will turn my attention to the sustained analysis of institutional authority that both Daly and Luther offer. Their respective assessments of the status of the human person is bound up with the problem of the institution that gets in the way between the person and God or authentic reality. Looking both at what the institution is and what it does according to the two reformers further reveals their parallel political theological task.

Finally in this section, chapter 6 zones in on the use and power of language as employed in revolutionary ways by these two theologians. Words and texts are vitally important for the worldview and the theological construction offered by both reformers as they name persons, institutions, and classes of people. Attention to their respective rhetorical styles ultimately suggests that there are crucial limitations to the political theologies of these two that will be attended to in the final section of the book.

4

Theological Anthropology
Freedom in Captivity and for Community

Be a sinner and sin boldly, but believe and rejoice in Christ even more boldly . . .[1]

Sin Big: The Mary Daly Defense Fund[2]

One nonnegotiable concept grounds the theological anthropology of both Martin Luther and Mary Daly: freedom. One problem limits this freedom: captivity. One ideal compels both reformers: community. Within their theological reflections on what it means to be human, each reformer envisions and works toward a community of equals where freedom for the individual is no longer restricted by a corrupt hierarchy. Comparing Luther's and Daly's ideas on freedom, captivity, and community reveals a set of parallels, differences, and inversions that draw them closer into conversation with one another and reveals in more detail how each emerges as a political theologian.

Freedom

For Luther, the freedom of a Christian was based on his radically simple reclamation of justification by grace through faith: The Christian is free from works-for-salvation and is freed for service to the neighbor. For Daly, the freedom of Original Woman was based on her emphasis on women's access to deep reserves of life-affirming power: Original Woman is free from fixation on falsified needs and is freed for authentic life in relationship with her Self and others. Both Luther and Daly rely on a dialectical

---

1. Luther, "To Philip Melanchthon" (1521), in *LW* 48:282.
2. Bumper sticker slogan, 1998.

world construction in order to fully explain their concept of freedom, and both are careful to make clear what freedom is and is not.

Freedom of a Christian

Luther's 1520 essay on "The Freedom of a Christian" provides clear insight into his dialectical worldview and his understanding of freedom. For Luther, we can understand "to be human" as meaning "to be Christian," for that was fundamental to his theological system. His anthropology embraces both a radical human freedom and a radical human obligation which he expresses in the often quoted dialectic: "A Christian is a perfectly free lord of all, subject to none. A Christian is a perfectly dutiful servant of all, subject to all."[3] He goes on to describe human nature in two dimensions: the inner spiritual person and the outer enfleshed person. With regard to the freedom of the inner person, Luther states that "the soul can do without anything except the Word of God."[4] The outer person, therefore, can be a dutiful servant because she is freed from everything other than God, free to serve others.

The dialectical character of this statement provides one example of Luther's twofold cosmology. Throughout his work he speaks of the temporal, earthly, physical realm and the eternal, transcendent, spiritual realm. They are not mutually exclusive or separate; in fact both are realms of God. In the same way that Augustine wrote about the "city of this world" and the "city of God," Luther assumes a binary reality for relationship with God, both at the level of the human person and at the level of the whole world. Both are important, as seen in his understanding of freedom and righteousness.

When he writes about Christian freedom, Luther distinguishes sharply between the role of works and the role of faith in human life. He insists that faith alone is needed to understand the word of God and to be in relationship with God made possible by God's grace. In context, it is important to emphasize here that he removes any and all need for the clerical class to guide, inform, and connect the Christian with God. Freedom from church hierarchy is what he allows and encourages with this idea. This becomes a theological political power play:

---

3. Luther, "The Freedom of a Christian" (1520), in *LW* 31:344.
4. Ibid., 345.

It is clear, then, that a Christian has all that he needs in faith and needs no works to justify him; and if he has no need of works, he has no need of the law; and if he has no need of the law, surely he is free from the law.[5]

If the Christian needs no works and is freed from the law with regard to his relationship with God, then he needs no intervention from the hierarchy of the church to dispense indulgences and provide means for other salvific works. Luther insists that "every Christian is by faith so exalted above all things that, by virtue of a spiritual power, he is lord of all things without exception, so that nothing can do him any harm."[6] The spiritual power identified here is the basis of freedom and the reason that every Christian is liberated from and has power over all things. This power is not limited to just some Christians, like priests; it defines every Christian.

The second part of Luther's dialectic builds on the first: The freedom that he emphasizes enables the Christian to serve the neighbor, as commanded in scripture. This makes Luther's anthropology one both grounded in freedom and moving toward community. He insists that the Christian "should be guided in all his works by this thought and contemplate this one thing alone, that he may serve and benefit others in all that he does, considering nothing except the need and advantage of his neighbor."[7] As dutiful servant, the Christian shows the fruit of her faith. Rather than be the *cause* of righteousness, good works are the *effect* of a person made righteous by the grace of God. Freedom *from* works frees the Christian *for* service to the neighbor. In both cases, the hierarchy of the church is unnecessary for a person's relationship with God and expression of faith through care of the neighbor.

Luther's concern in his essay on freedom is to further clarify what he previously wrote about righteousness, stating how the Christian was made right again and freed from sin. Luther has a deeply personal concept of sin throughout his theology, and he understands that sin is the fundamental characteristic of human nature. Sin is the disease with which every human being lives, and that with which he wrestled in his own conscience. The liberation that Luther found in the idea of justification by grace through faith leads him to write about freedom as a product of the righteousness brought

---

5. Ibid., 349.
6. Ibid., 354.
7. Ibid., 365.

by justification. In a 1519 sermon on "Two Kinds of Righteousness," Luther insists first that righteousness comes from God. The emphasis is once again on God and not on the hierarchy of the church. Like Luther's discussion of freedom, his discussion of righteousness presents a dialectical view: Righteousness is both alien and proper. Alien righteousness is that which comes from outside the person, and comes to him first: "Therefore everything which Christ has is ours, graciously bestowed on us unworthy men out of God's sheer mercy, although we have rather deserved wrath and condemnation, and hell also."[8] This grounds his idea of freedom from works, because righteousness comes not through anything the individual can do, rather it comes entirely from outside, from God through Christ.

Proper righteousness comes second for Luther, as a product of alien righteousness. Moving from one to the next works much in the same way that good works follow from justification: a justified person who has been made so by God's grace produces good works. A righteous person who has been made so by God shows this through proper righteousness: bringing herself under control, loving her neighbor, and fearing God. The actual things that the person does (works) are a consequence of alien righteousness (grace). Luther emphasizes the good of the community in this discussion also: "Therefore it [righteousness] hates itself and loves its neighbor; it does not seek its own good, but that of another, and in this its whole way of living consists."[9] The focus for the Christian is therefore on others because there is no longer a need to focus on oneself: God takes care of that.

Luther's entire theological system is dramatically shaped by his ideas about freedom from works as a means to salvation. However, this does not mean that the Christian is free to do whatever she or he wishes. A brief note about Luther's extensive critique of Erasmus' discussion of a free will helps illustrate what Christian freedom is not. In response to Erasmus' 1524 treatise *Diatribe seu collatio de libero arbitrio*, "Diatribe or Discussion on the Free Will," Luther produced in 1525 the lengthy *De Servo Arbitrio*, "On the Enslaved Will," or as it is popularly called, "The Bondage of the Will." In his argument for the bondage of the will and against Erasmus' idea of the free will, Luther articulates in yet another way the radical dependence on God that is the source of freedom from works

---

8. Luther, "Two Kinds of Righteousness" (1519), in *LW* 31:298.
9. Ibid., 300.

and the law for matters of salvation. Erasmus understood human life as a moral enterprise and argued that the human being was free to choose the good or to turn away from it. He shared Luther's emphasis on God as the first cause of salvation, but then suggested contrary to Luther that the human being could, by virtue of her free will, either choose or reject God and salvation.

Luther vehemently disagrees, certain that his understanding of justification by grace through faith was in fact the heart of the gospel. In this treatise, he develops his analogy of the human will as a beast standing between two riders, a beast who cannot choose a rider for itself. Its fate is dependent on its rider: "If God rides, it wills and goes where God wills . . . If Satan rides, it wills and goes where Satan wills. Nor may it choose to which rider it will run, or which it will seek; but the riders themselves fight to decide who shall have and hold it."[10] The reason for this inability to choose the good was sin, for Luther. Sin is the personal flaw that affects every human being; therefore, every human being needs righteousness bestowed from outside their own being, from God. In the same way, the beast cannot run to the good rider. The good rider must choose the beast. And, for Luther, since God *does* choose the human beast, then the human beast goes and does where and what God wills. Whatever the beast does is at the direction of the rider. Whatever the Christian does is because of and for God. At the same time, whatever mistakes the beast makes are its own fault, based on its own flawed nature. Christians are still sinful, according to Luther, but justification by God's grace makes it possible for them to do some good, God's good.

In the analogy, which demonstrates how little Luther actually thought of human beings, the beast is effectively free from having to discern and make the right choice. How is a beast to know which rider is right in the first place? The power and mercy of God is so great for Luther that the human being can be compelled to do God's work. This is another angle for describing the liberation that he found in the message of justification by grace. Because of the pervasive reality of sin, the human being is totally unable to do any right thing. God had to be the source of all righteousness and good work. Any errors that the human beast commits are its own fault; any good that it does is due to the grace of God. Luther thought very little of human nature and thought very much of God's power.

---

10. Luther, *The Bondage of the Will* (1525), 103–4.

With regard to cultural and political life, the effects of Luther's reclamation of the freedom of a Christian are manifest in another way. Freedom did not mean exemption from laws and responsibilities in the temporal world. He remains concerned about society in the temporal world, as seen in treatises and sermons on social issues like education, organized rebellion, the legitimacy of the military profession, and the authority of governing figures.[11]

In a treatise on temporal authority, Luther draws from Paul's letter to the Romans as well as 1 Peter to show that the word from God is for Christians to be subject to governing authority. This authority is itself derived from God. His Augustinian roots show through clearly here, as he works with Augustine's dialectical "city of God" and the "city of this world." For Luther, Christians are members of the spiritual kingdom of God as well as the temporal kingdom of the world. As members of the first spiritual realm, Christians have no need of law and are free from it. But, Christians are also members of the temporal world, so their freedom from the law for matters of eternal life does not mean exemption from laws now in matters of temporal life. The reason is flawed human nature, once again: "Now since no one is by nature Christian or righteous, but altogether sinful and wicked, God through the law puts them all under restraint so they dare not willfully implement their wickedness in actual deeds."[12] The emphasis on human sin is crucial here, as Luther reminds Christians that in and of themselves they are simply wild beasts requiring direction from someone else.

Because of this sinful nature, rebellion against the governing authority is ill-advised, and Luther first counsels resistance to a corrupt governing authority by confession of truth. Ultimately, in response to the question, "What if a prince is in the wrong? Are his people bound to follow him then too?" Luther responds: "No, for it is no one's duty to do wrong; we must obey God (who desires the right) rather than men [Acts 5:29]."[13] And thus he returns to the core Christian freedom that comes from God.

---

11. For example, "To the Christian Nobility of the German Nation," (1520); "A Sincere Admonition by Martin Luther to All Christians to Guard Against Insurrection and Rebellion," (1522); "Whether Soldiers, Too, Can be Saved," (1526); and "A Sermon on Keeping Children in School," (1530).

12. Luther, "Temporal Authority: To What Extent It Should Be Obeyed" (1523), in *LW* 45:90.

13. Ibid., 125.

The Christian is bound to and by God, which frees her from obligation to those things which are not from God. Because temporal authority comes from God, the Christian is bound to obey it. But, when temporal or even ecclesial authority acts in opposition to the word of God, the Christian is freed from it by God. This sets up the political nature of Luther's theology.

Freedom of Original Woman

Since Mary Daly is gravely concerned about the state of women's souls and the future of their lives, her theological anthropology focuses on women and what it means to be a woman. Daly's anthropology is also understood within the context of a dialectical worldview: the foreground and the Background. The foreground is the realm of patriarchy and the Background is the realm of Woman. Strategic capitalization demonstrates her assessment of these realms and her definitions of them showcase her play with language:

> **foreground** *n:* male centered and monodimensional arena where fabrication, objectification, and alienation take place; zone of fixed feeling, perceptions, behaviors; the elementary world: FLATLAND.[14]
>
> **Background** *n*: the Realm of Wild Reality; the Homeland of women's Selves and of all other Others; the Time/Space where auras of plants, planets, stars, animals and all Other animate beings connect.[15]

The Background is the level of existence that is below and behind the surface of a false foreground reality. At times Daly's descriptions make it sound like an actual place. At other times her discussions make it seem like a deep reservoir of dynamic energy. In her early theological work, she describes "this rushing of the waters of life that have been dammed and damned by our culture."[16] While she had not begun using the term Background in this 1973 comment, the idea of it was already present. Whether it is a place or an energy source, the Background is the source for women intuiting Be-ing, life itself which is Ultimate/Intimate Reality.

---

14. Daly, *Wickedary,* 76.
15. Ibid., 63.
16. Daly, *Beyond God the Father*, 159.

Though Daly ceases to call this reality God after 1973, she maintains the language of Ultimate Reality and speaks of it in much the same way that Luther speaks of the Christian connection to God.

The foreground is the one-dimensional reality which gains its power by inverting the life-force of the Background. It is false and fabricated. It is patriarchy, the ideology of the world as experienced on the surface. The Background has ultimate authority over the foreground in matters of the soul and be-ing. It is more complex and "Really Real." The foreground works tirelessly to cover and control the Background. Women inhabit both worlds for Daly, and distinguishing between them becomes important for distinguishing between their priorities. She calls on inhabitants of the Background to reverse the foreground's falsifications. Therefore, for Daly sin is understood as systemic. The flaw inherent in reality is not to be found in individual persons, rather it is to be found in the mechanisms of the foreground and patriarchy.

This dialectical world construction is the source and paradigm for much of Daly's theological and philosophical system, and is the reason for her patterns of capitalization and spelling. She uses visual clues like capitalization to distinguish between the realms in her writing. Because the Background is the realm of "the divine depth of the Self" and the foreground is mere surface consciousness, she capitalizes all words referring to inhabitants of the Background or concepts to describe elements therein. Dashes, slashes, and hyphens are used liberally to recapture and emphasize original meanings of terms like re-member (to put the members back in, literally).

Within this binary cosmology, Daly describes what it means to be human/woman. Two definitions from her *Wickedary* highlight themes in her anthropology:

> **Original Woman**: one who "charts her own beginnings from the deepest recesses of her Self and other women . . . [who] stands throughout history as the antithesis to the man-made females of patriarchal creation . . . [who] seizes the power to originate."[17]
>
> **Daughter** *n*: the Original Self; the Untouchable Integrity in every woman; the Wild Virgin within every woman who Lives beyond

---

17. Daly, *Wickedary*, 153.

the confines of patriarchal rules and roles, reveling in be-ing Alone and fiercely bonding with her own kind.[18]

Two words emerge in these definitions as key to understanding her anthropology: Original and Wild. Her repeated use of the term Original to describe Woman shows both what comes ordinally first and what is ideologically primary. The term original can be seen temporally, as in an *original* film, the one that comes first distinguishing it from its later remake or sequel. The term can also be read existentially, as in an *original* idea, one which has not existed before and is wholly new. Daly seems to move between the two as she describes the Background and its inhabitants as archaic and ancient, and as she describes original things as tapped into the deep well of life itself. She further describes any thought or deed that comes from this Original Self as being in harmony with one's final cause—and this is Original Movement. This is a "primal tendency toward the Good."[19] Both the temporal and the existential levels give the Original its meaning.

The second term that appears repeatedly in her descriptions of Woman is Wild. Much like the word primal, Wild is a term used to refer to things that are natural or uncivilized. There is a radical freedom involved in being Woman that originates from the Background and is Wild and uncontrollable by the inhabitants of the foreground. Her definition of the term actually replicates the traditional definition, but it takes on a completely new meaning when placed within her dialectical worldview. In fact, she cites the full definition of "wild" from *Webster's Third New International Dictionary of the English Language*, and then gives it her Websters' Intergalactic Seal of Approval.[20] The definition includes the following phrases:

> not tamed or domesticated . . . growing or produced without the aid and care of man . . . not amenable to control, restraint, or domestication . . . exceeding normal or conventional bounds in thought, design, conception, execution, or nature . . .[21]

---

18. Ibid., 70.
19. Ibid., 152.
20. Note the difference between the terms "Webster's" and "Websters'." It is slight but significant.
21. Daly, *Wickedary*, 100.

The connotation in *Webster's Dictionary* is negative and suggests that the wild is something to be feared: Wild is bad in the foreground, but good in the Background.

There is another entry in the *Wickedary* for "Wild" as a noun, following this adjective definition endorsed from *Webster's*. Daly's definition for the noun is:

> **Wild** *n*: the vast Realm of Reality outside of the pinoramic world view constructed by the bores and necrophiliacs of patriarchy; true Homeland of all Elemental be-ing, characterized by diversity, wonder, joy, beauty, Metamorphic Movement and Spirit.[22]

Wild—negative and feared in the foreground—has a positively sparkling meaning when used by Websters' in the Background, representing everything that is encouraged and celebrated. If wild describes anything not amenable to control, then the Wild is precisely that realm which is beyond restraint and domestication which women can and do inhabit. It is the Background. Yes!

Original Woman's freedom comes from the Background and it informs how she acts in the realm of the foreground. Writing early in the women's liberation movement of the late twentieth century, Daly describes the impact of women dis-covering their freedom: "The beginning of liberation comes when women refuse to be 'good' and/or healthy by prevailing standards. To be female is to be deviant by definition in the prevailing culture."[23] Women are *free from* this prevailing culture which seeks to smother, destroy, and silence them. To refuse to be silenced and destroyed is to resist this culture. Women are *free to* define themselves instead of being defined by another. If systemic sin defines the foreground, women are freed from it by the power of the Background.

The definitions of good and bad in the foreground, for Daly, are of course a central part of the problem. Resisting these definitions is an expression of real freedom that makes even greater freedom possible:

> In going beyond the imposed innocence which both the good woman and the bad woman have in common (i.e., lack of valuation and choice of identity by the self) women are gaining the

---

22. Ibid., 101.
23. Daly, *Beyond God the Father*, 65.

psychological freedom required to challenge the destructive false innocence that is characteristic of our age.[24]

Daly insists that women must come to understand Original freedom because if they do not, they have no reason to challenge the "imposed innocence" and definitions of the foreground. Challenging these impositions are critically important for the flourishing and development of Real life. This is why she calls it a

> Fall from false innocence into a new kind of adulthood. Unlike the old adulthood that required the arresting of growth, this demands a growing that is ever continuing, never completed. . . . the Fall now initiated by women becomes a Fall *into* the sacred and therefore into freedom.[25]

In this new understanding of the Fall, Daly insists that women are free in the way that adults are free. Instead of remaining subject to the patriarchal captivity like children subject to their fathers, women are fully capable adults who challenge foreground ideas freely and name reality creatively.

One final characteristic of Woman drawn from the Background is her ability to Re-member: "the power to transcend the categories of tidy time, to connect with the sources of instinctive, ecstatic knowledge."[26] Daly also calls this Elemental Memory or Metamemory, Deep knowledge that comes from the Background and challenges the foreground. Because of this, the "Choice to recall the empowering memories and to create in our daily lives future memories of Happiness is a continuing act of deviant defiance."[27] Channeling energy from the Background is one way that Women refuse to submit to the fabricated reality of the foreground. The memories which are re-called challenge the truth and authority of the prevailing culture. This ability and this connection shape a further level of the freedom of woman—a freedom from "frenzied foreground fixations."[28]

Throughout the body of her work, Daly routinely invokes the memories of historical women. In her 2006 book *Amazon Grace*, Daly and imagined conversation partners Annie and Sophie speak with Matilda Joslyn Gage, nineteenth-century activist for abolition and women's suffrage. In

24. Ibid., 66–67.
25. Ibid., 67.
26. Daly, *Wickedary*, 79.
27. Daly, *Pure Lust*, 358.
28. Ibid., xii.

doing so, they call forth the memories of women's captivity under patriarchy in the nineteenth century:

> Matilda and I then strode over to the center of the grass, and I was carrying *Woman, Church and State*. The cheering and clapping and thumping began again, but it subsided after a few signals from Anowa, Kate, and Sophie. Turning to Matilda, I asked, "Will you please be so kind, Matilda, as to tell us a bit about how you expressed your Wild Fury back in the nineteenth century?"[29]

As Matilda tells tales of how her book and work were attacked by Anthony Comstock, crusader against indecency, Daly and the others listen, nod in understanding, and are generally mesmerized. This conversation is one example of exchanges that take place in the Background, and Daly's 1998 book *Quintessence* contains many more. That book is where Daly first introduces Annie, or Anonyma. Anonyma is the character who writes the preface for what Daly calls the fiftieth anniversary edition of *Quintessence*, published in 2048 B.E., reflecting travel through time into the Biophilic Era (B.E.). These things showcase how Daly's creative world construction even defies the space-time continuum of the foreground.

The foreground remains the physical world that women inhabit, however, so how does Daly suggest that women survive a life in this world? Her descriptions of what she calls Elementals in the introduction to *Pure Lust* are descriptions of skills that challenge the foreground in many ways. Daly presents a litany of terms used to describe and control women, and she liberates and redefines the words: *websters* are female weavers; *virgins* are women who are never captured; *wantons* are those not susceptible to control; *sprites* are creatures inspired with courage; *muses* are those women who are embodied memories like Annie and Matilda; *shrews* scold malignant behavior; *scolds* tell the truth about perverse behavior; *soothsayers* are the truthsayers; *prudes* are proud, capable, and brave women; *dikes* are women as barriers excluding the undesirable; and *viragos* are loud overbearing women.[30] In reclaiming these terms and actions, Daly effectively describes how women should live in the world, to embody their connection to the Background and by virtue of their very existence challenge the foreground. A woman should be a virgin, a shrew, and a dike. Given Daly's cosmology, these things which are limitations and insults in the foreground become

---

29. Daly, *Amazon Grace*, 149.
30. Daly, *Pure Lust*, 12–14.

life-giving roles from the Background. Women embody the Passion of being and can reclaim Reality through speaking truth, scolding the perverse, and excluding malignant behaviors. This is what it means to be Original Woman, and what it means for Daly for women to be free.

Notes on Freedom

In two very different contexts, Luther and Daly both prize human freedom and use it as their starting points for theological criticism and political challenges. Both suggest that they are going to the heart of the matter, or to the more authentic reality, and this brings two very different theological anthropologies together. On the topic of freedom, both emphasize that human beings are free from something and freed for something else. In addition, both Luther and Daly rely heavily on a binary or a dialectical view of the world to fully explain freedom. Luther's temporal and spiritual function much like Daly's foreground and Background. There is a flaw in reality for both reformers that creates the need for freedom: for Luther sin is personal, while for Daly sin is systemic. Despite this difference, there are many comparable things to be said about their views of human freedom. They both discuss the human person as inhabiting both of the two realms of the world, and emphasize how the connection to the one, the kingdom of God and the Background, is the source of liberation from the fixations of the other, the kingdom of the world and the foreground. Of course, Luther focuses his criticism almost wholly on the corruption in the church and Daly focuses her criticism almost wholly on the corruption of patriarchy. Despite that difference, they both have a keen sense of the human person as captive under tyrannical authority.

Captivity

Captivity in an alien land is the central problem that brings Luther's and Daly's theological work fully into the political realm. They both see that the individual person lives captive to an imposed authority which tries to erase a natural connection to the spiritual kingdom or the Background. The memory or intuition of that other place remains, however. For Luther, this state of reality is reminiscent of the "Babylonian captivity." For Daly, there exists "some other dimension . . . the homeland of the Race of Women."³¹

The Babylonian Captivity

A defining reality for the freed Christian in Luther's time was the church's control over Christian life. Here the problems with institutional authority begin to emerge. In his 1520 treatise on "The Babylonian Captivity of the Church," Luther describes how spiritual captivity occurs when freedom from works is ignored:

> For where faith dies and the word of faith is silent, there works and the prescribing of works immediately crowd into their place. By them we have been carried away out of our own land, as into a Babylonian captivity, and despoiled of all our precious possessions.³²

One precious possession lost and carried away is spiritual freedom and with it the connection to God by means of grace. The "works" which he says crowd in here include the pomp and ceremony that the church has attached to the sacrament of the mass, rituals like buying indulgences, climbing the *Scala Sancta*, and viewing relics which he himself had done while in Rome, and having to ask a priest for forgiveness when in fact it is God who grants forgiveness. In contrast to the Roman Catholic system, Luther's sacramental theology described in this treatise and elsewhere relies completely on the twin criteria of God's promise and sign, received in faith alone. Man-made ordinances and rituals which have no basis in scripture (like climbing stairs to earn forgiveness and paying money for salvation) therefore get in the way of a full and free relationship with God through faith alone.

The title of Luther's piece and his image of the church carried away as if into a Babylonian captivity intentionally invokes the powerful memory of ancient Israel's exile in Babylon. The anguish of the period when the Israelites were removed from their promised land and prevented from freely expressing devotion to God is captured in Psalm 137:

---

31. Ibid., 6. I considered this dynamic of an envisioned homeland in both Luther and Daly initially in "From a Babylonian Captivity to the Otherworld."

32. Luther, "The Babylonian Captivity of the Church" (1520), in *LW* 36:47.

> By the rivers of Babylon—there we sat down and there we wept when we remembered Zion. On the willows there we hung up our harps. For there our captors asked us for songs, and our tormentors asked for mirth, saying, "Sing us one of the songs of Zion!" How could we sing the Lord's song in a foreign land? . . . O daughter Babylon, you devastator! Happy shall they be who pay you back what you have done to us! Happy shall they be who take your little ones and dash them against the rock! (Psalm 137:1–4, 8–9).

The words and images of the Psalm insist that the Babylonian captivity be seen not just as a political reality, but as a state of personal anguish. Weeping, an inability to sing the Lord's song, and a dramatic longing for retribution against the captors all reveal the memory of Babylon to be more than that of a nation's historical captivity. It is a memory of personal distress. Babylon is also used by the author of Revelation to symbolize a wicked regime: "Fallen, fallen is Babylon the great! It has become a dwelling place of demons, a haunt of every foul spirit, a haunt of every foul bird, a haunt of every foul and hateful beast." (Rev. 18:2). The psalmist recalls the historical Babylonian captivity, and the apocalyptic imagery used by the author of Revelation looks forward to the destruction of the evil empire that he knew, Rome. In this tradition, Luther likens yet another power structure to a tyrannical state that imprisons the faithful: the papacy.

The problem is clear: The freedom which Luther so carefully understands, explains, and applies to matters of both temporal and spiritual life is being held captive. This captivity may be one reason why the ideal of a Christian community that he envisions is not-yet a reality. In addition, there is cause for great concern for the individual Christians who are in this state of captivity. Not only are the church and its rightful practices under captivity, but the Christian soul which has already been freed from works by God is now being falsely instructed by tyrants who do not draw from the word of God. This state of things informs Luther's dramatic critique of that tyrannical authority which attempts to impose itself on the Christian conscience. In order to have full expression of Christian freedom, the state of captivity that exists under the Roman Catholic Church must end.

The Patriarchal Captivity

According to Mary Daly, the defining reality for women is the captivity of the foreground. This reality is what she calls the sado-society, a society fabricated by patriarchy which attempts to define and control all women. This is the reality against which women struggle, and the more they Realize their Selves the more struggle ensues. She calls for an

> exorcism of the internalized patriarchal presence, which carries with it feelings of guilt, inferiority, and self-hatred that extends itself to other women. It means recognition that women are in a real sense possessed by a demonic power within the psyche—the masculine subject within—that reduces the self to an object.[33]

Exorcism is necessary because the foreground is a demonic presence that possesses women. Patriarchy is "society manufactured and controlled by males"[34] and as such it manufactures and controls women. They are held captive and are rewarded for keeping themselves and others under control.

The paradigmatic woman enslaved to the sadostate is the token-torturer who is the ultimate instrument of the captors. These are women who buy in to the necrophilic system of patriarchy and pass on the ideals and wisdom that it implants in them. This is the extreme of internalizing the patriarchal presence, the extreme of captivity. Women as token torturers serve "the interests of fixers, framers, rakes and rippers, drones, and snools who applaud and promote such scenarios, such scapegoating."[35] The danger lies not only in the captivity of these women and the ways that they set out to enslave other women, but also in the ways that their presence obscures the identity of the real torturers. They are just tokens.[36]

Captivity under patriarchy threatens the freedom of women in physical as well as spiritual ways. As a system, patriarchy is described as "the prevailing religion of the entire planet, whose essential message is necrophilia."[37] In *Gyn/Ecology* Daly wrote "to expose the atrocities perpetrated against women under patriarchy on a planetary scale and to show the profound connections among these Goddess-murdering atrocities."[38] The atrocities she exposes include things like footbinding in China and genital mutilation in Africa. The book moves through example after example of

---

33. Daly, *Beyond God the Father*, 50.
34. Daly, *Wickedary*, 87.
35. Daly, *Pure Lust*, 71.
36. Daly, *Wickedary*, 231.
37. Ibid., 88.
38. Daly, *Gyn/Ecology*, xxv.

systems of thought and practice that seek to destroy and control women. It spirals around the globe and throughout time to expose rituals of what she calls the patriarchal religion. This is the exorcism she calls for, intending both the actual meaning of confronting and expelling demons and the presence of evil, as well as the metaphorical meaning of confronting and getting rid of ideas and thoughts that support and perpetuate the evil system.

The threat inherent in this patriarchal captivity is very real. However, Daly insists that the Self remains, even though it is captive, and this is the "Original core of one's being that cannot be contained within the State of Possession; living spirit/matter: the psyche that participates in Be-ing."[39] Because of this inner freedom, the struggle against captivity is driven to a revolution against the foreground itself. The patriarchal captivity cannot and will not have the last word for Daly. The struggle against the captors brings women together into a community, a covenant, a sisterhood.

Notes on Captivity

In discussing the problem of captivity, both Luther and Daly examine the use and misuse of rituals. Both the Roman church which Luther criticizes and the patriarchal foreground which Daly criticizes attempt to control and manipulate through their ritual systems. The church fabricates sacraments that they say give life and forgiveness, while patriarchy sacralizes rituals that enact physical destruction on women's bodies. Both Luther and Daly expose these systems as fraudulent and in doing so reduce the power of the captors. For both reformers, the metaphor of captivity was the specific idea that expressed their criticism of institutions that impeding human freedom. They use historical and practical references as evidence of this captivity: just as Babylon was the evil empire that took the Israelites captive, now Rome is the evil empire that takes Christian conscience captive; patriarchy was the evil system that bound the feet of women and mutilated their genitals, now women remain captive to a foreground that limits their freedom in physical, mental, and spiritual ways. Captivity is very acute for the two reformers, and the state of emergency which both perceive compels them to seek immediate change and articulate alternatives. Both Luther and Daly are ultimately driven to and by a vision of a community of equals, a utopian ideal of how the world should be.

39. Daly, *Wickedary*, 95.

Community

The utopian visions of each reformer reveal the hopes that sustain the individual even while in a state of captivity and a state of emergency. Both Luther and Daly have in their reforming theologies a sense of what type of community is possible and necessary, given the radical freedom of the human being. This is the place where freedom is fully realized, and captivity is overcome. However, as is often the case with idealistic visions, these communities are far from fully realized or realizable.

Christian Community

Service to the neighbor is the key to understanding Luther's ideas about community. Ideally, the Christian who is justified by God is freed from false notions concerning works as a means for salvation and happily does good works in service to the neighbor:

> Therefore he should be guided in all his works by this thought and contemplate this one thing along, that he may serve and benefit others in all that he does, considering nothing except the need and advantage of his neighbor.[40]

This vision of relations among Christians suggests a community wherein each person only looks out for the well-being of others. This is only possible because each individual is freed from worry about himself. The model of interpersonal relations in this Christian community is made possible by God and is an ideal which Luther holds up as the highest vision of what it is to be Christian.

Even caring for oneself is only done insofar as it aids the further service of others. Luther here articulates a radical selflessness that brings together the two natures of humans: the outer enfleshed person is brought under control so it can do the work of the justified inner spiritual person. The justified inner spiritual person's work is to serve the neighbor:

> This is what makes caring for the body a Christian work, that through its health and comfort we may be able to work, to acquire, and lay by funds with which to aid those who are in need . . . bearing one another's burdens and so fulfilling the law of Christ. This is a truly Christian life. Here faith is truly active through love,

---

40. Luther, "Freedom of a Christian" (1520), in *LW* 31:365.

that is, it finds expression in works of the freest service, cheerfully and lovingly done . . .[41]

This vision of a "truly Christian life" creates the community of persons who live merely for others, not for themselves. Luther insisted that Christians should seek to embody this life, basing his call on the words of Paul in his letters to the Galatians and the Philippians. Faith is not merely about trust in God, for Luther, because it is also active in love. Love of others is therefore a consequence of grace from God.

Because this community was a not-yet fully realized entity, and because Luther still understood that the Christian was bound to life in the temporal realm, he instructed Christians on the purpose of the law as part of what it meant to live in this world among papists and nonChristians. It also reveals his vision of what a community of "real Christians" would look like:

> If all the world were composed of real Christians, that is, true believers, there would be no need for or benefits from prince, king, lord, sword, or law. They would serve no purpose, since Christians have in their heart the Holy Spirit, who both teaches and makes them do injustice to no one, to love everyone, and to suffer injustice and even death willingly and cheerfully at the hands of anyone.[42]

Real Christians love everyone and suffer for others and even happily die for their neighbors. "Real Christians" are not alone in the world, however; in fact Luther suggests that there are not many "real Christians" in the world. This is the basis for his affirming both the spiritual kingdom as well as the temporal kingdom. Because the world is not in fact full of "real Christians," the law continues to serve a purpose to subject the body and to control the desires of the outer person. All human beings remain sinful, like the ignorant beast, and therefore need constant direction. That direction comes from God, like the rider of the beast, whether by means of the gospel or by means of temporal law and rulers.

Luther understood how idealistic his proposal was, and how rare the real Christian was. This pragmatic admission again reinforces the role of

---

41. Ibid., 365.
42. Luther, "Temporal Authority: To What Extent it Should Be Obeyed" (1523), in *LW* 45:89.

the temporal order and the secular law, because the spiritual law would not be able to effectively rule over the masses. He warns the temporal rulers:

> But take heed and first fill the world with real Christians before you attempt to rule it in a Christian and evangelical manner. This you will never accomplish; for the world and the masses are and always will be un-Christian, even if they are all baptized and Christian in name. Christians are few and far between.[43]

This warning shows the power and radicalism of his vision of an authentic Christian community. He recognized that such individuals are few and far between. But, because he had such a clear idea of who they are, what they would do, and how the world would be if it were full of them, he was painfully aware of how much it was not.

For these reasons, Luther involved himself in national political issues like a proposed church council, as well as several local political issues like public support for schools and education. He wrote a treatise to the Christian nobility of the German nation in 1520 with twenty-seven propositions on how they might in fact become better rulers of the nation. In doing so he wrote a thorough critique of papal claims to authority, attacking what he called the "three walls" that supported their claims. He wrote in 1524 to encourage the councilmen of Germany to maintain and support schools. Luther understood that some parents did not and some parents could not educate their children at home, and he understood the importance of education as a matter of the community's welfare. He preached a sermon in 1530 on the merits of keeping children in school. So while his vision of what a community of real Christians would look like was clear and powerful, and formed the goal toward which he worked, his concerns for practical temporal matters, basic survival, and communal well-being remained.

Luther's central focus however was always theological and specifically Christological. Everything that he said about how the individual ought to live in freedom, and about how the community ought to operate in terms of the relations among participants was for one reason: to follow the example of Christ. He insists that "Just as he himself did all things for us, not seeking his own good but ours only—and in this he was most obedient to God the Father—so he desires that we also should set the same

---

43. Ibid., 91.

example for our neighbors."⁴⁴ Further, freedom itself both comes from the justification achieved by Christ, and is modeled on the freedom that Christ had in his own life, "subject to none of the vices or sins to which all other men are subject."⁴⁵ Individual Christians are to be servants for one another in the same way that Christ was a servant for all of humanity. This radical selflessness is the fundamental characteristic of the ideal Christian community for Luther.

Luther's ideal Christian community here, however, is only for Christians and excludes all who are not Christian, or even all who are not "real Christians." Because of his intense focus on the gospel and on Christ, he ignores or eliminates all non-Christians in his utopian vision. So what about those who are not Christian? Luther's community of equals seems to have no place for them. We might even want to ask him what a "real Christian" is, and though he admits that there are very few of them in reality, he gives no indication as to how one finds these people. Probably only God can determine who real Christians are, and probably for Luther that is all that matters.

Feminist Community

Mary Daly's ideal community includes the "Race of Elemental be-ing: . . . the Elemental kinship of all Biophilic creatures, of all who participate in the Prance of Life."⁴⁶ This Race is composed of women, animals, Elemental creatures, Fore-Crones, and sisters in a cosmic covenant. Her utopian vision is creative and amusing, but is also politically savvy and radically feminist.

In the Background realm, women and Wild creatures come together in a life-affirming gathering. Daly describes her companions in the process of writing her *Wickedary*, including ducks, toads, cardinals, "and a special spider who said her Name was Sarah."⁴⁷ Daly's vision is fanciful, as she communicates with her Familiars, especially Ms. Wild Cat to whom readers are introduced as the author of the "cat/egorical" appendix to *Pure Lust*, "an allegory written by and for cats and their friends."⁴⁸ In the preliminary

---

44. Luther, "Two Kinds of Righteousness" (1519), in *LW* 31:300.
45. Ibid., 301.
46. Daly, *Wickedary*, 90.
47. Ibid., xv.
48. Daly, *Pure Lust*, 412–17.

"webs" or chapters for the *Wickedary*, she describes the animals' parade as a group of travelers embarks on the Intergalactic Journey into the Heart of the text:

> Instead of marching, the animals parade in different styles. They tumble, hop, leap, gallop, crawl, scamper. Some twirl widdershins as they walk. As the land animals parade on the edge of the sea, the sea animals swim alongside them. These dive and jump with joy.[49]

And so the parade continues with dolphins, birds, and butterflies. The collection also includes Elemental creatures like gnomes, pixies, and sprites. This imaginative scene begins to convey the sort of peaceable kingdom that Daly envisions existing in the Background.

Daly's ideal community consists not just of a harmony between women and animals, but also of a connection across generations to women in the past and women in the future. In addition to her affinity for Matilda Joslyn Gage noted earlier, she describes the presence of other historically significant women in this Journey into the *Wickedary*. This includes Sojourner Truth, Joan of Arc, Mary Wollstonecraft, Sappho, the Bronte sisters, and Rachel Carson among others. Transcending time and space, Journeys into the Background unify all Original Women into one community of Crones and Fore-Crones. This is possible because of what she names

> **Women's Space**: Space created by women who choose to separate our Selves from the State of Servitude: FREE SPACE; Space in which women actualize Archimagical Powers, releasing the flow of Gynergy; Space in which women Spin and Weave, creating cosmic tapestries; Space in which women find Rooms, Looms, Brooms of our Own.[50]

Intentionally playing on Virginia Woolf's longing for a room of her own, the desire of many early feminists and fore-crones, Daly understands its necessity and includes it within her vision of the Background community. Women's Space therefore is the location of her community of equals.

Daly envisions relationships among women in the foreground world as empowered by the Background. In discussions of sisterhood early in the

---

49. Daly, *Wickedary*, 53.
50. Ibid., 101.

1970s, she describes the origination of community: "The moving center which is the energy source of the new sisterhood as exodus community is the promise in ourselves. It is the promise in our foremothers whose history we are beginning to discover, and in our sisters whose voices have been stolen from them."[51] Forming community begins with tapping in to a source of energy that connects women to their own Selves and to their ancestors. This is an allusion to the Background as existential energy source. The connection to foremothers and to sisters is through their promises and energy, all of which is conducted through the Background, despite captivity in the foreground. The center of this community is moving, dynamic, and rushing like waters under the surface.

Daly understands that women continue to live in the foreground. She knows that women cannot actually live elsewhere than on this planet, despite her fanciful descriptions of other worlds. So, she describes a departure that fits the situation:

> We can depart mentally to some extent by refusing to be blinded by society's myths. We can depart physically and socially to a degree also. . . . The adequate exodus requires communication, community, and creation.[52]

A mental departure is first, while some physical and social departure from this foreground world is also possible. Daly's work is the very creative communication that she calls for. It is one venue through which women can escape, can journey away from and separate themselves from patriarchal reality. This is how women discover community; she said that they do not "form" it, because they are finding what is already there. The covenant that is sisterhood for her is a "profound agreement that is found."[53]

Her use of the term sisterhood was consistent with second-wave feminism, the movement in which her work represented the leading radical edge. Also consistent with the early 1970s political discussions about feminist utopian ideals, Daly was inevitably confronted with the question: what about men? On this question, there seems to be a shift in her position over the course of decades that will be discussed in depth in a later chapter, but she remained consistent throughout her work in her focus on the life and well-being of women. Early in her writing, seen in the 1973

---

51. Daly, *Beyond God the Father*, 158.
52. Ibid., 158.
53. Ibid., 159.

Beyond God the Father, Daly insisted that women and men inhabit different worlds: "Even though these are profoundly related emotionally, physically, economically, socially, there is a wall that is visible to those who almost have managed to achieve genuine interplanetary communication with the opposite sex."[54] But, because she insists that the covenant of sisterhood is one that is found, not formed, men can in fact find themselves in this space and therefore become part of the covenant. "The cosmic covenant means coming into living harmony with the self, the universe, and God."[55] Liberation for all "requires the breakdown of the obstacle to the flow of life within the divided self, the wall of the opposition of opposites. But it should not be forgotten that our situations are not the same."[56] What men and women need to do to be liberated is radically different, and she insists that men must first learn to listen before they can learn a new way of speaking. For Daly, this early discussion provided space in the covenant for men who are willing to learn to listen. She doubts that many want to, however.

In her later work, the nature of the discussion changes. No longer does she discuss women's liberation (a decidedly 1970s phrase) and whether or not men can participate. In the *Wickedary* fourteen years later in 1987, Daly defines Sisterhood:

> **Sisterhood** *n*: authentic bonding of women who Biophilically affirm individual freedom and Originality, refuse tokenism, and actively give primal loyalty to women. *Compare* **brotherhood**.[57]

> **brotherhood** *n*: transitory and shallow substitute for Friendship; condition dependent on emergencies, violence, and the existence of The Enemy; male merging in the communal "ecstasy" of self-loss; bonding of those who are malfunctioning/male-functioning as cells in a military organism: necrophilic comradeship.[58]

The reason for and focus of sisterhood is women, and it is based on the bonding of women. Active loyalty is to women. Men are simply not a factor in the discussion. Daly draws sharper distinctions between the worlds of men and women through her descriptions of their respective communi-

54. Ibid., 172.
55. Ibid., 173.
56. Ibid., 173.
57. Daly, *Wickedary*, 96.
58. Ibid., 186.

ties here. It is a further contextual note that the definition of brotherhood in the 1987 *Wickedary* reflects a rejection of the growing militarism in the middle of the Cold War Reagan-era defense build-up.

Notes on Community

Luther and Daly have such a keen sense of the captivity of the human being that they both rely heavily on a utopian vision of a community of equals as a survival strategy. This vision serves as mental escape and spiritual promise. For Luther it takes the form of the kingdom of God, and for Daly it takes the form of the Background, for both perhaps it is a peaceable kingdom. Because they are both reforming theologians compelled by their sense of authentic human freedom, they both seem to believe that if the obstacles were removed, all would live happily ever after. However, both of them are ultimately limited in their visions: They deliberately exclude classes of people from their utopian communities. Can there be a happy ever after when some are left out? Perhaps it is the leaving out of the others that creates a utopia. Is escape from the problem through a purification of the human community a good thing? This potential limitation of their visions will be explored in a later chapter, but must be noted here as a factor in these reforming visions of the community freed from captivity.

Parallels, Differences, Inversions

After reflecting on the theological anthropology of Martin Luther and Mary Daly individually, specific parallels, differences, and inversions in their understandings of what it means to be human emerge. Both have a keen sense that freedom constitutes the core of human existence, and both take seriously the captive state in which human beings currently exist. The context for their work remains radically different, thus the differences and inverted direction of some comparable ideas can be explained.

Parallel: Political Commentary and Exclusion

Luther's and Daly's visions of the ideal community both serve as political commentary insofar as they highlight what is wrong with the current power structure. In proposing how the human community *should* look, they suggest that how it currently exists is how it should *not* look. Each vision is firmly grounded in the cultural and religious context out of which it emerges. What Luther wanted was based on scripture and was contrasted with the church and the world of his experience. This is the reason for his focus on Christians and his exclusion of non-Christians. What Daly wanted was based on her intuition of be-ing and was contrasted with the destruction of women that was in the world of her experience. This is the reason for her focus on women and her exclusion of men. These utopian visions are also part of why each found himself/herself in conflict with the prevailing power structure of their day. Their visions threatened the power of specific institutions: Luther saw no need for exclusive clerical rights; Daly saw no need for exclusive male rights. Each reformer was in fact a threat to business as usual for those whom they criticized. They named captivity where they saw it, and called for a radically new way of being human and being in community. In context, their theologies were sharp political commentaries.

In addition, both reformers end up excluding an entire class of people from their communities. Why this should be the case raises interesting questions about the nature of utopian visions: Must they include everyone? What is their purpose? Luther and Daly perhaps leave a bit of room for everyone to be included (anyone can become Christian in Luther's mind, and if men can tune their consciences to the Background they might be welcome participants to Daly), but both seem relatively unconcerned with that because of their intense focus on one community of people. The purpose of these utopian visions is clearly to give an ideal toward which all can work. It is also to criticize extant reality by counterexample. In those goals, they succeed.

Difference: Dangers in Captivity

Luther was relentlessly focused on the spiritual life of human beings. Captivity for him was almost entirely a mental and spiritual reality. Daly was relentlessly focused on the actual concrete lives of women. Captivity for her included the mental limitations, but included the real physical dangers that constantly surrounded women in patriarchy. In this way, we can see that Daly's focus on actual experience in this world is very different than Luther's focus on eternal salvation and right relationship with God. Because of their different contexts and different status in those contexts, they have very different concerns. Luther was a priest and pastor in a Christian nation concerned about the Christian soul and the common good. Daly was a feminist activist in a male-dominated world concerned about the physical safety and well-being of all women. Even their discussion of rituals shows this notable difference: Luther writes about the sacraments of the Roman church and how they get in the way of a Christian's relationship with God; Daly writes about how women's feet and genitals have been mutilated to meet a male-imposed standard, how women have been killed because the patriarchal power structure declared them to be witches and threats to the community, and how the rape of women is legitimated by patriarchy and Christian myths. There is a major qualitative difference here in the types of dangers faced by the human beings with which Luther and Daly were concerned.

Inversion: Self and the Turn Inward/Outward

In Luther's ideal Christian community, individuals are enabled to live for the well-being of others because they are freed from having to focus only on themselves. In Daly's ideal feminist community, women are enabled to live for themselves because they are freed from having to focus only on others. Luther envisions a radical selflessness while Daly envisions a radical subjectivity. Luther's radical turn of the self outward and Daly's radical turn of the self inward are inverted expressions of the same thing: They both challenging the dominant theological understanding of what it means to be human, but in doing so they turn the focus of the human person in opposite directions.

In the church Luther was reforming, he saw a mistaken focus on works as a means to gain salvation for oneself and an emphasis on doing the right things for personal righteousness. This was a mistaken focus on the self. Because he re-emphasized with Paul that justification and righteousness come only from the grace of God through Christ, this inward-looking focus was all wrong and destructive for the soul. The Christian, freed from self-justification, was now able to focus outward on the neighbor. Ideally, everyone would be Christian, and would focus on everyone other than themselves, thereby bringing the fully egalitarian spiritual community into existence. In reality, everyone was not Christian and all Christians lived in the temporal world, so Luther wrote some about how to live subject to law and order.

In the world Daly was reforming, she saw that women were encouraged to only focus on others and their concerns. This was a mistaken focus on others. Because she understood the difference between false foreground fixations and real Background memories, this outward looking focus was all wrong and quite destructive for the soul. Women, freed from potted passions and plastic reality, were able to tap deeper into the reservoir of energy that they already knew. Ideally, everyone would fall into this freedom from the foreground, would focus on their own connections to life and each other, and would exist together in a biophilic realm of be-ing. In reality, women live in the foreground and so Daly wrote about strategies for survival and living on the margins.

Because Luther and Daly reclaimed the freedom inherent to being human, each saw that it existed in a state of captivity, and each worked with a vision of the community as it ought to be. In doing this, both present a reforming theological anthropology. The power of their visions of what it is to be human brought each into direct conflict with and into a deep criticism of that-which-gets-in-the-way: the institutionalized authority.

5

Institutional Authority
Corruption and Confusion

> *Recognizing that deep damage has been inflicted upon consciousness under phallocracy's myths and institutions, we continue to Name patriarchy as the perverted paradigm and source of other social evils.*[1]

> *Therefore the papacy is a veritable torture chamber of consciences and the very kingdom of the devil.*[2]

Because of the radical freedom illumined by each theologian's anthropology, both Mary Daly and Martin Luther have very specific critiques of the institution which hampers that freedom. For Daly, the problem is patriarchy; for Luther, the problem is the papacy. The comments above reveal how both understand the severity of the damage and torture inflicted upon the consciousness or the conscience, and how the institution is the source of evil and the kingdom of the devil. In addition, Daly defines a priest in her Wickedary as "a member of any of the hierarchies/liararchies of patriarchy"[3] and Luther claims at one point that "the ignorance of the papists has been revealed."[4] Focusing on their criticisms of institutional authority further reveals their brilliant and provocative use of language as each works to define and describe the enemy as vividly as possible.

Basic definitions and descriptions of the institutions that Daly and Luther criticize reveal fundamental characteristics of their theological criticisms. Daly defines patriarchy at length as

---

1. Daly, *Pure Lust*, xii.
2. Luther, "Commentary on Galatians 4:7," in *LW* 26:386
3. Daly, *Wickedary*, 220.
4. Luther, "A Sincere Admonition by Martin Luther" (1522), in *LW* 45:69.

> **patriarchy** n 1: society manufactured and controlled by males: FATHERLAND; society in which every legitimate institution is entirely in the hands of males and a few selected henchwomen; society characterized by oppression, repression, depressions, narcissism, cruelty, racism, classism, ageism, objectification, sadomasochism, necrophilia; joyless society, ruled by Godfather, Son, and Company; society fixated on proliferation, propagation, procreation, and bent on the destruction of all Life **2**: the prevailing religion of the entire planet, whose essential message is necrophilia.[5]

The problem of patriarchy defined by her is not just that it is male-dominated society; the problem is that it is the paradigm for and root of all evil enacted on a daily basis. With the same intense criticism, Luther understood the papacy as blasphemous because "one pope after the other . . . set himself up as the supreme head and light of Christendom."[6] For him, the "light" of the papacy and the pope

> shone like manure in a lantern. He, the chief and archheretic, hid the Gospel and buried it under a bushel. In its place he filled and flooded the world with his filth, stench, and dirty mess, that is, with his false and devilish doctrine, his loathsome decrees and decretals, his gross idolatry, his abomination, and with innumerable sects and schismatic spirits. All this he prescribed as necessary for salvation.[7]

The problem of the papacy described by Luther is not just the pope misusing power; the problem is the fundamental corruption of the gospel that it enacts on a daily basis. Side-by-side, these definitions show that Daly and Luther first have criticisms about what the institution is ("necrophilic"; "manure in a lantern"), and then about what it does (fixates on proliferation and procreation; fills the world with filth and "devilish doctrine"). By looking in depth at their critical assessment of institutional authority, examining both what the institution is and what it does, parallel tones and methods of criticism emerge, an inverse assessment of the overarching reality takes shape, and different assumptions and concerns regarding words and rituals are revealed.

---

5. Daly, *Wickedary*, 87–88.
6. Luther, "Commentary on The Gospel of St. John," in *LW* 22:58.
7. Ibid.

What It Is

Daly's definition of patriarchy identifies it as the root of all social injustice including "oppression, repression, depressions, narcissism, cruelty, racism, classism, ageism, objectification, sadomasochism, necrophilia."[8] This is the heart of the matter for her criticism of the institution: it is about the many ways that patriarchy oppresses and represses. Luther's description of the papacy suggests that the heart of the matter for him is that the Gospel is hidden and buried out of reach from all people. He sets out to use the Gospel to prove the papacy wrong in its doctrines and prescriptions for salvation. In the same way, there is nothing good in patriarchy, and nothing good comes from the papacy. A difference in focus already emerges, where Daly focuses much on physical human experiences of oppression and rejection, Luther focuses mostly on spiritual experience and salvation.

Patriarchy: The Root of All Evil

Daly's judgment that patriarchy is the root of all evil is criticized by other scholars, as we will see, but she continues to argue that it simply has multiple ways by which it dulls the intuition of life and perverts reality. Her intense focus on gender oppression may ultimately lead to a limitation of her work, but it also provides clarity to her analysis.

In Daly's early work she identifies sexism and sexist institutions as the source of harm for women and articulates a desire to reform some of those institutions. In her later work, she maintains the criticism in a much sharper and less charitable fashion. Throughout her first book in 1968, *The Church and the Second Sex*, she engages in rigorous analysis of biblical texts, philosophical treatises, and church history to show the way that all of these forces come together to make "it seem that the sociological fact of woman's subordination was inscribed in the heavens."[9] Daly incorporated and built on the then-relatively recent work of Simone deBeauvoir. DeBeauvoir wrote in 1949 about the ways that "woman" has been constructed as and understood to be "the second sex." She insisted that "it is civilization as a whole that produces this creature . . . which is described as feminine."[10] The notion that gender was socially constructed served as a

---

8. Daly, *Wickedary*, 88.
9. Daly, *The Church and the Second Sex*, 63.
10. deBeauvoir, *The Second Sex*, 267.

crucial jumping off point for much of the feminist analysis in subsequent generations, and it is where Daly began.

Nearly twenty years after deBeauvoir, Daly described views of women throughout history as "a record of contradictions."[11] This is a mild description of the problem in comparison to her later discussion of patriarchal society and its mechanisms. However, in this early work she provided a straightforward description of what she called "obstacles to theological development":

> Kept in ignorance of theology and canon law and of the political realities of the Church, women have until recently lacked even an awareness of their own situation. When questions did arise, they were intimidated by their lack of knowledge from challenging the situation of subservience imposed upon them. This is to some extent still true.[12]

This very basic description of how the Church holds and maintains power through controlling access to knowledge gives a clear sense of how the institution works against women. Keeping women ignorant serves to prevent them from asking questions about their situation, which would inevitably lead to asking questions about those who are in power. Since they are systematically denied access to both knowledge and power, women are kept out of decision-making positions. This occurred in Daly's lifetime as women were prevented access to higher education in theology and philosophy, barred from official church leadership positions, and prohibited full legal status in society.

At this point in her career, Daly articulates some hope that the Church would recognize the evils of sexism and act as an agent for change. Her hope is evident in the closing sentence of *The Church and The Second Sex*:

> Men and women, using their best talents, forgetful of self and intent upon the work, will with God's help mount together toward a higher order of consciousness and being, in which the alienating projections will have been defeated and wholeness, psychic integrity, achieved.[13]

Defeating the alienating forces is the goal, and it seems like a tangible reality at this stage of her work. This early proposal already had a deep sense

11. Daly, *The Church and the Second Sex*, 74.
12. Ibid., 190.
13. Ibid., 223.

of the way in which the institution was part of the problem. Here, she identifies God as an agent for change and one who may help all people, men and women, achieve psychic integrity.

However, Daly quickly moved beyond God in her analysis of institutional authority. By the time her second book, *Beyond God the Father*, emerged in 1973, the church was identified as merely one facet of the overarching religion of the planet: patriarchy:

> The entire conceptual systems of theology and ethics, developed under the conditions of patriarchy, have been the products of males and tend to serve the interests of sexist society.[14]

Patriarchy is thus named as the overarching systemic evil that is the cause of all other evils; theology and the church exist under this male-produced umbrella and therefore serve the interests of sexism. In this move, she locates "the problem" as beyond just the church, and even "beyond God the father." The problem is patriarchy, an ideology based on "an artificial polarization of human qualities" according to sexist stereotyping.[15]

Daly suggests then that patriarchy merely uses religion and theology to legitimate itself. Her analysis of the Christian myth of the Fall reveals how this occurs:

> In a real sense the projection of guilt upon women is patriarchy's Fall, the primordial lie. Together with its offspring—the theology of "original sin"—the myth reveals the "fall" of religion into the role of patriarchy's prostitute.[16]

Daly claims from this point forward in her work that the real problem lies with the institution of patriarchy. Religion merely serves as its whore. Original sin is found in what she calls the sexual caste system, not in some primordial choice in paradise. This caste system comes from patriarchal ideology and infects every institution that patriarchy controls, including religion.

In describing sexist institutions, Daly proposes a general categorization of various ways through which they co-opt women's energy and distract them from the real problem of this sexual caste system. The categories of institutions include obviously sexist antifeminine organizations, which

---

14. Daly, *Beyond God the Father*, 4.
15. Ibid., 15.
16. Ibid., 47.

women are to avoid at all costs. In this category Daly gives an example of an organization that worked specifically to oppose the right of women to vote in Switzerland. There are also institutions that are explicitly sexist but are not defined by it, and about which women must decide if any merits outweigh the sexism. The Catholic church might fall into either one of these first two categories; it is obviously sexist in that it bars women from full participation in leadership and seeks to control their lives and reproductive capability. At the same time, its theological emphasis on love and life with God need not be sexist. Institutions like this have potential for change, but she cautions women to not expend too much energy in bringing about this change.

Then she notes institutions whose sexism is "indirect and implicit," like the American college or university. For these organizations or institutions, sexism is not acknowledged or overtly stated, but it exists as part of the culture. Finally, she identifies countercultural institutions that actually say they are for liberation and for the oppressed, but which focus "all their attention upon some deformity within patriarchy—for example, racism, war, poverty—rather than patriarchy itself, without recognizing sexism as root and paradigm of the various forms of oppression they seek to eradicate."[17] Daly insists in this discussion that any institution in patriarchal society is always patriarchal, so women are best counseled to live on the margins of that institution and that society.

As evident in the example of these countercultural institutions, Daly places gender as the prime category of analysis for social injustices, including racism and poverty. She sees race and class oppression as real, but as mere expressions of the ideology of patriarchy. One specific example that she gives to show this is the black liberation movement in the United States, including the Southern Christian Leadership Conference (led by Martin Luther King Jr.), which was "wholly male dominated," and the Nation of Islam movement (led by Elijah Muhammed).[18] These groups are expressly for the liberation of oppressed people, but Daly points out that they ignore the problem of sexism. She refers to particular black women whose voices in those movements have been largely ignored, women who "proclaim links between racism and sexism."[19] Pauli Murray, Angela Davis,

---

17. Ibid., 55–56.
18. Ibid., 163.
19. Ibid., 164.

and Florynce Kennedy are three black feminist activists whom she names here as being largely ignored in the movements for black liberation.

Eventually, Daly was challenged by other scholars who suggested that she had a limited view of the complex nature of social injustice, especially in the nexus of race, class, and gender oppressions. The now famous interchange between Daly and Audre Lorde centered around precisely this issue. In 1979, Lorde wrote an open letter to Mary Daly in response to Daly's third book, *Gyn/Ecology: The Metaethics of Radical Feminism*. Lorde challenged Daly's use of goddesses and myths that were only "white, western european, judeo-christian."[20] She pushed further than just Daly's scholarship and methodology, however, to probe the nature of racism in feminism more broadly:

> I ask that you be aware of how this serves the destructive forces of racism and separation between women—the assumption that the herstory and myth of white women is the legitimate and sole herstory of all women . . . [D]ifferences expose all women to various forms and degrees of patriarchal oppression, some of which we share and some of which we do not. . . . [B]eyond sisterhood is still racism.[21]

Lorde points out what she sees as Daly's blind spot: there are forms of difference beyond gender that have real and oppressive effects on women's lives.

An account of what happened after this letter was published is provided by Daly in her 2006 book *Amazon Grace*. She describes there that she wrote a letter responding to Audre Lorde in 1979, several months after reading Lorde's open letter. This was not acknowledged or made public until Lorde's biographer, Alexis DeVeaux, found the letter among other papers after Lorde's death. DeVeaux contacted Daly about her letter in June 2003, and sent her a copy. Daly reprints her own letter to Lorde in *Amazon Grace*. In the 1979 letter, she acknowledged that there was no simple response to the issues Lorde raised, that "you most definitely do have a point," and that she hopes that they can look forward together, "constantly expanding the vision."[22] At the end of the letter, she offered to meet with Lorde and talk in person at an upcoming conference. In

20. Lorde, "An Open Letter to Mary Daly," 67.
21. Ibid., 69–70.
22. Daly, *Amazon Grace*, 25–26.

2006, it is clear that Daly is primarily concerned with setting the historical record of their interaction straight. She felt for decades that her work was one-sidedly condemned by those who only read Lorde's criticism, widely anthologized in readers and collections of feminist writings, and not Daly's work or her subsequent response to Lorde. Regardless of her intent in printing the letter in her book, it does show that Daly in 1979 saw at least some truth in Lorde's challenge to include sources beyond the western, European, and Judeo-Christian, and that she articulated a hope for women working together for future justice. Some of her work throughout the 1980s and 1990s did attempt to be more inclusive of race and class oppression among women, but she remained ultimately convinced that patriarchy was the root source and main model of unjust relations.

So while Daly's definition of patriarchy includes the basic "rule of the father" meaning of the term patriarchy, it expands on that and includes all forms of social injustice under its influence. Where her concept and her analysis can still be challenged is precisely where Audre Lorde started: Do all women suffer equally under the rule of men? Is racism always a product of patriarchy? Is classism solely a product of male domination? Complex and nuanced analysis of the interplay between race, class, gender, sexuality, and other categories of socially constructed identity shows that there is rarely one category that supersedes all others when it comes to oppression of the other. For this reason, Daly's essentialist focus on gender remains a possible limitation to her work.

Papacy: Hiding and Blaspheming the Gospel

Defining the institution that is the problem for Martin Luther is relatively easy. The papacy is the system wherein the pope is the head of the Roman Church as successor to Peter, an institution claimed to have been established by Jesus as recorded in the gospel of Matthew. Explaining *why* it is the problem is Luther's main task. He relies on scripture to do this because of his consistent methodological insistence that everything valid for Christian life must be established on the basis of scripture alone.

Luther demonstrates at great length that in fact the papacy was not based on scripture. He revisits this theme in multiple places in his sermons, in his exegetical work, and in polemical treatises, insisting that the Roman church's interpretation of Matthew 16 is "the pope's first rascality and blasphemy against God's holy words."²³ In Luther's original German he used the words *"die erste Spitzbuberei des Papstes und Gottes Lasterung in seinen heiligen Worten"*²⁴ (the first rascality of the papists in blaspheming God in his holy word). From this first *Spitzbuberei*, rascality or roguishness, in exegeting the text, he says that the papists build and strengthen their evil institution in ways that are destructive for the Christian conscience. Luther engages in careful exegesis of his own to show how this passage, when read in concert with other passages in scripture, does not effectively establish the authority of the papacy and does not effectively show that Jesus gave "the power of the keys," or the power to forgive sin, to Peter alone.

Luther interprets Matthew 16 with Matthew 18 and John 20, reading scripture in relationship to other scripture. The latter two passages, consistent with each other, not only outnumber the first but they and others support his contention that the power of the keys, or the power to forgive sins and distribute punishment, is in fact given to the whole community, not just to Peter as an individual. The passages in question are worth reading fully here to appreciate Luther's interpretation. First, the passage on which the Roman church claimed and continues to claim that the Petrine line of succession was established:

> And I tell you, you are Peter, and on this rock I will build my church, and the gates of Hades will not prevail against it. I will give you the keys of the kingdom of heaven, and whatever you bind on earth will be bound in heaven, and whatever you loose on earth will be loosed in heaven. (Matthew 16:18–20)

Then, the two passages with which Luther interprets the first:

> Truly I tell you, whatever you bind on earth will be bound in heaven, and whatever you loose on earth will be loosed in heaven. Again, truly I tell you, if two of you agree on earth about anything you ask, it will be done for you by my Father in heaven. For where two or three are gathered in my name, I am there among them. (Matthew 18:18–20)

> Jesus said to them again, "Peace be with you. As the Father has sent me, so I send you." When he had said this, he breathed on them and said to them, "Receive the Holy Spirit. If you forgive the sins

---

23. Luther, "Against the Roman Papacy," (1545) in *LW* 41:291.
24. Martin Luther, *Gesammelte Werke*, 1655. Translation mine.

of any, they are forgiven them; if you retain the sins of any, they are retained." (John 20:21–23)

Luther's very basic point was that in the second Matthew passage, and in the John passage, Jesus gives power to the community, to the gathered body of the faithful, and not just to one individual. As for the first Matthew passage, on which the papacy claims authority, Luther insists that "Peter received the keys not as Peter, but in place of the community."[25] Beyond this, Luther notes that the papacy seeks power to rule in addition to the power to forgive, clearly violating the text. He raises the important question of who on earth forgives the pope if and when he sins, and dismisses those who say that either the pope does not sin or that there is a difference between the person and the office.

What Luther emphasizes in his exegesis of these three texts is the power of the community: "The words of Christ are nothing but gracious promises to the whole community, given to all of Christendom."[26] He rejects the "Romanists" who insisted that power is given to Peter alone and his successors as individuals. Reading the three passages in concert with one another gave Luther the assurance that he had a fuller and more adequate understanding of God's word. The latter two texts reveal Jesus speaking basically the same words to a gathered group of disciples. In addition, Matthew 18 specifically states the necessity for a minimum of two people to do this work, and John 20 shows Jesus breathing the Spirit on all of the gathered disciples to whom he has appeared after his crucifixion. Luther highlights the communal nature of the audiences in these texts. Jesus' specific renaming of Simon as Peter in the Matthew 16 text was therefore not sufficient evidence to outweigh the clear intent of other texts to provide authority to the community of believers. Luther certainly did not believe that it carried enough scriptural weight to support the vast powers claimed by the papacy.

Not only did scripture simply not provide a basis for the papacy's authority, but Luther relies on scripture to criticize the institution itself: "For this light shines so powerfully before the eyes of the pope, bishops, cardinals, and other knaves that it reveals to them their own darkness."[27]

---

25. Luther, "On the Papacy in Rome" (1520), in *LW* 39:89.
26. Ibid., 90.
27. Luther, "Commentary on The Gospel of John," in *LW* 22:35.

For him, the Word pointed out how the papacy was wrong in the same way that Christ's light illumined and challenged darkness.

In addition, he uses this light imagery from the gospel of John to show how failing to attend properly to the Word of God brings tragic consequences: He warns that "the inevitable result of any disregard for God's Word is this, that the people will believe a lie to their own damnation . . . . For—God be merciful—who can say how many false lights were ignited in the papacy?"[28] Because the papacy was an institution which he believed lied to Christians, it lit "false lights" and was an agent of the devil, leading Christians to hell. Luther had deep concern for individuals who believed what they were taught by the institution, because those teachings were not based in scripture and they could lead to damnation. Not only was he concerned with exposing the false claims of the institution, he remained concerned with the spiritual well-being of Christians who were convinced to follow its lies.

Several times Luther appears to insist that if the papacy followed the Word of God, if it taught Christ, then he would find authority in it. In a sermon on the gospel of John he says "if they teach Christ properly, I, too, shall believe and trust her; for in Christ I know no sin, no error, no lie."[29] As a pastor and preacher, he took great care to establish the true source of authority, Christ as the Word of God. It was necessary then that anyone or any institution that adhered to it should be obeyed. God made known in Jesus Christ accessed through scripture is the true source of authority. The papacy could exist properly under it, but unfortunately it did not. This hope for its redemption may have been sincere since he occasionally acknowledged the harsh nature of some of his writings:

> But our heart is certainly not bitter or envious or vindictive against our opponents. On the contrary, there is in us a godly agitation and sorrow of spirit. I do not hate papists and other erring spirits in such a way that I invoke evil upon them or wish that they would perish. No, I would wish that they would return to the way and be saved together with us.[30]

This spirit of generosity is not always evident in Luther's writings on the papacy, but here in the midst of commentary on Paul's letter to the

---

28. Ibid., 58.
29. Ibid., 259.
30. Luther, "Commentary on Galatians 4:12," in *LW* 26:416.

Galatians, he indicates that if the papacy could operate under the true authority of Christ and God's word, then it too could "be saved" from its erring ways.

Ten years after this generous comment in his Galatians commentary, however, Luther writes his polemic "Against the Roman Papacy, An Institution of the Devil." This piece was written in 1545, the last year of his life, and seems to do away with any earlier optimistic Christian hope. He begins the polemical piece referring to the "Most Hellish Father" (*der aller hellischt Vater*) and throughout the piece referred to the pope as "Your Hellishness" (*ihr Hellischeit*).[31] In the treatise, Luther expresses outrage at the convening of a council in Trent that would be none of the things it should be: free, Christian, and German. The council would take place at the command of the pope "with the condition that no one attend except his own scum, the Epicureans and those agreeable to him."[32] Luther lambasts the council throughout the treatise, showing how it was not even consistent with the early councils of the church at Nicea and Constantinople that were convened not by popes but by emperors, and took place with representatives not only from the church but from outside of it.

Luther turns to personal insults in this treatise as he challenges not only the theological and scriptural basis for the council, but also the character of those charged with leading it:

> You are Epicurean sows, just like all the popes, your predecessors . . . . you and your children commit abominable unchastity, for the cardinals and the Sodomists and hermaphrodites of your court lead such horrible lives that heaven and earth quake and tremble before them. . . . thus it would be found that the pope and his cardinals are crude asses, unlearned in the Scriptures.[33]

He goes on to refer to the "pope of Sodomists," the "bishop of hermaphrodites," and the "*Huren- und Hermaphroditenkirche,*" church of whores and hermaphrodites.[34] The intent of all of these crude and belittling terms clearly was to mock and humiliate his adversaries. It is fairly clear throughout this treatise that the spirit of Christian generosity is all but gone, and that Luther imagines himself in a fight with an irredeemably evil and

---

31. German phrases from *WA* 54, 206–7, translation mine.
32. Luther, "Against the Roman Papacy" (1545), in *LW* 41:263.
33. Ibid., 287–88.
34. German phrase from *Gesammelte Werke*, 1657; translation mine.

corrupt enemy. His passionate defense is angry and makes extensive use of scatological rhetorical flourish to insult, illustrate atrocity, and invoke the truth of God's Word showing the falsity of the papal abominations. It is here that we finally see what Luther understood the papacy to be: blasphemous.

Notes on Root Issues

Daly's central criticism of patriarchy is that it is the root of all evil; Luther's central criticism of the papacy is that it is the greatest blasphemy ever perpetrated against Christianity. The root issues for both reformers are so vitally important that they bring out extremist rhetoric and impassioned defense of truths they see being covered and obscured. As each defines more and more clearly what the core problem of the institution is, each descends deeper into the layers of falsehoods that it has constructed. The criticisms leveled at patriarchy and the papacy are vast and sweeping because the stakes for both reformers are very high: basic human freedom is threatened. They both go on to examine how the respective institutions perpetrate their tyranny to expose the atrocities further.

What It Does

Examples of how patriarchy and the papacy imprison people with their lies can be found throughout the work of Daly and Luther. Daly describes "snooldom, the place/time where the air is filled with the crowing of cocks, the joking of jocks, the droning of clones, the sniveling of snookers and snudges, the noisy parades and processions of prickers."[35] Luther asks people to "listen and look first at what the pope teaches in his books, what poisonous and frightful doctrines are contained in the holy canon law, and what until the present time we have worshipped instead of the truth."[36] Both pay keen attention to what the institutions say and what they teach, along with what they do and what they insist that their followers do. Language and ritual, word and sacraments are central methods in the war on freedom identified by Daly and Luther. The institutions tell lies in order to create a false dependence on them, and then construct ritual reenactments of that dependence in order to solidify their power. Both

---

35. Daly, *Pure Lust*, 24.
36. Luther, "Why the Books of the Pope and His Disciples Were Burned" (1520), in *LW* 31:384.

understand here what sociologists of religion argue: myth and ritual go together to create a reality and foster participation in it. Emile Durkheim observed that "religious phenomena are naturally arranged in two fundamental categories: beliefs and rites. . . . It is possible to define the rite only after we have defined the belief."[37] Language as it reflects a set of beliefs and rituals as they reflect those beliefs are inextricably linked for Daly and Luther.

Language and Ritual in Patriarchy

LANGUAGE

Knowing the power of language, Daly notes the many ways that it is used by patriarchy and how it becomes another tool of deception and destruction: "Multi-leveled communication is of course not unknown to all men, but the rules of patriarchy try to write it out as much as possible."[38] She examines communication as a tool with which the institution of patriarchy maintains itself and its ideas. She also engages in manipulation of language herself to counter the institution and reclaim the freedom she insists had been lost.

Daly's work focuses on revealing the way that words effectively control not only women's minds but their bodies as well. In her 1978 book *Gyn/Ecology*, she focuses on the word which she adapted for the title as an example of how patriarchy uses language to its own ends: "The fact that most gynecologists are males is in itself a colossal comment on 'our' society. It is a symptom and example of male control over women and over language."[39] This is why she titles the text with that word, but changes the capitalization and writes it with a slash through the middle:

> I am using the term Gyn/Ecology very loosely, that is freely, to describe the science, that is the process of know-ing, of "loose" women who choose to be subjects and not mere objects of enquiry. Gyn/Ecology is by and about women a-mazing all the male-authored "sciences of womankind" and weaving world tapestries of our own kind.[40]

---

37. Durkheim, *The Elementary Forms of Religious Life*, 51.
38. Daly, *Beyond God the Father*, 151.
39. Daly, *Gyn/Ecology*, 9.
40. Ibid., 10.

In one move, she challenges not only the male dominated medical practice known as gynecology, but also the system in which it makes sense that men can be the scientists best trained in the study of women. The words themselves suggest the irony of the situation. This is for her one fundamental way in which patriarchy controls women, by making them objects about which someone other than a woman can be an expert. Their words are an obvious clue to this dangerous reality.

Words are like women for Daly, in that both are captive to patriarchy and have liberating potential within them. She describes "the patriarchal control of women's creativity" with which "our speech is curtailed by manners and lethal custom into polite, shallow verbiage."[41] Patriarchy uses words as tools for its false instruction, and she argues that it commits "verbicide, that is, 'deliberate distortion or destruction of the sense of a word.'"[42] The word "gynecology" is an example of this distortion of the sense of a word. Patriarchy commits verbicide: it kills words. Because of her equivocation of words and women, verbicide leads eventually to gynocide.

Daly's focus on how patriarchy uses words leads her to recover their power and use them for her own purposes: "But when we wield words to dis-close the inner beauty, the radiance of the Race of Lusty Women, we/they blaze open pathways to our Background/homeland."[43] Daly uses the image of the labrys, the two edged axe, extensively in her work to illustrate how women are simultaneously cutting away the falsehoods of patriarchy and blazing pathways to "our Background/homeland." She calls Labryses "our double-axes of divination"[44] and speaks of the labrys as a tool in the same way that words were tools. Language has been misused by the patriarchs to construct a false reality, and Daly moves to take the words back to their Original liberating meaning. In doing so, she moves to liberate women, taking them back to their Original liberating potential.

Ritual

Beyond merely using language to deceive and create a false dependence, patriarchy creates ways to ritually reenact and reinforce the dependence of women on men. Daly examines the myriad ways that patriarchy infects

---

41. Daly, *Pure Lust*, 18.
42. Ibid., 94.
43. Ibid., 4.
44. Ibid., 1.

culture and rules through fear and physical control. In *Gyn/Ecology*, she sets off on a journey to expose the practices and rituals through which patriarchy destroys women. This follows her exposé on language and words:

> Having uncovered the patterns of patriarchal myth, the Voyager must now dis-cover the global dimensions of its gynocidal re-enactments. As she moves through this Passage, she finds multiple manifestations of the lethal *intent* of patriarchy.[45]

Daly's lengthy discussion includes the rituals of Indian suttee, Chinese footbinding, African genital mutilation, European witch burning, and American gynecology. All reveal the destructive practices inherent in patriarchy, and her analysis of them serves in part as "exorcism of the internalized Godfather."[46] She wants to name and expel the demonic patriarchal ideas and practices that infect societies around the globe.

The connection between myth and ritual in religion is widely recognized by sociologists, and Daly mentions Emile Durkheim and Mircea Eliade who "unwittingly elucidate the oppressive function of the rituals which re-create and re-enforce" myth.[47] Her chief concern is of course the myth of "gynocidal patriarchy" as itself a religion; and, therefore, she analyzes specific rituals that are part of what she calls its sado-ritual syndrome:

> Thus the psyches of the performers are conditioned so that they become carriers and perpetrators of patriarchal myth. In giving the myth reality by acting it out, the participants become re-producers and "living proof" of the deceptive myths. The scene is set for the ritual de-legitimation and destruction of the be-ing of female-identified Furious women.[48]

The ancient and modern rituals that she analyzes "unmask the very real, existential meaning of Goddess murder in the concrete lives of women."[49] The rituals are drawn from cultures around the world, India, China, Africa, the U.S., and Europe, and attentive to possible charges of cultural racism, she notes "those who claim to see racism and/or imperialism in

45. Daly, *Gyn/Ecology*, 112.
46. Ibid., 1.
47. Ibid., 109–10. She specifically cites Durkehim's *The Elementary Forms of Religious Life*, and Eliade's *The Sacred and the Profane*.
48. Daly, *Gyn/Ecology*, 109.
49. Ibid., 111.

my indictment of these atrocities can do so only by blinding themselves to the fact that the oppression of women knows no ethnic, national, or religious bounds."[50] It is interesting to note that Daly writes this before Audre Lorde's public criticism, revealing that she understood the changing discourse around her, and the possibility for the very criticism that did in fact emerge.

In her analysis of the rituals of patriarchy, Daly also attends to the temporal dimension of reality because "to be caught up in these institutions is to be living in time past. This is strikingly evident in the liturgies and rituals that legitimate them."[51] The institutions that fall under patriarchy not only have rituals to legitimate their existence and to reinforce their worldview, but they do other things too: "The rituals of patriarchy do create false needs, such as the need to lean on father-figures instead of finding strength in the self, or the need for compulsive 'self-sacrifice' because one is brainwashed into thinking that one is sinful and 'unworthy.'"[52] These needs for father-figures are met by patriarchy, and therefore false notions of dependence and dangerous ideas about sacrifice in women's lives and minds are perpetuated. Daly insists that it is women who suffer most under such a system. As a religion itself, patriarchy creates myth and uses ritual to reinforce it. Daly understands that specific religions like Christianity are part of the work of reinforcing patriarchal myths of dependence and rituals of destruction.

In her work, Daly also moves toward the construction of new rituals to counter those of patriarchy. At the end of *Gyn/Ecology*'s journey through the sado-ritual syndrome, Daly describes a convocation of Crones as a sort of counter-ritual. In the scene, seven demonic groups of patriarchs try to address the Chaircrone with their solutions and suggestions for improving women's lives. The seven groups embody and recast the seven deadly sins of the Catholic tradition. Again, Daly turns the meaning of words and intention of practices on their head. In a Procession, they come forward: The Professionals, doctors, researchers, and therapists, personify *pride*, and the Possessors who sell every type of insurance personify *avarice*. The Aggressors are virile *anger* and violence who propose to protect and defend, while the Obsessors sell objects of *lust* like nylons, heels, and "chokers."

50. Ibid.
51. Daly, *Beyond God the Father*, 42.
52. Ibid., 143.

The Assimilators embody *gluttony* as they propose to include women and minorities in their work, and the Eliminators operate based on *envy* as they insist that there are not many talented feminist writers anyway. The final group of Fragmenters are experts in *sloth* as they divide the personal and political, and seek to divide and conquer.[53] This personification of the traditional typology of sins is Daly's creative way of showing how the institution of patriarchy is ruled by the very sins that Roman Catholic Christianity purports to heal. The scene interweaves creative characterization of the problems of patriarchy, and social criticism of the various institutions that distract, distort, and destroy women.

For Mary Daly, patriarchy is the source of all evil and oppression, and it perpetuates itself through myth and ritual that creates a false dependence of women on men and reenacts that dependence in various ways. In order to fully understand anything about the theological and philosophical work of Mary Daly, one must fully understand her analysis of patriarchy. It is *the* problem.

Word and Sacrament in the Papacy

Throughout his varied works, Luther amasses a lengthy list of crimes that he charges to the papacy. Their errors begin with "rascally exegesis" and continue in their false instruction of consciences and leading Christians to hell. He opines in his commentary on Isaiah: "I wish someone would take the time to make a collection of papistic monstrosities struck down by the Word. Such a collection should strengthen our consciences. . . ."[54] Luther may have wished that someone else would do this, but it seems that he does an effective job of collecting and exposing "papistic monstrosities" himself. They can be generally lumped under the problem of tyrannical claims to power that produce wrong interpretation of scripture and take the sacraments captive. Of course, for Luther, word and sacrament were the indisputable foundation and structure of all of Christianity. Proper understanding of both are therefore essential.

Word

Luther found the base for his own calling and work in pointing out that the papacy is a false authority, and that the words of scripture are the only

---

53. Daly, *Gyn/Ecology*, 420–21.
54. Luther, "Commentary on Isaiah 44:8," in *LW* 17:106.

way by which Christians can know God in Christ: "This we preach daily in order to inculcate respect for the Word of God, which was very much despised in the papacy. It was never taught or understood there. Instead, there was a deep contempt for the divine Word."[55] Luther insists that the Word encompasses all institutions and persons in the world. Because of this, the papacy was subject to it as much as individuals. He saw that the papacy was not acting subject to the Word and therefore was despising it. This was a major problem, so Luther uses the words of scripture to challenge their false claims.

Luther points out that the pope "uses" the words of scripture, but does not understand the Word of God. For Luther, there is a power behind the words that is the source of their power and authority: "To be sure, the pope retains the bare words of this text in the Gospel, but he denies their power altogether."[56] This meant for him that the words could be spoken or read, but their real meaning not fully apprehended. Various groups in fact make this mistake, for Luther, and he regularly lumps together criticism of "Jews, Turks, and papists."[57] Each of these groups fails to understand the true power of the Word according to him, and therefore was subject to scathing critique insofar as they not only failed to see the truth themselves, but as they actively prevented Christians from understanding it.

Luther's theological critique of the papacy, beyond the fact that the institution had no basis in scripture on which it could claim authority, was ultimately that it countered the heart of the gospel. He centers all of his theological claims on Paul's explanation that "the law was our disciplinarian until Christ came, so that we might be justified by faith." (Gal. 3:24). In his commentary on Galatians, Luther insists that "although these words of Paul are clear enough, they are altogether obscure and unknown to the papists."[58] Not only do they not really know the meaning of these words, they in fact teach and act contrary to them: "These words of Paul are changed and read in all the churches of the papacy, and yet the teaching and life in these churches are the very opposite."[59] Luther declares himself as standing with Paul on this matter as witness to the truth of God

---

55. Luther, "Commentary on The Gospel of John," in *LW* 22:312.
56. Ibid., 333.
57. Ibid., 333.
58. Luther, "Commentary on Galatians 3:21," in *LW* 26:330.
59. Ibid.

in Christ. The papacy acted against the saving power of faith because it taught that works could save and that laws and traditions have more power than the words of scripture.

In the same way that he rejected the Roman church's interpretation of Matthew 16 as its foundation, Luther challenges the papacy's claims to mete out forgiveness, also known as the power of the keys:

> As if this were not enough, they apply the words of Christ used about the keys neither to the keys nor to their use but to their own usurped might and power over the keys. Consequently, the power of the keys, freely given by Christ, is now imprisoned in the power of the Romanists.[60]

They don't just get it wrong, for Luther, they actively promote a twisted view of the power that Christ intended to establish. He uses the actions of the popes themselves to show that they could not possibly be the true authority of Christ on earth. After stating that some popes have been heretics and set up heretical laws, he concludes: "That is why the rock [of Peter] cannot mean an authority which is unable to prevail against the gates of hell; it can only mean Christ alone and the faith against which no power can do anything."[61] Christ is the one true authority of the church, and a claim to power that is not based on him is false and dangerous. Luther refuses to accept the Romanist interpretation based on the content of other texts and based on the actual actions and history of the papacy. He reasserts a willingness at one point to consider the legitimacy of the pope, if he were ruling for and under Christ: "I shall accept whatever the pope establishes and does, on condition that I judge it first on the basis of Holy Scripture."[62] The overarching authority is clear: scripture, the Word of God, the words of Christ. Anything that is based squarely on that is to be accepted—even the papacy.

These moments of generosity on Luther's part are curious. Did he really allow for the possibility that the papacy could be legitimate, if it was shown to be based on the word of God? Logically, this is possible. We can take Luther at his word when he repeatedly asserts that anything based on scripture was to be adhered to. However, the rhetorical purpose of these charitable offerings is perhaps more the point. He was so certain that there

---

60. Luther, "On the Papacy in Rome" (1520), in *LW* 39:91.
61. Ibid., 92.
62. Ibid., 101.

was indeed no word of scripture that could be properly shown as the basis for the papacy that his suggestion of allowing the truth of the papacy may in fact be an empty gesture. Like his personal defense at the Diet of Worms in 1521, where he said that he would recant if he could be shown with scripture where he was wrong, these supposedly generous words were no more than rhetorical devices offered to show himself as a truer interpreter of the Word of God.

This strong adherence to and use of the words of Christ are exemplified in Luther's challenge to Jerome Emser whom he called in an eponymous piece "the goat of Leipzig." Emser had been a papal legate and had done extensive work for the Roman church, so he and Luther engaged in a public theological feud on the authority of the papacy and the form of the church. Luther claims several times that Emser had no ability to read scripture adequately and uses the goat symbol from Emser's coat of arms to level personal as well as professional insults against him:

> What do you, stupid goat, want to accomplish with Holy Scripture? ... Your canon law is not going to teach it to you, and your goat's brain will not discover it either. This is one more indication that you have put off the man and put on the goat: you are a "licentiate of canon law" and a "prohibitor of Holy Scripture," and this you will certainly remain.[63]

Luther's invectives against Emser stem from his conviction that Emser was unable to interpret scripture properly, and because of this he was doing damage to the word of God. Through lambasting Emser, Luther challenges the authority of all of the writings of the pope primarily because of their lack of basis in scripture.

He also suggests that the writings could not adhere to the Word of God because they were received too peacefully: "They entered the world in peace and honor, without opposition, and they have been feared more and considered higher than the holy gospel."[64] God's word inevitably upends the order of the world for Luther, and this is one sort of test for the words of the pope. He proclaims that "the discord, dissension, and disturbance produced by God's word are blessed events. With them a true faith begins and struggles against false faith."[65] Because the words of the

---

63. Luther, "To the Goat in Leipzig" (1521), in *LW* 39:111–12.
64. Luther, "Concerning the Answer of the Goat" (1521), in *LW* 39:133.
65. Ibid.

pope caused and allowed no disturbance, they could not be part of the true faith. Luther clearly identifies the words of the pope as false words, and faith in the papacy as false faith insofar as it gets in the way of authentic Christian freedom.

Insufficient knowledge of scripture was the charge that Luther leveled against his enemies repeatedly. This was because the Word was the only acceptable authority and the only sure source of truth. God's grace was reaffirmed over and over again for Luther, and his reliance on and understanding of the role of scripture is yet another area where that is expressed. He allows for interpretation of scripture by those who truly understand it, and he judges those who truly understand it as those who read scripture on its own terms. His own method for interpreting Matthew 16 with other passages in scripture reflects how teachers of scripture can have authority:

> When they interpret a passage in Scripture they do not do so with their own sense or words . . . Instead, they add another passage which is clearer and thus illumine and interpret Scripture with Scripture, as my goats would certainly discover if they would read the fathers correctly."[66]

For Luther, when the Word is unclear or in dispute, one does not rely on one's own senses or preferences. Rather, one relies even more on scripture. Luther firmly insists that it is the only way to access true knowledge of God, so in order to understand scripture, one looks to God and to scripture all the more. Not doing this is precisely the fatal error of Emser and all other Romanists.

SACRAMENTS

All of Luther's theology follows from his intense focus on the words of scripture. He defines the sacraments in the Augustinian tradition as visible signs of an invisible grace. His conclusion that five of the Roman church's sacraments were not in fact truly sacraments emerges directly out of his reading of scripture. For him, the Word provided no basis for practicing penance, marriage, anointing of the sick, ordination, and confirmation *as sacraments*. They could and should still be part of Christian life, he insisted, but were not means of grace. The captivity of the true sacraments of baptism and eucharist, then, becomes a vital concern for Luther. This is most extensively discussed in his treatise on "The Babylonian Captivity

---

66. Luther, "Answer to the HyperChristian Book" (1521), in *LW* 39:164.

of the Church" and is noted in a variety of sermons and instructional writings. He believed that the papacy built on the myths they created by misusing the word, concocting these other "sacraments" as ritual reenactment of the dependence of Christians on their institution.

The crime of holding the sacraments of the church captive was among the worst possible crimes Luther imagined. They "have been subjected to a miserable captivity by the Roman curia, and the church has been robbed of all her liberty."[67] This is such a violation because of the role that the sacraments play in Christian faith. Luther claims that God deals with humans only and always through the promise, and that human beings respond to God and deal with God only and always through faith. He insists that the two go together, promise and faith, and shows how the true sacraments are signs of that promise received in faith. For him they are the means by which Christians express their faith in God: They receive the true promises administered in the sacraments of baptism and the eucharist:

> And so in baptism, to the words of promise he adds the sign of immersion in water. We may learn from this that in every promise of God two things are presented to us, the word and the sign, so that we are to understand the word to be the testament, but the sign to be the sacrament. Thus, in the mass, the word of Christ is the testament, and the bread and wine are the sacrament.[68]

Luther describes the captivity of the mass or the eucharist as threefold. First, in withholding the cup from the laity, the Roman church takes the completeness of the sacrament captive. The institution does not allow the full experience of the promise and sign when it does not allow all Christians to take both the wine and the bread, as instituted by Christ in scripture. Second, the Roman church engages in a slippery debate about the presence of Christ in the bread and wine through its promotion of the doctrine of transubstantiation. Luther dismisses the scholastic metaphysical arguments as not found in scripture, and returns again to a reading of the simple sense of the words of Christ. Third, Luther declares the sacrament of the eucharist to be captive insofar as the Roman church claims it to be a work and a sacrifice. This runs counter to the witness of the gospel for him, and he explains how the sacrament is participation in the testament of Christ, in the promises he made to fully be with his follow-

---

67. Luther, "The Babylonian Captivity of the Church," (1520) in *LW* 36:18.
68. Ibid., 44.

ers. Faith alone is needed to understand this sacrament, and faith alone justifies, therefore to speak of it as a work is to misunderstand its content and to misunderstand the words of Christ in scripture.[69]

While Luther's analysis of the captivity of the sacrament of baptism is not as systematically organized as his examination of the eucharist, he clearly identifies the way in which the institution has corrupted them. He considers the meaning of baptism as tied to the power of death and resurrection, reenacting the process of justification. He notes that it is effective through faith. And, he deals with the practical issues of administering the sacrament which have been challenged and misunderstood by the Roman church. Luther insists that it is not the priest who baptizes, rather it is God who baptizes, and the priest is simply the representative of God. Baptism, he says, is not done in the name of the priest, rather it is done in the name of God. Because it is a work of God and not of humans, it is effective when it is done, regardless of the age or ability of the Christian baptized. Luther is responding here to the challenge of the Anabaptists who advocated the efficacy of baptism only when received by consenting believers, and he is making allowance for the practice of baptizing infants. Insisting that it is a work of God dismisses all of the debate about the nature of the priest and the necessity of articulated belief for the efficacy of the sacrament. It is effective because it is done by God.[70]

In these ways, we see that Luther reclaims and reinvents rituals for his own purposes, insofar as they reinforce his own myth and theological narrative. Word and sacrament are two specific areas where Luther's criticism of the papacy is practically applied, and where his constructive response takes shape. Through a misuse of the Word, the sacraments are taken captive. Through their faulty use of and teaching about scripture, the papacy corrupts Christian consciences and disallows the connections with God that take place through not only scripture but also through the sacraments. By liberating the word and clarifying the sacraments with the tool of scripture, Luther reclaims them for use by free and faithful Christians.

---

69. The three captivities are discussed in greater detail in ibid., 19–57.
70. I am summarizing here his discussion of baptism found in ibid., 57–74.

Notes on Words and Rituals

Daly's and Luther's focus on the central power of words and myths is simultaneously critical and constructive. They intensely focus on the misuse of words by the institution because this is one major thing that the institution does wrong. It spins myths and narratives that create a false dependence on it. The words do not exist in the abstract, however, and both Daly and Luther tie this criticism directly into their criticism of the ritual reenactment of that dependence. Both seek not to abolish words and rituals, rather they seek to reinvent them and use them for liberating purposes. This is why Daly describes such rituals as a convocation of crones, and Luther takes great pains to establish the truths and legitimacy of baptism and the eucharist. Both use "tools" in order to do this: Daly's labrys and Luther's scripture both function as double-edged weapons to cut away lies and to blaze clear paths to the truth.

More substantively, both understand what Durkheim described: "The rites are a manner of acting which take rise in the midst of the assembled groups and which are destined to excite, maintain or recreate certain mental states in these groups."[71] Rituals reinforce myths accepted by the group, or by the dominant institution. Patriarchy and the papacy both use rituals to reinforce the false dependence they have taught, and Daly and Luther expose that before moving on to present their own understandings of rituals which support their worldviews. We can notice that the two reformers do not escape the basic fact that rituals reinforce myth; rather they both claim to expose the damaging rituals and myths, and present more effective, more correct, and more appropriate rituals and myths.

Parallels, Differences, and Inversions

Mary Daly and Martin Luther make parallel moves throughout their criticism of institutional authority, beginning mildly with some hope for change in the institution under scrutiny, and ending with harsh diatribes against the evils from which there is no recovery. However, their analyses of patriarchy and the papacy reveal fundamental aspects of their theological systems and they rely on inverse conclusions: For Daly, the overarching reality of patriarchy is evil. For Luther, the overarching reality of the Word

---

71. Durkheim, *The Elementary Forms of the Religious Life*, 22.

of God is good. Finally, their assessment of the role of words is a key difference. For Daly words are tools. For Luther, the Word is holy.

Parallel: Early Positive Hopes and Eventual Bitter Conclusions

As seen in the examination of Daly's and Luther's writings on the institutions that they say are corrupt, each begins with a modest proposal based on a key insight. Daly sees how patriarchy has blinded and corrupted the church, and the men and women within it. Initially, she voices a hope for real change, citing men and women working together, and God as an agent of change. Ultimately, she moves away from this reformist agenda into a radical ideology. Her feminist utopia of the twenty-first century bears little resemblance to her androgynous articulations in the mid to late twentieth century. Likewise, Luther's supposed allowance for the papacy to be a bearer of Christ earlier in his career is hard to find in the writings of his final years. In fact, because of the harsh polemical nature of his later writings on the papacy, a note of sarcasm may appropriately be read into his statements that if it adhered to the Word of God, the papacy could be a force for good, or his claim that if he is shown to be wrong with scripture that he will recant his own writings. Luther's Christian utopia ultimately has no room for "the pope of Sodomists" and "the bishop of hermaphrodites." Both Daly and Luther make at least some attempt at concession and reform early in their criticisms of the institutions they identify as the problem. Both conclude that the institution is beyond hope, and that the only hope for authentic personhood and community lies beyond and outside of it.

In addition to this shift of tone over the course of their reforming careers, Daly and Luther share a methodological similarity in wielding their weapon of choice: Daly's labrys and Luther's scripture serve to criticize everything from institutional claims to power and damaging rituals, while also serving to illuminate the true source of authority and construct appropriate rituals that reinforce its liberating core. These parallels show how these two remarkably different theologians are engaged in similar work criticizing an institution based on their insights into a core freedom, and reconstructing reality based on an uncovered truth.

Difference: Words and Rituals

Daly's and Luther's assessment of words and the types of rituals and damage with which they are concerned are notably different. Both use words as tools, but do it with different presuppositions. Both focus on rituals, but do it with different ultimate concerns.

For Daly, words are tools by which patriarchy defines and justifies itself, tools used to falsely instruct and dull consciences. She makes a move into the future by recapturing the words that have been used, and reconceiving their meaning. Occasionally, she also goes back to original meanings, but for the purposes of complexifying rather than simplifying. She wants to liberate the words themselves from the limitations of patriarchy, and constructs webs and worlds where they take on entirely new or discovered meanings. Words are a subjective reality for Daly, something that have a life of their own.

For Luther, since the Word is good, holy, and from God, it is to be returned to by relying only on scripture (words) for knowledge of God, and by relying on Christ (the Word) for justification. Luther repeatedly insists that the simplest sense of scripture is to be retained at all costs. He makes a move back to the basics, back to the original revelation found in scripture and found in Christ himself. Words are an objective reality for Luther, something to which he must adhere.

The rituals that Daly and Luther both criticize and re-construct have very different concerns. Daly is specifically concerned with material rituals of patriarchy that damage and destroy women's bodies, threatening their basic physical safety. Her ultimate concern is women's lives in the present, and her evidence is the destruction of women's bodies reenacted in the past and around the globe. Luther is specifically concerned with rituals of the Christian church that have to do with the salvation of souls. His ultimate concern is Christian spiritual life not only now but in the future afterlife and eternal communion with God, and his evidence is the metaphoric captivity of the rituals and the conscience of each Christians. For both, this reveals what is most crucial and what is most important in their theological systems. Focus on the interplay between words and rituals is something that they share, but substantial differences in assumptions and goals exist because of the different contexts in which they live and work.

Inversion: An Overarching Reality

Daly sees patriarchy as the overarching reality under which all things exist, and by which all evils come to exist. In an inverse way, Luther sees the Word of God as the overarching reality under which all things exist, and by which all things ought to be judged. For Daly, the overarching reality is evil and demonic, while for Luther, the overarching reality is good and holy. Structurally the two imagine similar paradigms; but the content of the two worldviews is inverse. For Daly, all persons are captive under patriarchy, the religion of the planet. Nothing can escape it and all institutions under it are evil. Women must find ways to live as far on the margins of it as they can. For Luther, all of reality is subject to the Word of God. Nothing can escape its judgment and all things that adhere to it are good and holy. The Christian who is captive under the institution of the papacy can be liberated from it because the Word of God is a more powerful authority. Daly's umbrella of patriarchy is the ultimate evil, Luther's umbrella of the Word of God is the ultimate good. Extended analysis of their often common rhetorical strategies in speaking about this reality continues in depth in the next chapter.

6

Snools and Snot
Reforming Rhetoric and Wicked Words

If only someone would stroke you, you ass, abecedarian, and bacchanal, with a whip until the blood flowed from your arse, and teach you the Donat and to decline the pronoun meum. I must give crass examples to the crass ass.[1]

To succumb to this seductive invitation is to become incorporated into the Mystical Body of Maledom, that is, to become "living" dead women, forever pumping our own blood into the Heavenly Head, giving head to the Holy Host, losing our heads.[2]

Martin Luther and Mary Daly share a stylistic sharpness that is apparent while examining the substance of their theologies. Both rely heavily on creative and even scatological use of words to expose atrocity and name evil. Both occasionally intend to shock their readers with their choice of words. The previous chapters showed how each reformer understood the individual person as a free subject, and how that subject could freely engage in criticism of the institution which threatens her conscience and existence. One of the ways by which Luther and Daly enact their criticism and this freedom is through their employment of words. They differ insofar as Luther focuses on the Word of God, revealed in Christ and known in scripture, while the only authoritative text Daly sometimes uses is the dictionary. Both demonstrate real reverence for the power of words, and both see them as a liberating force. An introduction to their respective worldviews and methods will show how their naming of individuals and

---

1. Luther, "Against the Roman Papacy" (1545), in *LW* 41:350.
2. Daly, *Gyn/Ecology*, 67.

institutions, and their exclusion of groups of people take shape within a particular perception of reality.

Worldview and Method

Luther and Daly each have a worldview and a theological method that makes space for their work with language and words. Various reasons from the medical to the strategic have been posed to explain why Luther and Daly make such dramatic use of language in their work, and while those elements may be contributing factors, I believe that it is their respective understandings of the world that lead them to their rhetorical revolts. As noted in the previous chapter, both envision an overarching reality that exerts some control over all things underneath it. Both identify a liberating force that is equated with words, and both see that speaking the unspeakable is a necessary move in the battles they are waging.

Luther, The Irascible

Luther demonstrates a skill with languages and wordplay gleaned from his years of study and reinforced with his time in the Augustinian order. Walter Altmann describes Luther as "an irascible human being." He goes on to say that "he did sometimes concede his excesses—often slanderous—in accusing his adversaries. The epithet 'ass' applied by Luther to the pope was doubtless very tame; 'spoon of snot' is surely a better example of his lexical creativity."[3] Altmann is referring here to Luther's frequent use of terms like "ass" and "snot-nose" throughout his polemical writings. "Snot-nose" appears five times in two essays and Luther refers to Catholic theologian Johann Cochlaeus as "Dr. Snotty-Nose." The German word, *Rotzlöffel*, is used here and described in a footnote in the American Edition of Luther's works as a term referring to an inexperienced person. *Rotz* is nose, and *löffel* is a play on Cochlaeus' name, which in Latin, *cochlear*, means spoon.[4] Whether it is read as snot-nose, snotty-nose or spoon of snot, the effect of the title is to demean to one of Luther's many adversaries.

A search of the 55 volumes of the American Edition of Luther's Works on CDROM[5] reveals that the following terms appear with some frequency:

3. Altmann, *Luther and Liberation*, 2.
4. Luther, "On Translating: An Open Letter" (1530), in *LW* 35:187.
5. *Luther's Works on CD-ROM*.

- Ass   606
- Antichrist   479
- Fart   34
- Hermaphrodite   12
- Snot-nose   5
- Sodomist   5

The majority of the uses of these terms are in the context of criticism and polemic, though a few of the references to "ass," for example, refer to actual animals. This accounts for only some of the uses, however. Luther clearly felt free to be excessive, slanderous, and creative in his assessment of the pope, the Roman church, and his theological enemies. He uses the Word of God to show that the papacy had no true claim to authority, and he uses his own words to mock, belittle, and challenge his public opponents. He uses the Word of God to show the guiding principles of Christian life and the life of the church, and uses his own words to shock and insult his adversaries, as well as educate his public.

Reasons for this style and this approach are tied to his understanding of the power of words themselves. For Luther, the words of scripture were the best connection that a Christian could have with God. Translating the biblical texts from ancient and scholarly languages into his vernacular, German, was a monumental achievement. What this endeavor represented was his belief that every person in Germany deserved to have access to the Word of God for himself or herself because the Word itself was liberating. The words also were tools by which Luther revealed the truth of Christian freedom and challenged the authority of the papacy and the priests. He took the words of scripture from their exclusive control, and scattered them around the countryside through his translation work as well as his treatises, sermons, and polemics. He made it easier for people to have access to scripture and therefore to God not only because of his push to translate the Bible into common languages, but also because of the newly invented printing press of Johann Gutenberg which facilitated wider distribution of texts and treatises.

Beyond enabling the dissemination of scripture in the vernacular, Luther himself became a master of words as he criticized and challenged the authority of nearly everyone associated with the papacy. Speculation about Luther's mental and physical health has often informed scholarly examination of his rhetorical harshness as discussed initially in chapter one. Mark Edwards suggests that "excesses of language and argument that cannot be explained by his theology or by his apocalyptic world view are generally attributed to ill health and the effects of aging."[6] He goes on to argue that such an approach is limited and does not take Luther's context and humanity into account. Luther did deal with various physical and mental distresses throughout his life as Gritsch details, and Edwards similarly describes everything from hemorrhoids, fainting spells, ear infections, and arthritis to depression, rage, and visions that afflicted Luther in his later years. The case that Edwards makes, however, is that these ailments alone were not enough to account for his enraged polemics and the vilification of his enemies.[7] Contextual realities like an increasingly secular audience influenced the tone of his work, and Luther's keen sense of his present age as apocalyptic in nature gave an urgency to his work. These factors especially contribute to the political impact of his work.

Edwards is right to include the broader context of Luther's work to an understanding of his rhetorical strategy. However, I believe that Luther's overall worldview is what ultimately makes this possible and necessary. He insists that the Word of God is the overarching authority under which the papacy was falsely asserting control. This paints a picture of a shoddily built house (papacy) under a great transcendent sky (Word of God). The inhabitants of the house try mightily to exert control over everyone around them, bringing them into their shoddy structure, but they are ultimately unsuccessful because the transcendent Word of God is visible and available to all, like a great sky. Luther becomes so convinced of the power of this Word that he is able to speak boldly against the flawed and corrupt institution of the papacy, the shoddily built house and its inhabitants.

Words then become not only the source of liberation and the grounding for criticism, but also the tools with which Luther names the evils for what they are. In speaking of what it means to be a theologian, Luther states in his "Heidelberg Disputation" that "a theologian of glory calls evil good and good evil. A theologian of the cross calls the thing what it actually is."[8] This is the American Edition translation, while the original German reads slightly different: "*der Theologe des Kreuzes nennt die Dinge*

---

6. Edwards, *Luther's Last Battles*, 4.
7. Ibid., 6–19.
8. Luther, "Heidelberg Disputation," (1518) in *LW* 31:40.

beim rechten Namen."⁹ The theologian of the cross *calls things by their right names*. Calling the thing *by its right name* becomes not only his theological point about the cross and about God's revelation in the life and death of Jesus, but also a methodological point about doing theology. It is this view of the world and of theology that allows and even necessitates his diatribes. Luther was compelled to call things by their right names, and he drew his understanding of what the right names were from none other than the transcendent Word of God. This point of his provides a tool by which we can evaluate the merits and limits of Luther's own work. When he writes of individuals, institutions, and classes of people, is he calling things by their right names?

Daly, the Conjurer

As soon as Mary Daly moved "beyond God the father," she decisively moved beyond the boundaries of patriarchal language. Frances Gray argues that Daly's use of language is both subversive and strategic. It is subversive because she "seeks to overthrow the purported neutrality of patriarchal discourses" and strategic because "she acknowledges that language always operates within sociopolitical contexts."¹⁰ The context within which language as we know it has been constructed and used has been a patriarchal context, so it has served the interests of the dominant males. Daly works to create a new space, a gynocentric space where new words are conjured, old words take on new meanings and where old meanings are revealed as destructive and hypocritical. Her use and crafting of language is both creative and critical; it is a tool with which women have been controlled and it is a tool with which women can regain control.

Daly links women and words in her worldview both as captives under patriarchal interests. She recognizes that "the liberation of language is rooted in the liberation of ourselves."¹¹ She makes this connection because she recognizes the overarching reality of patriarchy. She envisions it as the system which attempts to envelop all of reality. Under the shoddily constructed canopy of patriarchy, words and women have been co-opted to serve the interests of the elite ruling males. The liberation of one demands

---

9. Luther, "*Die Heidelberger Disputation*" (1518), in *Gesammelte Werke*, 984; translation mine.

10. Gray, "Elemental Philosophy," 223.

11. Daly, *Beyond God the Father*, 8.

the liberation of the other. Neither words nor women, for Daly, are authentically themselves under this canopy, under the rule of the patriarchs, and both words and women have a truth about them that she seeks to dis-cover, reveal, and set free.

After identifying liberation as the first step in her philosophy, Daly then advocates the actual castration of language, "cutting away the phallocentric value system imposed by patriarchy."[12] She insists that the system has castrated women and nonelite males, and that now the "primordial eunuchs" need to rise up to castrate the system itself. For Daly, this castration or cutting away has to be mental as well as physical, because that is the nature of the damage that has been done to women and men who were of little social value. Now, these "eunuchs" are set to rise up against the system of domination in order to bring it down.

Exorcism is the final piece of this three-fold method: liberation-castration-exorcism. This step involves expelling the demons of the phallic society that have possessed the minds and lives of women: "The machismo ethos . . . is essentially demonic in that it cuts off the power of human becoming."[13] This three-step method is how the shoddily built canopy that is patriarchy will be brought down. Words and women will be liberated, castrated, and exorcized.

Daly understands that the effect of this method is monumental:

> Women's new hearing and naming is cosmic upheaval, in contrast to this charism which is a controllable and cooptable ripple of protest. Feminist naming is a deliberate confrontation with language structures of our heritage. It transcends the split between nonrational . . . and the merely rational . . ., for it is a break out of the deafening noise of sexist language that has kept us from hearing our own word.[14]

In order for the world to change, women must speak. When women speak, patriarchal traditions are unmasked and challenged. When patriarchal traditions are unmasked, the structures that support them begin to crumble. Daly works with a keen sense of the revolutionary power of words and women, and bringing new consciousness to them both brings nothing short of cosmic upheaval. She also recognizes that as tools of the

---

12. Ibid., 9.
13. Ibid., 10.
14. Ibid., 167.

patriarchs, words and sexist language have been used to silence women and prevent them from hearing and from naming.

In addition to liberation-castration-exorcism, Daly consistently insists on a broader and more basic method of hearing and naming as crucial for bringing about this cosmic upheaval. Hearing only the sexist language of patriarchy is the most basic limitation she calls women to overcome. If women can exist on the margins of patriarchy, then they have a better chance of hearing things that come from outside or beyond patriarchy. They have a better chance of hearing from deep within themselves, listening to the element that might not be totally captive to the patriarchs: "The essential thing is to hear our *own* words, always giving prior attention to our *own* experience, never letting prefabricated theory have *authority* over us."[15] Women's words reflect women's experiences. Paying attention to women's experience is a fundamental insistence of feminism generally, and Daly grounds her reclamation of language in women's experience. Listening to one's self is the first step. The second step is speaking about that experience, using one's own words. Hearing leads to naming. Naming gives rise to further hearing by other women, who in turn speak their own reality. And the revolution begins as women not only hear the right things, but then call things by their right names.

Daly showcases her methods in a more developed way in *Gyn/Ecology* in 1978. AnaLouise Keating suggests that Daly's use of language at this stage of her work was not only metaphorical and substantive, but it also was performative. She said that Daly uses "metaphoric writing to activate language's performative effects, its ability to bring about individual and collective change."[16] Daly primarily seeks to change individuals and systems, and writing is a major tool for this transformation. The shifting spelling, capitalization, hyphenation and definition of words take visible shape in her work from this point forward. Her worldview provides the reason: "When I play with words I do this attentively, deeply, paying attention to etymology, to varied dimensions of meaning, to deep Background meanings and subliminal associations."[17] In the same way that Luther plays with the names of Cochleus' and other adversaries, Daly routinely plays with words and their root meanings. This reveals that for her, under the shoddy canopy of patriarchy, words have become fixed tools with one or perhaps

---

15. Ibid., 189.
16. Keating, "Back to the Mother?" 368.
17. Daly, *Gyn/Ecology*, 24.

two acceptable meanings, usually only one correct spelling, and no depth. She pays attention to the experience of the *word* itself in the same way that she insists on paying attention to the experience of *women* themselves. She insists that words need to be heard back into existence, as women need to be heard back into existence.

Daly even described words as entities unto themselves: "the words themselves seem to have a life of their own. They seem to want to break the bonds of conventional usage, to break the silence imposed upon their own Backgrounds."[18] Her references to the Background when writing about words and women demonstrate that not only does she have a sense of the overarching reality that is the shoddily constructed canopy of patriarchy, but also that there is a deeper reality that surrounds or is behind all of it: a Background. Daly seems to understand herself as a conduit to this Background, having dis-covered it (literally, removed the cover). Things like her capitalization practices also perform this worldview insofar as she not only challenges convention but also emphasizes what is really important: "I have no need to consistently capitalize christian or god, being much more inclined to capitalize Crone and Goddess. This is obviously a matter not only of 'taste' but of evaluation."[19] Capitalization confers power and importance, and Daly therefore performs the words and her evaluation of them. Foreground (patriarchal) words are not capitalized, while Background words are always capitalized.

Recognizing the patriarchal context for the publication of her own work, and anticipating "anti-male" criticism commonly leveled against feminist authors, Daly reclaims the very label that would be intended to frighten her. She acknowledges that "the courage to be logical—the courage to name—would require that we admit to ourselves that males and males only are the originators, planners, controllers, and legitimators of patriarchy."[20] In this way specifically, the book *Gyn/Ecology* and her work are decidedly anti-male. She disallows any rationalization that this man or that man could be the exception because her analysis and worldview are thoroughly focused on the systemic and institutional reality of patriarchy. Its power is systemic and institutional, therefore that is how it must be understood, criticized, and debunked.

18. Ibid.
19. Ibid., 26.
20. Ibid., 28.

Daly encapsulates her understanding of language and the power of words in her 1987 book *Wickedary*, "conjured by Mary Daly in cahoots with Jane Caputi."[21] Even the organization of the text challenges the hierarchical ordering characteristic of patriarchal books and scholarly work: She divides her "metadictionary" into webs rather than into linear chapters. Five preliminary webs serve as explanations of the text and her worldview. Three word-webs follow, first identifying Elemental Philosophical Words, then naming the Inhabitants of the Background, and finally naming the inhabitants of the foreground. The text concludes with four appendicular webs that expose patriarchal manipulations of words and narrate stories of be-laughing, spinning, and jumping off the doomsday clock. This text is a marvelous example of Daly performing her words and her worldview. In order to get to the heart of the text, the definitions of the words themselves, the reader has to wind through the five preliminary webs of explanation, contextualization, and symbol keys. After the reader is exposed to the "core" in the three word webs, she has to be led out through the appendices and ultimately led "off the clock" to Thirteen:

> *Thirteen* is when/where a Positively Revolting Hag Hears her own Name and finds the Courage to Be, to See, to Live, to Grieve, to Rage, and to Laugh Out Loud. And that is the End and the Beginning . . . .[22]

Daly's alpha and omega is thirteen, the time that is off the clock, on the margin of patriarchal time, the number and place that is beyond the false boundaries controlled by the system of male domination. It is the end and the beginning. This time/place is where and when her liberation of words (and women) takes place, and where she names individuals, institutions, and classes of people.

Notes on Worldview and Method

Worldviews make all the difference in the work of these two reformers. Without reading their harsh critiques as reflective of and consistent with their overall picture of reality, one could conclude from statements like the two that headline this chapter that these two reformers were unnecessarily angry or merely crazy. However, comments like those make sense within their worldviews and are consistent with the rest of their theological work.

21. Daly, *Wickedary*.
22. Ibid., 284.

For Luther, the Word of God transcends all and therefore is the source of criticism, emboldening the reformer to call things by their right names. For Daly, patriarchy envelops all of reality and therefore a new space-time reality has to be found in order for liberation to take place, leading her to the Background. Both employ a method of speaking what has previously been unspoken: Luther wants to call things by their right names, while Daly insists that women name their own experience.

Luther can and does continue to live and work in the world as he knows it because the Word of God makes it possible for him to spawn a whole new theological movement: Protestantism. Daly tries mightily to live and work in the world as she knows it, but it is so irretrievably patriarchal that she is forced to work on the margins and to inhabit the Background. Context, personality, and strategy all influence Luther's and Daly's use of language, but seeing how each works with a very particular view of how the world is currently structured sheds new light on evaluations of their respective rhetorical flourish.

Getting Personal

Luther and Daly single out particular individuals for focused criticism throughout the course of their careers. Criticism gets personal very quickly for both of them in part because both reformers were sharply criticized by their contemporaries. Because of their worldviews and methodologies, both felt free to respond by naming names and speaking the unspeakable.

Goats, Sows, and Sodomists

Many different individuals are singled out in Luther's writings for his mocking, attack, and general insult. Usually these are individuals with whom Luther was in dispute publicly, and often people to whom he was responding. Luther himself was the victim of occasionally vicious and slanderous verbal attacks by various church and secular leaders, so many of his writings about individuals must be seen as part of broader dialogue and debate. His interchanges with Johann Eck and Jerome Emser provide two examples of note.

In "The Leipzig Debate," Luther engages Eck on the issues of indulgences and of papal authority. Eck had publicly challenged thirty-one of the ninety-five theses that Luther had published, and Luther responded, eventually leading to a debate at Leipzig in 1519. This event is of particular significance for a study of Luther's understanding of the Word of God and his use of words because, as Harold Grimm states,

> he on that occasion publicly stated his evangelical conception of the church in unmistakable terms and showed that in the last analysis his sole authority in matters of faith was the Word of God. Therefore he could state without reservations that not only the papacy but also church councils could err.[23]

Luther could make bold claims about the mistakes of his adversaries because of his worldview and confidence of one true authoritative source transcending all things: the Word of God. When he emerged as a public reformer, he emerged with a certainty gleaned from years of struggling with tremendous doubt and weighty fear. The Leipzig Debate showcases his convictions about the Word of God, and reveals the growing creativity in the use of his own words.

It was personal, for Luther. He notes how Eck had been speaking of him "as a heretic and a Bohemian," and insists that "I cannot let this sort of name-calling pass unnoticed."[24] He claims that Eck was one of the "adversaries of Christian grace [who try to] terrify . . . with their flattery and consecrations."[25] He went on to state thirteen theses on the nature and authority of the church in his attempt to defend truth against the many errors in Eck's work. Eck was one early target of Luther's reforming rhetoric, and this debate reveals Luther's fundamental goal of showing the truth from the Word of God. Since Luther's adversary engaged in personal insults, he returns the favor, referring to Eck in two later essays as Dr. Sow.[26] In many ways, Luther was engaging in the debate and disputation style of his era, but more importantly he was acting based on his understanding of the problem that confronted Christians.

Jerome Emser was another of Luther's foes with whom he also engaged substantively on the issues of indulgences and the authority of the church, and one who received even more colorful naming at the pen of the reformer. Luther makes much out of the symbol on Emser's coat of arms,

---

23. Harold J. Grimm, "Introduction to The Leipzig Debate," in *LW* 31:311.
24. Luther, "The Leipzig Debate" (1519), in *LW* 31:314.
25. Ibid., 316.
26. Luther, "Against Hanswurst" (1541), in *LW* 41:235; "Against the Roman Papacy" (1545), in *LW* 41:293.

a shield and helmet with a goat, referring to him as the "goat of Leipzig."[27] He calls him a stupid goat, a dear goat, tells him to quit lying, and accuses Emser of trying to "soil Holy Scripture with your goatish snout."[28] In a lengthy piece with a lengthy title, the apex of their written interchange over a course of years, Luther thoroughly explicates his understanding of the Word of God as sole and ultimate authority for all that he says. His "Answer to the HyperChristian, Hyperspiritual, and Hyperlearned Book by Goat Emser in Leipzig—Including Some Thoughts Regarding His Companion, the Fool Murner" appeared in 1521 and deals at length with the role of scripture in church tradition, the understanding of the priestly role, and the authority of the pope. As if the title of the essay were not enough insult, Luther jabs at Emser throughout:

> Look here! Is he not the greatest blasphemer ever known? Who indeed has ever heard more blasphemous, poisonous, hellish, heretical, raging, and nonsensical words than those Emser here pours from his poisonous and hellish mouth and lets stink to heaven? This poor creature spits and sprays his spit at God his Creator so terribly and gruesomely that it is abominable to listen to or speak of.[29]

In this way, Emser serves as a personal target for Luther's criticism, epitomizing all those who did not base their writing and teaching on the Word of God. To not do this was blasphemy, and it was the crime with which Luther charged Emser and others.

The pope and the bishops and all "papists" come under direct and sustained rhetorical attack by Luther. Luther coyly says about the pope in his 1545 treatise "Against the Roman Papacy" that "I would not dream of judging or punishing him either," and then goes on to say that the pope

> was born from the behind of the devil, is full of devils, lies, blasphemy, and idolatry; is the instigator of these things, God's enemy, Antichrist, desolator of Christendom, church-robber, key-thief, brothel-keeper, steward of Sodom; and everything else that was said above.[30]

---

27. Eric W. Gritsch, "Introduction to 'To the Goat in Leipzig'" (1521), in *LW* 39:107.

28. Luther, "To the Goat in Leipzig" (1521), in *LW* 39:111–13.

29. Luther, "Answer to the HyperChristian Book" (1521), in *LW* 39:199.

30. Luther, "Against the Roman Papacy" (1545), in *LW* 41:363.

Woodcut cartoons by Lucas Cranach accompanied Luther's writings on the papacy at his most polemically vulgar here in the last year of his life. The cartoons depict the pope and the cardinals in a variety of disgusting situations including being "born from the behind of the devil" in a cartoon titled *"Ortus et origo Papae"* (Origin and Birth of the Pope).

1. Ortus et origo Papae

Further cartoons show the pope holding a steaming pile of excrement that represented the Council he proposed, two men bent over with dropped trousers farting at the pope, and the pope defecating into a crown, the crown of Christ.[31] These visual images of Luther's scatological descriptions of the pope and his cardinals "each said a whole book's worth of what ought to be written about the papacy."[32] These cartoons expressed Luther's written criticism in a much more vivid and effective way. Speaking of the pope himself, Luther says that Paul III was a "shameful fop" and calls him "His Hellishness" and "the Most Hellish Father" instead of the Holy

---

31. In *WA* 54:531ff; The cartoons are also reprinted in Edwards, *Luther's Last Battles*, 190–98.

32. Edwards, *Luther's Last Battles*, 199.

Father.³³ He degrades papists "as the arch-whore of the devil [who] have abandoned the ancient church and its ancient bridegroom"³⁴ Luther's criticisms ranged from merely calling them liars to humiliating them with personal insults that carried what he saw as sexually perverse overtones: His phrases "pope of Sodomists" and "bishop of hermaphrodites" are the most descriptive, and somewhat puzzling. In Luther's original language of German, the phrase is *"der hermaphroditen Bischoff und Puseronen Papst."*³⁵ Luther uses the term *puseron* here, which is from the Latin meaning "little boy," but in the authoritative Weimar edition it is footnoted *"Sodomit"* with no further reference as to why *puseron* would mean *sodomit*. The use of this word and its translation are curious, and perhaps explained elsewhere when Luther is describing the sexual abominations of the papacy, and refers to them using what he says is the Italian term *"buseron,* which is the chastity of Sodom and Gomorrah."³⁶ He clearly intended to portray them as what he saw as shameful: men who had intercourse with other men. Whether or not "pope of Sodomists" is the most accurate rendering perhaps remains lost in translation. It is clear though that in every place, Luther's intent was to mock and humiliate the cardinals, bishops, and papists as perverse and less than human because of what they did with the Word of God.

The Papal Bully and an Old Maid

The individuals who come under sharp criticism in Daly's third word-web in the *Wickedary* are usually those males who control, shape, and benefit from patriarchy. Prime examples that reveal her naming to the church as chief agent of patriarchy are found in the following definitions:

> **bully, papal**: the supreme sacred bully. *Example*: pope John Paul II, who told an audience of 4,000 women from around the world who work as maids for priests that they can never thank the Lord enough for letting them serve the clergy.³⁷

---

33. Luther, "Against the Roman Papacy" (1545), in *LW* 41:263ff.
34. Luther, "Against Hanswurst" (1541), in *LW* 41:205.
35. Luther, *"Wider das Papsttum zu Rom"* (1545), in *WA* 54:227.
36. Luther, "Dr. Martin Luther's Warning to his Dear German People" (1531), in *LW* 47:37.
37. Daly, *Wickedary*, 187–88.

> **cardinals** *n*: foppish popocrats; pontifically chosen members of the Sacred Men's Club; colorless pretenders to the beauty and status of colorful songbirds; favored sons of the papal bully; pompous hypocrites who unflaggingly lobby in favor of the most flagrant abuses and atrocities, under the aegis of their respective national flags. *Examples* **a**: the war-mongering prelate Francis cardinal Spellman, who ceaselessly agitated for the escalation of the United States' genocidal/biocidal devastation of Vietnam **b**: Terrence cardinal Cooke, who blathered in 1981: "Nuclear deterrence can be morally tolerated if a nation is sincerely trying to come up with a rational alternative."[38]

These two definitions showcase Daly's basic method of hearing and naming as it is used throughout her work. First, she "hears" by using conventional phrases and words, giving them a revealing twist. A papal "bully" and a cardinal as "colorless" play on the literal meaning of words themselves and invoke the reality of experiencing them as mean persons (bully), a red bird (cardinal), or an authoritative document (a papal bull). Second, she "names" and calls the thing what it is, to use Luther's phrase, insisting that the pope is a bully and that the cardinals are hypocrites and actually without vibrant color, among other things. Finally, she gives specific examples and names names: Pope John Paul II, and Cardinals Spellman and Cooke. She hears their own words and cites them in order to properly name their abuses. The definition of papal bully is followed by a lengthy note, not included here, about John Paul II's visit to Australia when he was met with numerous protesters, some of whom were subsequently arrested and sent to psychiatric hospitals for their actions. And as seen above, the definition of cardinals includes Cooke's own words on nuclear deterrence.

Daly's naming and hearing are not limited to individuals within the church since she seeks to identify all of the individuals who were perpetrators under patriarchy. In doing so, Daly freely employs terms that are normally "considered vulgar":

> **dick** *n* ["PENIS—usu. considered vulgar" —*Webster's*] **1**: the second person (member) of the vulgar trinity—tom, dick, and harry **2**: a common member of the thrusting throng. *Examples*: tricky dick nixon, dick tracy.[39]

---

38. Ibid., 188.
39. Ibid., 193.

Here Daly again calls the thing what it is. In common vulgar speech "dick" refers to the penis and that is how she means to mock it here. She names individuals who fall under the definition and in doing so seeks to denigrate them. Her words themselves are vivid, including her onomatopoetic use of "thrusting throng," her play on the synonyms of person and member, member and penis, and her use of the triad of common male names (Tom, Dick, and Harry) to describe "the vulgar trinity." In doing so, she ends up back at a criticism of the church, denigrating the Christian theological idea of trinity.

Acutely aware of the political reality in which she hears and names, Daly also names political figures as examples, like "tricky dick nixon" above. She further criticizes the presidency and the person who holds the office at the time of the *Wickedary's* publication:

> **presbot** *n*: the president as he appears on television: the Talking Head of State; the president as robot: mechanical imitation of a political leader capable of experiencing emotion and thought processes. *Example par excellence*: Ronald Reagan.[40]

Daly's definitions are thus a mix of convention and creativity. In one sense she is describing things as they are: the president existed for most people in the late twentieth-century on television as a two-dimensional figure, a talking head, a head of state. The 1980s was dominated by the two-term presidency of a former film actor, Ronald Reagan. In another sense, then, she is speaking the unspeakable: Her suggestion that the "presbot" was only imitating emotions and thoughts rather than actually having them amounts to a scathing critique.

One final example shows how Daly incorporates all of her hearing and naming techniques: calling the thing what it is, using conventional definitions to reveal hidden truth, giving examples from the patriarchal world, and finally invoking the words of historically significant women:

> **snool** *n* [*snool n* "*Scot* a cringing person"; also *snool v* "to reduce to submission: COW, BULLY ... CRINGE, COWER" —*Webster's*; also *snool n* "a tame, abject, or mean-spirited person" —*O.E.D.*]: normal inhabitant of sadosociety, characterized by sadism and masochism combined; stereotypic hero and/or saint of the sadostate. *Examples*: Adam; saint Paul; the Marquis de Sade. *Canny Comment*: "Remember all Men would be tyrants if they could." —Abigail Adams (1776).

---

40. Ibid., 220.

First, Daly affirms the traditional definitions of snool from both *Webster's* and the *Oxford English Dictionary* insofar as they support her insight and experience of these individuals. Then, she gives examples that are individuals who are loaded with religious and cultural significance—Adam (the first man), saint Paul (the first Christian evangelist), and the Marquis de Sade (the eponymous sadist). Finally, the "canny comment" with which she concludes the definition comes from one of the first ladies of American history, a woman who had the ability to name reality as she saw it. Daly concurs with what Abigail Adams already knew in the eighteenth century: "all men would be tyrants if they could."

Daly's naming is not only critical; it also becomes constructive as she reclaims names typically given to demean women, like Hag, Crone, and Old Maid.

> **Crone** *n*: Great Hag of History, long-lasting one; Survivor of the perpetual witchcraze of patriarchy, whose status is determined not merely by chronological age, but by Crone-logical considerations; one who has survived early states of the Otherworld Journey and who therefore has Dis-covered depths of Courage, Strength, and Wisdom in her Self. *Examples*: **a**: Harriet Tubman, rescuer of slaves, psychically/physically fearless Foresister **b**: Ding Ling, twentieth-century feminist activist and author, Survivor of multiple political purges, one of China's best-known and most prolific female writers.[41]
>
> **Old Maid** *n*: a Crone who has steadfastly resisted imprisonments in the comatose State of matrimony: SURVIVOR, SPINSTER.[42]

Her style of defining, challenging, and giving examples remains. The difference is that her discussion of individuals who are inhabitants of the Background is creative and constructive. It is a positive reclamation of the words that have been captive under patriarchy:

> These are Original words Naming the Background and the foreground from the perspective of the Background. That is, they Name Wild Reality and its patriarchal counterfeits from the perspective of those who choose the Background as our Homeland, electing to be members of the Outsiders' Society, and Living on the Boundary between the worlds.[43]

41. Ibid., 114.
42. Ibid., 150.
43. Ibid., 59.

In the above examples, Daly plays on the fact that women are frequently demeaned by being called a hag or an old maid. Within her worldview, however, to be an older unmarried woman is to have survived patriarchy and resisted marriage which she describes as a comatose state. This is a great thing to be celebrated in her feminist utopia. Likewise, a crone is usually an old ugly woman. This too is to be celebrated in Daly's view, as surviving patriarchy and resisting beauty ideals demands a strength and wisdom that few women really possess. The examples she gives, including Harriet Tubman and Ding Ling, embody her point.

These positive and lively definitions of women and other inhabitants of the Background are the subject of the illustrations that accompany the *Wickedary*. Artist Sudie Rakusin contributed thirty cartoons for the book, depicting actions from Be-Witching to X-ing, and persons from Angel to Virgin. These are all activities or inhabitants of the Background, and the images accompany Daly's descriptions throughout the text, but especially in Word-web two where the Background comes to life. The illustration for Virgin depicts a woman whose head is turned to face the reader, who is wearing wide legged striped pants, soft boots, a vividly decorated jacket, and a necklace with a labrys pendant. She is running alongside a cheetah, with a butterfly trailing above her flowing ponytail. The caption is "Wild, Lusty, Never-captured, Unsubdued old Maid; Marriage Resister."[44]

44. Ibid., 177.

Images like these reinforce the definitions and bring them to life. We can presume that the subjects of Rakusin's illustrations are only from the Background because the foreground is already seen and experienced far too much in reality. In order to make the Background emerge as a Really Real place and to make these characters and activities Real, the inclusion of images becomes another strategy of communication and performance in Daly's work.

Notes on Getting Personal

This final point about Daly's work with language shows one of the differences between her and Luther in their use of words to name individuals: Both subvert dominant meanings of words and texts, and both are intensely critical of their adversaries, but only Daly also shifts conventionally negative terms into positive meanings. Luther remains intensely polarized against the persons who represent the ideas that he criticizes. Daly does this also, but because she moves into and beyond the margins of reality, she has to construct new persons and new activities. In order to do that she has to construct new meanings of old words. In both cases, the two reformers use names and plays on the names of people who are in their estimation part of the problem. Daly offers more positive construction than Luther in this regard, though both are consistently enacting their worldviews and methodologies.

Institutional Criticism

The institutions of the papacy and patriarchy remain the problem for both Luther and Daly throughout their careers as the previous chapter showed in depth. Their analyses of the institutions showcase their creative and constructive rhetoric dramatically. The choice of words that each makes reveals very clearly their substantive theological problems with these evil institutions.

The Antichrist

Luther consistently associates the pope, bishops, cardinals, et.al. with evil, the devil, Satan, and/or the Antichrist. In 1545 he asks "do you almost believe that the Roman See, pope and cardinals, are possessed of all the devils and their rascally gibberish has neither bottom, end, nor measure?"[45] He actually did believe that this was the case. Emboldened by the Word of God, he seeks over and over again to make and reinforce his case that not only were the pope and cardinals not acting and teaching according to scripture, but they acted and taught according to some nefarious authority. Because it was clear to him that they were actually enemies of God's word, they logically were associates of the devil. Just as Daly insisted that exorcism needed to go along with working for liberation, Luther identified the demonic character of the institution that he railed against.

Luther's understanding of the papacy as an institution of the devil is first articulated in "The Freedom of a Christian" and "To the Christian Nobility of the German Nation" in 1520, and it emerged fully formed in his 1545 polemic "Against the Roman Papacy." His early treatises present the pope as antichrist with a relatively mild and somewhat logical explanation: The pope and his teachings have been without the words of Christ. Anything without Christ is against Christ. Therefore, he is the antichrist. Luther uses the papacy's own claim about representing Christ against the pope himself:

> A man is a vicar only when his superior is absent. If the pope rules, while Christ is absent and does not dwell in his heart, what else is he but a vicar of Christ? What is the church under such a vicar but a mass of people without Christ? Indeed what is such a vicar but an antichrist and an idol?[46]

The danger of which Luther was keenly aware in 1520 was that a large number of people believed in and were being led by this vicar. Later in the same treatise he suggests that they were being dragged down to hell. He continues presenting the pope as antichrist as a logical conclusion: "But if an authority does anything against Christ, then that authority is the power of Antichrist and the devil."[47] Anyone who does anything against Christ serves the interests of those powers against Christ, and therefore he is the antichrist. The pope and papacy are anti-Christ.

Naming the pope as Antichrist would have been intensely shocking to Luther's audience. The term may have lost some of its bite over the intervening centuries, but at the time, Luther was speaking the unspeakable:

---

45. Luther, "Against the Roman Papacy," (1545), in *LW* 41:285.
46. Luther, "The Freedom of a Christian" (1520), in *LW* 31:342.
47. Luther, "To the Christian Nobility" (1520), in *LW* 44:138.

He equated the Holy Father, the head of the Roman Catholic Church, with the devil himself. Because of this, Luther found justification for burning the pope's books and the papal bull that excommunicated him. To be against Christ is to be the antichrist, and to teach contrary to Christ is to be unchristian. Luther sees more and more danger to Christians as the years of these teachings continue. His boldness in naming is derived again from his worldview and his certainty about the authority he derived from the Word of God.

"Against the Roman Papacy" appeared in 1545 and is the most sustained and intense example of Luther's rhetorical revolt. Logic, humility, and generosity are all but gone in this text. Toward the end of that treatise, he insists that "this devilish popery is the last misfortune on earth, nearest to that which all the devils can do with all their might."[48] As the previous chapter showed, the treatise is a combination of exegetical work on Matthew 16, debunking the papal interpretation that the power of the keys is given directly to Peter and all of his successors, as well as a political ranting against the summons to a council that Luther insists will be neither free, Christian, or German. Sprinkled liberally throughout are vitriolic statements like "this damned ass-pope"[49] showing that Luther's criticism of the institution is intimately bound up with his criticisms of the individuals within it.

Luther was able to be verbally abusive and crass because of his sense of the urgency of the situation. He sincerely believed and understood that this institution of the papacy was a means by which the devil was gaining power in the world, preventing Christians from seeing the transcendent Word of God and providing false assurances to Christians for its own selfish gain. Because of the clarity of his vision about the evil institution, he had fewer and fewer hesitations about speaking his mind to the fullest extent. This is where Edwards identifies the apocalyptic strain in Luther's writings. Luther was convinced that the evil Roman Empire had emerged as the wicked majority power once again, and that he was part of the righteous minority that had to speak truth in the face of overwhelming danger. Edwards makes this connection: "The papacy was the antichrist alluded to in the eleventh chapter of Daniel. . . . The appearance of the papal antichrist . . . left no doubt in Luther's mind that the apocalyptic

---

48. Luther, "Against the Roman Papacy" (1545), in *LW* 41:376.
49. Ibid., 323.

drama was in its final act."⁵⁰ Because this was the ultimate drama playing out in his time, Luther spoke more and more as a righteous prophet and less like a pastor with every passing year. Again, I think that his worldview which envisioned the transcendent reality of the Word of God made this possible. Whether or not he thought that the end was imminent, Luther was consistently driven by and driven back to the Word of God. Words and images were naturally the tools on which Luther relied to attempt to really "call things by their right names."

Separatism from Dummydom

Daly has many names for the institutions under the canopy of patriarchy which thrive on and feed off of it. These all can be found under the heading of:

> **phallo-institutions** *n*: the building blocks of the Phallic State: sadosystems erected to block process, to confuse, ensnare, deceive, and defeat Journeyers; the major institutions of patriarchy, e.g., the all-male family, elementary schooling, necromantic luv, sado-religion, missile envy, apartheid.⁵¹

Daly argues that all of the institutions alluded to here, including the family, the state, the educational system, religion, and segregated political systems, erase women, promote a culture of death, and reinforce the tyrannical rule of males. These institutions are the problem because they are part of or supporters of patriarchy. Individuals were the perpetrators of the system, and institutions were the ways that they organized themselves in order to further exert their control.

A few of Daly's specific examples of phallo-institutions reveal how almost no dimension of reality is left uncriticized:

> **dummydom** *n*: any domain of dummies. *Examples*: wall street, the pentagon, harvard university.⁵²
>
> **family, patriarchal** *n* [(derived fr. L *familia* servants of a household): "*archaic*: a group of persons in the service of an individual (he had a great family, that is to say . . . many slaves . . .)"—*Webster's*]: primary unit of the sadosociety, consisting of slaves organized in

---

50. Edwards, *Luther's Last Battles*, 97.
51. Daly, *Wickedary*, 217.
52. Ibid., 196.

domestic and sexual service to a snool as their head. *Cockaludicrous Comments*:

> This order [of domestic society] includes both the primacy of the husband with regard to the wife and children, the ready subjection of the wife and her willing obedience.
> —pope Pius XI

> Wives are young men's mistresses, companions for middle age, and old men's nurses.
> —Francis Bacon[53]

Institutions that are common and famous, mundane and popular are specifically named in Daly's webs of words. Systems of economic life are represented by her inclusion of Wall Street, while the Pentagon embodies US military power. The etymology and archaic definitions of "family" reveal for Daly what was really at the heart of this institution of patriarchy. The words of Bacon and Pope Pius XI simply reinforce the real values in patriarchal families: women's obedience and subjection. The "sadosociety" to which she refers here is defined elsewhere as "the sum of places/times where the beliefs and practices of sadomasochism are The Rule."[54] Defined in these ways, these institutions serve the interests of only the male heads, which makes them prime targets for feminist criticism.

Like her naming of individuals, Daly's naming of institutions also takes a constructive turn as she envisions new institutions and communities of women who took leave of patriarchy. Including Harvard University as a "domain of dummies" in the previous definition has particular significance in her work. In 1971, Mary Daly was the first woman to preach at Harvard Memorial Church, and the text of that sermon is now widely anthologized as an effective expression of the second-wave feminist call to depart from patriarchal institutions. Before the exodus described in chapter two, she concluded the sermon with a critical naming of the institution in which she was speaking:

> We cannot really belong to institutional religion as it exists. It isn't good enough to be token preachers. It isn't good enough to have our energies drained and co-opted. Singing sexist hymns, praying to a male god breaks our spirit, makes us less than human. The

---

53. Ibid., 197
54. Ibid., 94.

crushing weight of this tradition, of this power structure, tells us that we do not even exist.[55]

Several participants wrote about the experience later: "We walked *together*, not so much out of Memorial Church, as *toward* possibility and strength in sisterhood."[56] Daly understood Sisterhood as a bonding and a mode of relating, and saw Women's Space as physical and psychic. Once departing the silence and darkness of patriarchal traditions, women are called to live on the Boundary: The Boundary has "Time and Space created by women Surviving and Spinning"[57] Patriarchy is the overarching problem, the shoddy canopy trying to envelop reality, and conventional institutions that hold it up, like churches and universities, must be abandoned in order to bring the canopy down and to create this new space.

This is where the feminist utopia takes shape in Daly's vision. She defines her separatist philosophy as it informs this marginal living:

> **Separatism, Radical Feminist:** theory and actions of Radical Feminists who choose separation from the Dissociated State of patriarchy in order to release the flow of elemental energy and Gynophilic communication; radical withdrawal of energy from warring patriarchy and transferral of this energy to women's Selves.[58]

While Daly regularly alludes to and imagines a space and place set apart, it is also clear that the fundamental characteristic of her feminist separatist utopia is a redirection of energy. This is why she focuses much of her construction on the actions that take place "in" the Background, like Spinning, Re-membering, and Be-Musing. Old institutions of patriarchy therefore lose the reservoir of women's energy from which they have been stealing, and Women's Selves are re-energized as authentic Beings hearing their own words and naming their own reality.

Notes on Institutional Criticism

In word and in action, Daly left the institutions she criticized, both church and patriarchy. Luther never did leave the church, though his words and actions clearly indicate his desire to end the papacy as he knew it. Both

---

55. Daly, "The Women's Movement," 332.
56. Barufaldi, "Letters from the Exodus Community," 334.
57. Daly, *Wickedary*, 67.
58. Ibid., 96.

reformers focused on the words used to name the institutions that they criticized, and the words used by those institutions. They were both empowered to write increasingly harsh things against tremendously powerful institutions like the Roman See and the Pentagon because both were very certain of a higher authority or a deeper reality with which they were in touch. Both take on powerful authorities, and both eventually pay for that by risking their lives and reputations.

Group Exclusion

The certainty that defines Luther's and Daly's criticisms of powerful institutions also leads them both to definitively exclude groups of people from their idealized communities. Language that Luther used about the Jews and his recommendations on how to deal with them reveals his low estimation of their worth in the world, and Daly's reclamation of the word "anti-male" and claim of it as a valid descriptor reveals her low estimation of their role in the future. Are the two reformers calling things by their right names when they essentialize human identity in their rhetoric about entire classes of people?

Theologically Anti-Semitic

Luther writes about the Jews at various times throughout his career. In 1523 he writes "That Jesus Christ Was Born a Jew" in part to further criticize the papacy and to protect Jews and Christians from believing that the papal authorities spoke truth about Christianity. He ostensibly seeks to protect the Jews in this essay, recognizing a kinship between Jews and Christians, and suggesting "that one deal gently with them and instruct them from Scripture; then some of them may come along."[59] He wants them to recognize the truth as he saw it and join the Christian community. While these words are in fact quite gentle judging by his later work, they show that his concerns about Jews are fundamentally consistent with the rest of his worldview where everything is guided and judged by one true authority: the Word of God.

Twenty years later, in 1543, Luther published the extremist piece "On the Jews and Their Lies." In the introduction to its translation and publication in the American Edition, Martin Bertram acknowledged the potential misuse of the treatise even as it is reprinted in 1971. The rhetoric

---

59. Luther, "That Jesus Christ Was Born a Jew" (1523), in *LW* 45:229.

about the Jews in the text is so problematic that he felt it important to include the disclaimer:

> Such publication is in no way intended as an endorsement of the distorted views of Jewish faith and practice or the defamation of the Jewish people which this treatise contains.[60]

The inclusion of such a disclaimer vividly demonstrates awareness of the impact of Luther's thought on anti-Semitism, and the practical reality of such anti-Semitism witnessed throughout Western history. The awareness of the impact, though, was not Luther's, it was a later editor's. Understanding the treatise as a whole shows how it largely remains methodologically and substantively consistent with the rest of Luther's work and his rhetorical style.

The treatise has four sections that grow increasingly violent and specific. In the first section, Luther analyzes the "lies" that Jews tell about their lineage, homeland, and national identity. He then spends an extensive part of the treatise on the "lies" about the Messiah as they understand it, and eventually moves to examine their "lies against persons."[61] Here, he invokes numerous superstitions and stereotypes about Jews popular in the sixteenth century, before he concludes with a call to action in seven steps, spelled out in political and theological terms for both the princes and the Christians in Germany. In every section of the polemical writing, Luther relies heavily on exegesis of scripture to show how the Jews were wrong, and to show how he was right.

One example of this use of the Word of God to challenge the teachings and actions of the Jews focused on the practice of circumcision as sign of the covenant. Luther states that

> it is not a clever and ingenious, but a clumsy, foolish, and stupid lie when the Jews boast of their circumcision before God, presuming that God should regard them graciously for that reason, though they should certainly know from Scripture that they are not the only race circumcised in compliance with God's decree, and that they cannot on that account be God's special people.[62]

---

60. Martin Bertram, "Introduction to 'On the Jews and Their Lies,'" in *LW* 47:123.
61. Luther, "On the Jews and Their Lies" (1543), in *LW* 47:254.
62. Ibid., 152.

He goes on to show how they should know from scripture that they are not the only chosen people, and further, how texts in Deuteronomy, Leviticus, and Jeremiah speak about a circumcision of the heart. Luther mocks and belittles Jews as he points out these texts and concludes that

> these and similar passages prove irrefutably that the Jews' arrogance and boast of circumcision over against the uncircumcised Gentiles are null and void, and, unless accompanied by something else, deserves nothing but God's wrath.[63]

As he had little patience for the papists and their misuse of scripture to justify their selfish and arrogant actions, Luther had little patience for the Jews' claim of a special heritage based on scripture.

His rhetoric against the Jews reaches its most specific when it becomes the most violent in the fourth section of the treatise. He outlines in seven steps what ought to be done about the Jews:

> First, to set fire to their synagogues or schools. . . . Second, that their houses also be razed and destroyed. . . . Third, I advise that all their prayer books and Talmudic writings . . . be taken from them. . . . Fourth, I advise that their rabbis be forbidden to teach henceforth on pain of loss of life and limb. . . . Fifth, I advise that safe-conduct on the highways be abolished completely for the Jews. . . . Sixth, I advise that usury be prohibited to them. . . . Seventh, I recommend putting a flail, an ax, a hoe . . . into the hands of young strong Jews and Jewesses and letting them earn their bread . . .[64]

The editors of the American edition note how similar these proposals are to "the actions of the National Socialist regime in Germany in the 1930's and 1940's."[65] Because of this, it is usually this section of this treatise that receives the most attention for its shocking and eerily prescient calls for burning synagogues, destroying Jewish texts, and enslaving young Jews to work. In context, the build-up to the calls to action can be seen as theologically motivated, albeit deeply anti-Semitic.

Luther was an anti-Semite in several ways. A current definition of anti-Semitism includes several bases for prejudice and discrimination against Jews, all of which have been seen throughout history: "their re-

63. Ibid., 155.
64. Ibid., 268–72.
65. Ibid., 268 n73.

ligious beliefs, their group membership (ethnicity) and sometimes . . . the erroneous belief that Jews are a 'race.'"[66] Luther demonstrates this erroneous understanding of Jews as a race, seen in the comment below, exemplary of many others throughout his treatise:

> They let us work in the sweat of our brow to earn money and property while they sit behind the stove, idle away the time, fart, and roast pears. They stuff themselves, guzzle, and live in luxury and ease from our hard-earned goods. With their accursed usury they hold us and our property captive.[67]

The stereotypes invoked here are typical of much racist rhetoric: the minority group in a culture is "known" to be greedy, lazy, a burden on society, and detrimental to the hard-working, god-fearing, dominant people. Luther's misplaced racism, his anti-Semitism, is theologically motivated, however, and seems consistent with his rhetoric about the papists as well as the Turks. All three groups—Jews, papists, and Turks—blaspheme the Word of God and this violates God and confuses Christians. He says that

> we have seen this happen in the case of the papacy and of Muhammad. The example of the Jews demonstrates clearly how easily the devil can mislead people, after they once have digressed from the proper understanding of Scripture, into such blindness and darkness that it can be readily grasped and perceived simply by natural reason, yes, even by irrational beasts.[68]

In all three cases, the devil is at work, masked as the Jew, the Muslim, or the papist, because each of those groups misuses the Word of God, fails to understand it, and gives false assurances to the masses.

Within his own system of thought, this rhetoric is mostly consistent with his worldview and method. He uses his exegesis of several different biblical texts to debunk the claims of the Jews, he uses scripture to interpret scripture, and he is concerned first and foremost with being true to the Word of God. Where it differs, though, is with his specific calls to action. In his diatribes against the papists, Luther never calls for the destruction of their homes and cities, and never seeks to prohibit their free travel as he did with the Jews. He did hurl personal insults at them and call for the destruction of their texts. Luther spoke directly about burning

66. Anti-Defamation League, "101 Ways to Combat Prejudice."
67. Luther, "On the Jews and Their Lies" (1543), in *LW* 47:266.
68. Ibid., 253.

the papal bulls and writings, much in the same way that he called for a destruction of Jewish prayer books and Talmudic writings. Luther's theological critiques of the papists and the Jews are similar. The difference is the anti-Semitic element he finally reveals in his critique of the Jews. This is one glaring example where Luther fails his own theological criterion and calls something by its wrong name. He did not understand that Jews were not a race and he made the same error when using the word "Turks" when he likely meant Muslims, not all of whom are Turkish. We can use Luther to read Luther on this matter, and recognize his limitation. The problem that this introduces as a limitation to his work will be dealt with at length in the next chapter.

Philosophically Anti-Male

Mary Daly understands that there are classes of people in the world, and she herself identifies with a "Race of Women." She essentializes gender as the prime category of identification, while allowing for the fact that race, class, sexuality, age, and other identifiers are used to oppress classes of people, albeit under the control of patriarchy. She becomes increasingly aware throughout the course of her work that it was criticized for being anti-male. If we use her reclaimed definition of anti-male described in *Gyn/Ecology*, where she insists that since she is staunchly opposed to patriarchy, and males are the only ones who control and benefit from patriarchy, then it is easy to see how she is anti-male. The question of her treatment of men as a class of people leads to complex answers, in part because her engagement with the "issue" of men shifted over time. The shifts were both strategic and substantive.

We must remember that Daly's critical work was thoroughly systemic: She focused on the institutional reality of patriarchy rather than only on the perpetrators of it. The system was the main problem, and she criticized anyone who participated in it. This included women, and she famously named women who buy in to and help justify patriarchy the "token torturers." These are the women who believe, for example, that binding the feet of their daughters will be good for them, who buy in to the idea that a 4-inch debilitated foot or a mutilated clitoris is what is necessary to ensure a girl's future marriage and life.[69] Women can clearly be part of the problem of patriarchy, buying in to their own domination

---

69. Daly, *Gyn/Ecology*, 134–52.

and oppression as well as perpetrating it on others. So can men be part of the solution, the revolution?

Daly's answers shift throughout the course of her work, and might follow in this sequence: yes, maybe, no, and ultimately, who cares? A snapshot of her language about men shows this transformation. In *The Church and the Second Sex*, Daly seems to allow and even call for the participation of men in a reformation of the church and its practices. The final chapter is titled "Toward Partnership" and in the conclusion of that 1968 text she speaks of men and women working together against sexism and prejudice. In *Beyond God the Father*, her language shifts to a discussion of androgyny. Androgyny in 1973 signifies for her a sort of hope for transcending what she then called the sexual caste system; but she also warns against universalizing the problem: "One frequently hears: 'But isn't the real problem human liberation?' The difficulty with this approach is that the words used may be 'true,' but when used to avoid confronting the specific problems of sexism they are radically untruthful."[70] Here, while overcoming categories of gender identity and sexual caste is the goal, she insists that we not forget who the real victims of sexism are. Men are not systemically paid less, barred from educational institutions, or threatened with sexual violence every day. Women are. This is what I would call the "maybe" phase of Daly's inclusion of or attention to men as part of the revolution.

As her work continued to develop, her words shift from partnership to androgyny and ultimately to gynocentrism. She more fiercely focuses on women and their actions and relations as the decades pass. They are what receive almost all of her attention after 1975, and the question of men becomes a nonquestion. The reason for this is tied to her keen sense of the dynamics of male privilege that function in any place where men and women are together. This included her classroom. In *Amazon Grace* in 2006, she discusses the incident that eventually ended her teaching career: "For about twenty-five years I'd had a classroom policy of teaching women and men separately in my Feminist Ethics classes. I developed this method during the early 1970s, after I saw the dulling of women's participation that occurred in mixed classes."[71] While she insists that she never refused to teach a student who met the prerequisites for any of her classes, Daly was aware of the effect of men's presence on women's consciousness.

---

70. Daly, *Beyond God the Father*, 5–6.
71. Daly, *Amazon Grace*, 70.

Further performing her worldview and her words, Daly's separate sections of Feminist Ethics eventually became targets for a lawsuit funded by the Center for Individual Rights. This will be described in more detail in the next chapter, but here it provides a concrete example of how she enacted what it means for her to be anti-male. In a classroom, it means to actively work against the privileges that patriarchy bestows on men. Daly had observed the tendency of the female students to either silence themselves or focus their energy on educating the male students, and she found this utterly counterproductive to a course in feminist ethics.

This embodies what I describe as being philosophically anti-male. It is not necessarily to be against men individually. This concept makes sense and can be justified only within the systemic reality of patriarchy: To be philosophically anti-male is to intentionally view and respond to the male sex in specific ways designed to combat the privilege that they enjoy under patriarchy. This idea is consistent with the rest of her theological and philosophical system which carefully analyzes the overt and covert ways that patriarchy exerts control over the minds and lives of all who live within it. Women are better equipped to realize this and move to the margins because there is *no* benefit for them under patriarchy. Men are less able to realize this because there *are* benefits for them under patriarchy, whether they want them or not. Their possible participation in the revolution, then, cannot be the concern of women. If they are able to, good, but that has to be determined by them. One of the chief sins of women in the patriarchal past has been excessive focus on the needs and well-being of men. Daly insists that this must cease immediately, even and especially in the work of dismantling patriarchy.

Notes on Group Exclusion

Both Luther and Daly were unashamed and even arrogant about their exclusion of a group of people from their vision of liberation and the struggle required to achieve it. Neither was apologetic or ever wavered as witnessed in their very specific words and actions regarding the group they excluded. This is because for both, the exclusion of the particular group of people was consistent with their worldview and method, and it reflected their growing certainty throughout the decades of their work that their insight into reality was insight into a greater truth that justified all of their actions and rhetoric. Both end up essentializing human identity in accord with their vision, however. Luther saw the world in terms of Christians and Daly saw the world in terms of women. Both had good reasons for doing this, but for both this exclusionary move leads to a particular limitation that will be explored in the following chapter.

Parallels, Differences, and Inversions

Focusing on Luther's and Daly's use of words to name people, institutions, and groups and their polemic rhetorical strategies and styles reveals a depth to the ideological system of each. Their use of words and their methods reveal their conceptualizations in parallel, different, and inverse ways.

Parallel Equations: Word/Words = God/Women

Both Luther and Daly equate words/Word with the agent of liberation: God and women. These are things that exist outside of the institution which is sharply critiqued, though the institution has attempted to co-opt them. For Luther, the Word (logos, Christ) is God. Words are one of the devices by which humans can access The Word, and words are resources for calling the thing what it is. For Daly, words and women are equated insofar as they have all been taken captive and now can be resources for unmasking patriarchy. Both words and women connect to a Background level of reality that the foreground attempts to shut out. God for Luther and women for Daly are sacred, true, authentic, and free. In the same way that the papacy has misused and distorted the Word (Christ) and the words (of scripture), patriarchy has abused and manipulated women and falsely fixed meanings of words. By liberating the words, Luther and Daly seek to liberate humanity from the tyrannical institution.

In the same way that Luther and Daly equate the positive resources of God and women with words, they extensively employ rhetoric about evil, the devil, and exorcism in describing and responding to their adversaries. The papacy is the antichrist for Luther while patriarchy is the root of evil for Daly. Luther speaks of the devilish pope while Daly seeks to exorcize words who are possessed with demonic meanings. Both freely employ language that upholds a paradigm of good versus evil because both are completely convinced that they recognize true evil as well as true good. Only a person who has no semblance of doubt about his or her worldview can speak so freely about such massive realities.

Difference: Use of the Bible

The obvious difference between Luther and Daly in the area of words and their understanding and use of them is Luther's defining claim to rest all of his convictions on scripture, the Word of God. Daly almost never uses scripture, and the few references to it that do appear in *Beyond God the Father* serve only to show the problems that exist in religious traditions. In no way is it a definitive source or text for her work. This is in sharp contrast to the way in which it is *the* definitive source and text for Luther. Daly has no external authoritative text on which she draws or grounds her work, other than her creative employment of the dictionary. In fact, she creates her own corpus of work to which she refers repeatedly. In the *Wickedary* she indicates with a moon phase symbol in which text of hers the word being defined originally appears. Luther is continually bound by and pulled back to the external authoritative texts of the Bible in every moment of his work. He sees himself as a mere servant to the Word of God revealed in scripture, and will say (almost) nothing unless it is grounded there. Both Luther and Daly use words as tools, but Luther is bound to an external source, the Bible as the revealed Word of God: The Word is completely objective for Luther while words are completely subjective for Daly.

This difference frees Daly to be more positively creative—she invents words and ideas to describe the world that she imagines, the feminist utopia, the Background. The positive Christian utopia that Luther envisions is already described by God in scripture, and therefore his rhetoric and creative application of language remains largely negative and critical. Daly becomes creatively positive as she imagines a whole Otherworld that is yet unrealized. This difference also allows us to criticize Luther for potential abuse of the external source, when he uses the Word of God as his justification for destroying the Jews. If he is beholden to scripture, then it is the perfect resource with which we can critically debunk his own writing against the Jews in the next chapter.

Inverse Imaging and Exclusion

In the later polemics of Luther and Daly, they both incorporate artwork from a contemporary artist to express and embody key ideas. However, the images accompanying Luther's criticism of the papacy are of the papacy and are critical and disgusting representations of the pope and cardinals. The images accompanying Daly's work are of the created world that she envisions, the inhabitants and activities of the Background. Cranach's images for Luther are grotesque and negative representations of his adversaries. Rakusin's images for Daly are delightful and positive representations of creatures with whom she imaginatively cavorts. In addition to the inversion of positive and negative imagery, the images for Luther are of actual people and institutions, while for Daly they are imagined people and activities.

Another inversion lies in the group exclusion that emerges for each reformer. Luther writes as a theological anti-Semite and Daly writes as philosophically anti-male. Both arrive here at a limitation to their method and style, which will be considered more fully in the next chapter. The essentialism of both is consistent with the rest of their systems of thought, but Luther's is based on erroneous ideas about race and has theological motivation while Daly's is based on systemic and real gender politics and has philosophical justification. They both can be seen as categorically excluding a class of people from their revolutions. For both, the group in question (Jews and men) could theoretically be part of the reformed world, but practically, Luther and Daly don't seem to care much in the end.

The major inversion here is that the group Luther isolates and marginalizes is a minority group already subject to discrimination and violence, while the group that Daly isolates and marginalizes is the group who holds the majority of power in a patriarchal world. This dramatically affects how we can evaluate this group exclusion element: Luther's theological anti-Semitism is part of a shameful legacy of Christian prejudice and systematic genocide, while Daly's philosophically anti-male practice is a source of empowerment for women seeking to compensate for centuries of injustice perpetrated against women. The controversies that arise here for both reformers give final concrete form to the political relevance of their theologies, a proposal now worth considering at length.

PART THREE

Interpretation and Analysis

The final three chapters of the book move into more sustained comparative analysis of Mary Daly's and Martin Luther's reforming theological work. Some evaluation of their limitations and legacies is necessary before returning to the proposal that they be thought of as political theologians as a way to understand the parallels, differences, and inversions noticed throughout this book.

At the end, the question of whether or not it was all worth it is posed, and we find two unlikely conversation partners pointing us in new directions as we continue the work of understanding and constructing the world. What did they get right? What did they get wrong? And of course, why? What can we learn from two disaffected Catholics who abandon reality with hopes for a utopian community of equals?

7

Legacies and Limitations

Even if I were the only one, I would still be a Radical Feminist![1]

In the first place, I ask that men make no reference to my name; let them call themselves Christians, not Lutherans.[2]

They failed. Mary Daly did not reform the Catholic tradition she first engaged. The Roman Catholic Church tempered its reforming spirit by 1965 after the Second Vatican Council ended, it did not enact male-female partnership in its leadership models, and it has yet to be the fully egalitarian community demanded by Daly and others. Daly made a conscious decision in the 1970s to fully abandon efforts to reform not only the Catholic church, but also Christianity itself. By that time feminism was a wave beginning to crest and this was a definitive moment in U.S. history, but it was not the one that Daly sought. Likewise, Martin Luther did not reform all of Christianity in the way that he intended. The Roman Catholic Church defensively circled the wagons by 1545 with the Council of Trent, declared no salvation outside the Church, and refused to engage in the reforms demanded by Luther and others. An entirely new branch of Christianity, Protestantism, grew from this split. This was a definitive moment in the Christian tradition but it was not the one that Luther sought.

Each reformer reached a limit to his or her work. At the same time that their failures are obvious, the legacy of each is remarkable. Both Daly and Luther were igniting forces for the social, political, and ecclesial tinder that enveloped them. The second wave of the women's movement in the United States remains a marker of distinctive social and cultural shifts

---

1. Daly, *Quintessence*, xi.
2. Luther, "A Sincere Admonition by Martin Luther" (1522), in *LW* 45:70.

to which Christianity around the world is still responding and engaging. Daly's role in this movement was pioneering and revolutionary, raising just as many questions as providing answers. The reformation of the sixteenth century is a definitive moment in the development of the Christian tradition, and Luther's role in it was indisputably central.

Before fully considering Mary Daly and Martin Luther as political theologians, we need to consider the limitations and the legacies of their theological work. For Daly, this requires examining her philosophically anti-male view, understanding why she left the church and Christianity as irredeemable, and seeing how she viewed the definition and expansion of feminism during and after the second wave. For Luther, this requires examining why he expressed anti-Semitic attitudes, understanding why he called for the suppression of the "murdering hordes of peasants," and seeing how he responded to the emergence of "Lutherans."

Anti-Male and Anti-Semitic

As discussed briefly in the previous chapter, Daly and Luther each systemically exclude an entire class of people from their reforming visions. How and why they do this is best examined in historical context. Daly's early affirmations of partnership and androgyny fade away as she realizes and articulates the overwhelming physical and spiritual destruction wrought by patriarchy. The liberation of males and the participation of males in the liberation of women becomes a nonissue for her as she deliberately works to de-emphasize the male in society, in her classroom and in her philosophy. They and their comfort are not her concern, and she insists that they do not merit the energy of women's attention. Luther's anti-Judaism morphs into an anti-Semitism based on his flawed understanding of Jews as a race, and what began for him as a passionate defense of the truth and grace of God revealed in Christ becomes a dangerous call for violence against a minority group. His religious concerns get mixed up in political realities and he ultimately relies on his more privileged social status to pass judgment on the Jews.

Daly: Anti-patriarchy and Anti-male

As described in the previous chapter: To be philosophically anti-male is to intentionally view and respond to the male sex in specific ways designed to combat the privilege that men enjoy under patriarchy. I emphasize this because the label of "anti-male" is one that is commonly used to deride and denigrate feminist work. Clearly that is not my intention here. For using and interpreting this label as a limitation and a legacy, I take cues from Daly herself in her discussions of it and in her reflections on the practice of female-only feminist ethics classes.

Daly recognized that such a label as "anti-male" would be leveled against her work. Anticipating criticism of *Gyn/Ecology* in 1978, she writes, "This will of course be called an 'anti-male' book. Even the most cautious and circumspect feminist writings are described in this way."[3] The intent of this label when applied by men and other supporters of patriarchy is to discredit the work in question and deny the author legitimacy. She refers to this label as an unimaginative cliché that makes "real hearing of what radical feminists are saying difficult, at times even for ourselves."[4] Use of this label is meant to block thinking, trigger fears, and freeze minds, "for to write an 'anti-male' book is to utter the ultimate blasphemy."[5] The threat of being seen as blasphemous did not deter Daly in the least. On the contrary, it is actually logical to be anti-male if you are combating patriarchy:

> Thus women continue to be intimidated by the label *anti-male*. Some feel a false need to draw distinctions, for example: 'I am anti-patriarchal but not anti-male.' The courage to be logical [requires] that we admit to ourselves that males and males only are the originators . . . of patriarchy.[6]

In the context of her own thought and in the context of patriarchy, it makes perfect sense to be anti-male. She goes on in the same passage to emphasize that we live in a "profoundly anti-female society" in which males repeatedly and collectively victimize women. In such a world, she insists that her work is "beyond the limitations of the label *anti-male*, it is absolutely Anti-androcrat, A-mazingly Anti-male, Furiously and Finally Female."[7] Not only does she reclaim the label, anti-male, she pushes it beyond the boundaries of its own meaning.

3. Daly, *Gyn/Ecology*, 27.
4. Ibid., 28.
5. Ibid.
6. Ibid.
7. Ibid., 29.

As logical as this is within her own philosophical system, Daly eventually runs into the limits of being Anti-male in her daily work as a professor at Boston College. As mentioned briefly in the preceding chapter, Daly ended her teaching career at the Jesuit institution amid controversy over her practice of excluding men from her Introduction to Feminist Ethics class.[8] A male student was enrolled in her class without her consent and without the prerequisites for the Spring 1999 semester. After noticing this, Daly was informed in December 1998 by her department chair that the student was supported by a conservative law firm in Washington D.C., the Center for Individual Rights. The student and the CIR threatened a sex discrimination lawsuit if he was not allowed in the class. Daly notes that she'd had a policy and practice of teaching men and women separately in her Feminist Ethics classes for about twenty-five years, "after I saw the dulling of women's participation that occurred in mixed classes." She emphatically states that she "never refused to teach a student, female or male, who expressed interest and had completed the course prerequisites."[9] If men were interested in and prepared for the class, she would teach them separately from the women.

Nevertheless and ironically, CIR cited Title IX legislation in their suit and used legislation that was originally passed to ensure women's access to education to force the college to enroll a male student in Daly's Feminist Ethics course. Boston College agreed to settle with the student and CIR in 1998 before Daly was notified. One of the stipulations of the settlement was that the student in question be allowed to enroll. Daly's response was to first take a leave of absence rather than being forced into violating her classroom standards. During subsequent meetings with administrators, she recalls "I must have blurted out something like 'I'd rather resign than teach under these conditions,' and they jumped at this chance to take me at my word."[10] They asked her to sign a retirement agreement that included a gag order at that time, and she refused. In February 1999 she filed a lawsuit against Boston College for breach of contract and violation of academic freedom and tenure. Her name and courses were removed from the 1999–2000 college catalog without notice.[11] The case proceeded and four

8. Daly discusses this at length in *Amazon Grace*, 69–77. My description is taken from her recollections there.

9. Daly, *Amazon Grace*, 70.

10. Ibid., 73.

11. During this period of time, Daly spoke about her case at a session titled "Feminist

days before it was scheduled to go to trial in February 2001, a settlement was reached and the announcement was that Daly had agreed to retire from the college. The Boston College press release gives the impression of a concession by Daly, stating that "Daly and her attorney, Gretchen Van Ness, approached the University for a settlement."[12] However, Daly's own discussion in *Amazon Grace* provides a somewhat different picture:

> It was not until the end of the twentieth century, the time when the ultraconservative takeover of power in the US and in the catholic church was rapidly encroaching, that they reached the point of savagely and illegally disappearing me. . . . What they perpetrated against me was an act of rapism . . . "the fundamental ideology and practice of patriarchy, characterized by invasion, violation, degradation . . ."[13]

Daly's resolute and perhaps philosophically justifiable Anti-male practices thus were permanently moved off campus in 2001, ending her 35 year teaching career at Boston College.

To hear her tell it, these events confirmed the irretrievability of patriarchy and all of the institutions that support it. She had managed to successfully teach and live just on the margins over the course of four decades. She gives the impression that it was no longer sustainable because of the rise of conservatism as a massive social force in the late twentieth century, and the loss of the age of protests and demonstrations that originally saved her position amid controversy in the late 1960s. She also describes it as a systemic maneuver intended to not only remove her from the college but also to remind all women that they are not really welcome in a male dominated space. In the words of Anowa, a character with whom Daly has imagined conversation in *Amazon Grace*,

> By invading and violating your classroom and taking away your job, they were trying to shut you up and destroy the possibility of Women's Space at that school—as far as their tentacles could reach. Yuk!"[14]

Pedagogies and Academic Freedom" at the American Academy of Religion Annual Meeting in Boston, November 22, 1999. I attended the session which also included remarks from her lawyer Gretchen Van Ness.

12. Boston College Office of Public Affairs, "Mary Daly Ends Suit, Agrees to Retire."
13. Daly, *Amazon Grace*, 74.
14. Ibid., 76.

While Daly was the target and her career was a casualty of this attack, she recognizes that it is simply one more instance where patriarchy reasserted the power of the male over any space within reach of its "tentacles."

Given all of this, Daly's Anti-male ideology and practice can be seen as both a limitation and as a legacy. It is a limitation insofar as it had practical consequences for her own employment and freedom to continue teaching at the institution where she had done so for most of her professional career. It is a limitation insofar as it prejudices certain audiences against her work if they have not taken the time to understand it in depth. It is a limitation because it may or may not remain the most effective strategy for dismantling patriarchy in the twenty-first century. Her stance remains invaluable, however, and is also a legacy of her work. It is the logical conclusion of everything for which she writes and argues. It is a radical response to a world in which radical violation of women at the hands of men occurs on a daily and hourly basis. It is a necessary strategy in some instances and at some times for the well-being and preservation of women. In the same way that Alice Walker describes a womanist as "Not a separatist, except periodically for health,"[15] Daly's feminist separatism is almost entirely for the purposes of women's physical and psychic health. The legacy of Mary Daly as Anti-male is compelling and mixed.

Luther: Anti-Jewish and Anti-Semitic

In order to fully and somewhat fairly examine Luther's anti-Semitism, we should note the meaning of terms and remember the historical context of the era in which he was living and working. A distinction can be made between being anti-Jewish, which is a religious and theological position, and being anti-Semitic, previously defined as prejudice and discrimination against Jews based on any number of factors including religion, group identity, or the erroneous belief that Jews are a race. Luther's work predates the use of some of these terms, but contains evidence of both of these problematic attitudes.[16] As noted, Luther's writings about the Jews shift through the course of his life, and initially are more evangelical and welcoming in tone, focused on convincing the Jews to not believe that the

---

15. Walker, *In Search of Our Mother's Gardens*, xi.

16. The term Anti-Semitism did not come into use until the nineteenth century, appearing in 1879 in the work of a journalist named Wilhelm Marr. See Lewis, "Anti-Semites," 17–41.

papacy is an authentic representation of Christ on earth, and convincing them that he and others more fully understand the scriptures and welcome them to join in living the gospel.

In 1523, he wrote "That Jesus Christ was Born a Jew" to refute a persistent rumor that he believed that Jesus was not born of the virgin Mary, was from the lineage of Joseph and was therefore not a Jew. In addition to defending his work and clarifying his views that Mary was indeed a virgin and that Jesus was in the lineage of Abraham, the essay moves in the second part into instruction for the Jews about the nature of Jesus as the messiah.

Luther focuses on several passages in scripture to establish that Jesus was a Jew and to show that he is in fact the messiah, including texts from Genesis, 2 Samuel, Isaiah, Daniel, and Psalms. The evidence is overwhelming for him, and he thinks that it should be for anyone who reads it:

> It is amazing that the Jews are not moved to believe in this Jesus, their own flesh and blood, with whom the prophecies of Scripture actually square so powerfully and exactly, when they see that we Gentiles cling to him so hard and fast and in such numbers that many thousands have shed their blood for his sake.[17]

He communicates patience at this stage of his work, suggesting later in the essay that the Jews "have been led astray so long and so far that one must deal gently with them."[18] Instruction seems to be his goal in this piece. He still has in mind of course that the papal methods of teaching are wrong, and he points that out several times. At this point for Luther in 1523, it is safe to say that his prejudice against the Jews is mainly theological, motivated by his focused passion for the word of God revealed in Christ. He simply thinks that they are wrong in believing that the messiah has not yet come, and he wants to correct them based on scripture. At this point, Luther is anti-Jewish.

By the time that "On the Jews and Their Lies" is written in 1543, however, Luther reveals an attitude toward the Jews that will later be called anti-Semitism. This treatise was more fully examined in the preceding chapter, and we can now consider its troubling legacy. Though the term anti-Semitism comes later, hatred of the Jews predates even Luther, going back to the origins of Christianity. Prior to the fifteenth century anti-

17. Luther, "That Jesus Christ Was Born a Jew" (1523), in *LW* 46:220.
18. Ibid., 229.

Judaism dominated, but after the fifteenth century, anti-Semitism took on a new character:

> In medieval times hostility to the Jew, whatever its underlying social or psychological motivations, was defined primarily in religious terms. From the fifteenth century onward this was no longer true, and Jew hatred was redefined, becoming at first partly, and then, at least in theory, wholly racial.[19]

Luther was part of this shift in the early sixteenth century, when his theological problems with Jews and Judaism transformed into a hostility that began taking on racial overtones. Where Luther in 1523 "simply" says that Jewish beliefs are wrong and uses scripture to make his case, Luther in 1543 says that Jews slander God, that preaching to them is like preaching to a sow, and that they are blind and immovable. In the later piece he also uses scripture to make his case, but toward a different and more violent end. The recommendations for action that come at the end of the 1543 piece, examined fully in the preceding chapter, go far beyond exegesis of scripture. This is perhaps where Luther goes most lamentably astray, when he is no longer focused on scripture and its own recommendations.

Luther's early 1523 ideas about the Jews and their religious "wrongness" laid the groundwork for his 1543 recommendations for burning down their houses of worship and destroying their sacred texts. The political implications of these views realized in later centuries inevitably affects our reading of them in the twenty-first century, but trying to set that aside, the question worth exploring is this: Why did Luther move from articulating a theological anti-Judaism to recommending a course of action informed by a hateful anti-Semitism?

As we saw in the preceding chapter, Luther's rhetoric overall grows more harsh and more scatological as the years pass and as some of his efforts at reform are frustrated. His declining health and a changing cultural context perhaps affected his views on the Jews also. I believe that one central problem not yet emphasized is that Luther moves away from relying wholly on scripture for discerning truth and recommending Christian action. When he does this, he clearly reveals culturally and historically conditioned prejudices: Burning the Talmud is beyond any claims made in scripture. Restricting the travel of entire groups of people is in no way consistent with the word of God on which Luther relies elsewhere. The

---

19. Lewis, "Anti-Semites," 17.

limitation he reaches here is wholly his own: When he speaks of things that are not in fact based in scripture, he commits grave and dangerous errors. In addition to this methodological flaw, his social position and personal hubris are other factors to consider. Luther's method and style of critique of the Jews is nearly consistent with his critique of the papacy, as noted in the previous chapter, but his criticism changes based on his position of power in relation to the group. In relation to the papacy, Luther saw himself in the righteous minority. In relation to the Jews, Luther was part of the more powerful majority culture and religion. Because of this, he had the freedom and power to deal with them as he saw fit.

He fell prey, then, to a human tendency to subjugate those who are deemed inferior, either based on religion (Jewish beliefs are wrong) or based on identity (Jews are lazy people). This may serve as a warning for how human beings relate to others with whom they disagree. Luther's crude references to the bishops as hermaphrodites have far fewer implications than his references to the Jews as "irrational beasts"[20] because of his political and cultural position and privilege in Germany at the time. The papists still had more power than he did while the Jews had less. Because of these things, Luther's anti-Semitism stands as a tragic limitation to his work not the least because of the consequences of anti-Semitism realized in later centuries.

Notes on Exclusions

Daly's Anti-male ideology remains far less problematic than Luther's anti-Semitism in part because of the consequences of each. As noted, Luther's exclusion of the Jews had far more damaging results because of his power position and status as an educated and ordained church leader in a society which was already prejudiced against the minority community. Daly's exclusion or even ignoring of men has its own limitations which have been noted, but it also has its legitimate reasons and its effective use in combating patriarchy. It is important to note that at no time does Daly advocate violence, hatred, or limiting of male rights. This contrasts her exclusionary move with that of Luther quite dramatically.

---

20. Luther, "On the Jews and Their Lies" (1543), in *LW* 47:253.

Abandoning Those Who Take You Seriously

A curious moment in the life and work of Mary Daly and Martin Luther is the point at which they effectively turn their backs on groups of people who take their calls for equality and freedom seriously and put their criticisms of institutions into practice. Daly inspired and continues to inspire generations of women to work for change in the Christian church, yet she herself abandons it entirely. German peasants who wanted to get rid of the church's financial dominance and corruption found in Luther's writing a helpful criticism of the ecclesiastical authorities and their tyrannical control, but Luther is appalled at their methods of insurrection and calls for their immediate suppression by any means necessary. Daly's and Luther's messages seem to be used in ways that they do not intend them to be used. This illustrates how both have powerful legacies that transcend the limitations that they themselves impose on their visions.

In one way, Daly does what Luther counseled the peasants to do. Luther said:

> It is true, of course, that the rulers may suppress the gospel in cities or places where the gospel is, or where there are preachers; but you can leave these cities or places and follow the gospel to some other place. It is not necessary, for the gospel's sake, for you to capture or occupy the city or place; on the contrary, let the ruler have his city; you follow the gospel.[21]

Luther counsels the peasants to leave the city where a corrupt prince is in power and follow the gospel elsewhere. Daly leaves the patriarchal world where corruption is the only power. She describes her move beyond Christianity in the following way:

> Certainly, there had been other women who had "left the church." Simone deBeauvoir had become an atheist and saw little or no value in religion. But "Postchristian," to me, did not mean merely "atheist." I longed passionately for the transcendence that was held prisoner and choked by religion and theology and for the emergence of Feminist philosophy/theology.[22]

For Daly and Luther, what is at stake and what is valued is truth. Truth transcends structures and institutions as they are encountered in this mate-

---

21. Luther, "Admonition to Peace" (1525), in *LW* 46:36.
22. Daly, *Outercourse*, 174.

rial world. The two reformers agree on the matter of not getting too caught up in systems that squelch truth, and of not wasting one's energy and soul on changing things that will not change. Move on, they say.

Daly: Beyond Christianity

Daly moves on to where she believes truth is and seeks to reclaim the sense of transcendence that has been lost to a suffocating patriarchal religion and theology. A broad view of her work shows that after 1975 she ceases systematic consideration of theological questions and stops using Christian words and concepts in her philosophy. Even with the publication of *Beyond God the Father* in 1973, she describes being pleased with the editorial recommendation that the subtitle be "toward a *philosophy* of women's liberation" rather than a *theology* of women's liberation. This reveals the shift that she knew was already in progress, a shift beyond the constraints and boundaries of the discipline of theology and words like God, androgyny, and homosexuality.[23] She calls this a postchristian ideology.

Daly's postchristianity includes rejecting certain questions and battles that many feminist theologians who follow her take seriously. The issue of women's ordination is one example of an issue that she abandons. Commenting on her earlier self, Daly notes:

> The early Daly had fought for the ordination of women to the catholic priesthood, because she saw the denial of this possibility as deeply connected with all the other injustices perpetrated by the church. This perception of connection was, of course, accurate.[24]

This is the basic underlying idea that continues to inform much of the ongoing battles over the ordained leadership of women, not only in the Catholic church but even in Protestant churches that do now officially ordain women as pastors and priests. In this way, the early Daly remains an important critical source for those advocating for women's ordination. But, Daly continues describing her own views in this passage and ultimately describes the idea as one whose time has come and gone:

> However, since the early seventies I had seen the idea of women's ordination in the catholic church as an absurd contradiction and

23. Ibid., 160–64, 174–80.
24. Ibid., 181.

had often publicly compared it to the idea of a Black person seeking office in the Ku Klux Klan.[25]

She abandons the idea of women priests, and therefore abandons all those who think the idea is a good one. Women who seek positions like that of priest or pastor in the Christian church do not go far enough for Daly in their criticism of patriarchy and its institutions. If they are still operating within the structure, then they are part of the destruction that it spawns.

Daly describes the subsequent phase of her work, after 1975, in the following way:

> My analysis was no longer restricted to christianity or to the "judeo-christian" tradition, but extended to the omnipresence of patriarchal myths and symbols on this planet and to the atrocities legitimated by them.[26]

This is when she does the focused research and writing of her book, *Gyn/Ecology*, which moves beyond Christianity and beyond the western world for examples of patriarchal myth, symbol, and practice. The work is powerful and compelling, but the question of the legacy of Daly's work for women and others who do not leave the church remains. Is meaningful change within the Christian church possible? Is it necessary?

Daly's answer is emphatically No. In a futuristic conversation between Daly and Anonyma in the year 2048 B.E. (biophilic era), the following exchange explains what "happens" in the years 1998–2048:

> "Are you saying that men who insisted on clinging to patriarchal beliefs and behaviors became obsolete and 'died off'" asked Mary.
> "Yes, they rapidly became extinct," I said.
> "And what became of the patriarchally assimilated women who identified with the roles and rules of patriarchy?" asked Mary.
> I answered, "Those women who refused to release themselves from the phallocratic dependencies and habits that had been embedded in them under the old system were in effect refusing to evolve. So they also could not survive in the New energy field."[27]

Women who stay in the church and seek roles like that of ordained priest are patriarchal women for Daly. They are women who are trapped by rules

---

25. Ibid., 181–82.
26. Ibid., 195.
27. Daly, *Quintessence*, 66.

that inevitably seek their destruction, and therefore they can never evolve and be truly liberated and free. When the "New energy field" of biophilic existence breaks through, all those who cling to patriarchal and necrophilic systems and beliefs will perish.

There can be no more obvious rejection of the work of Christian feminist women who stay within the parameters of the religion to work for change in practice and belief than this description of them as refusing to evolve and therefore not surviving in a new biophilic era. Daly would interpret their failure to leave the church as a failure to truly understand its irredeemable patriarchal nature. Once patriarchy is fully understood, for her, it is clear that there is nothing good and nothing worth saving in it.

Daly describes these women as "tokenized," failing to see the systems that trap them, and working within it, unwittingly perpetuating its destructive aims:

> A woman in this situation cannot bond deeply with other women, because she fails to be Present to herSelf. Having chosen not to Realize Elemental Feminist Genius in herSelf, she may (ill)logically work to block and destroy this in others.[28]

The consequences of refusing to evolve and choosing to stay within the bounds of patriarchy are destructive not only for the individual woman, but for all women and other creatures with whom she has contact. The real danger emerges because a woman in such a situation, in the church or in academia for example, is often blind to the ways that she inhibits the growth of others. These women do not take the dangers of patriarchy seriously.

The legacy of Daly's sharp move beyond Christianity is that she follows her own radical critiques to their logical end: abandoning patriarchy. Her work represents some of the most thorough and most challenging criticism leveled against a male-dominated world. Nothing escapes unscathed: systems of religion, family, education, medicine, and research all serve the interests of the male dominators. If one takes this seriously, one must abandon real hope of transforming such powerful systems. The limitation of this move beyond Christianity, though, is that without reformers, patriarchal systems will obviously continue to do their work. Daly reveals an apocalyptic strain in her work here, especially in the futuristic conversations that take place in another realm of time and space. It is a realm where

---

28. Ibid., 169.

she and several others inhabit a time after patriarchy has destroyed itself and a place beyond the world we presently know. She leaves patriarchy and Christianity to their own devices and their own destruction. She gets out while she can, trying to "save" as many others as she is able.

Daly's hopelessness as revealed here is lamentable, however, and can be identified as a limitation of her work. While her philosophy is infused with a creative and compelling hope for another realm, recognizing the Background and moving into the biophilic era, it is at the same time infused with this dark death sentence for the world as we know it. If that is the case, why bother working for justice in this world at all? Why work to eradicate violence against women? Why raise money to build schools and hospitals in impoverished communities? If this patriarchal world is simply destined for destruction, there is no impetus to act in order to make it more habitable and just.

No great change has occurred in human history without the enormous struggles of those who appear to be trapped by their circumstances. In the history of the United States, the oppressive system of slavery is one that was irretrievably flawed and destructive. But those trapped by it, both slave and free, did not accept that it was irredeemable and did not leave the perpetrators and the victims to their own devices to spiral into destruction and demise. Also, for most of its history this country did not recognize basic rights of women to be full and free participants in its legal and political systems. Again, those living within it did not abandon it to its certain collapse. They stood up, spoke out, and began the slow process of changing attitudes, ideas, and laws. Daly herself is part of this work as it continued through the end of the twentieth century. Civil rights activism has brought about some of the most compelling legal and political changes of the twentieth century, precisely for those who are oppressed within racist and patriarchal cultures.

So is Mary Daly crazy, or tired of fighting, or just plain frustrated? Rather than attribute this limitation to personal characteristics, it makes sense to describe this aspect of Daly's work as a limitation for her and not necessarily a limitation for those who are inspired by her work. She may be understandably at the limit of what she can and will do in this time and place, but others are not and they continue the work of naming evils and revealing atrocities. Women (and men) who take her seriously can be true to the spirit of her work while being true to the contexts of their own lives and work. Daly's work transcends the second wave of feminism. Its effects continue to drive new generations of feminism, and this is a powerful legacy. She created a system that transcends the boundaries of philosophy and theology, precisely the thing for which she longed thirty years earlier.

Luther: Beyond Insurrection

Martin Luther's writings on Christian freedom and the limitations of power and authority of the church were welcome support for the causes of peasants in Europe. Unrest among the peasant class had been a reality throughout the continent for decades, and reached a violent apex in Germany in 1525. This is the context where Luther's work had consequences that he did not intend: "To the peasants, it seemed that Luther's teachings pointed out a way whereby the vested financial institutions of the church might be overthrown without forfeiting the spiritual benefits the church claimed to confer."[29] Other reformers at the time like Thomas Münzer and Balthasar Hübmaier influenced the peasants as they argued that all ecclesiastical institutions be abolished. Luther disagreed with their approach, but the combination of their calls to revolution and Luther's theological criticisms of the papacy fed the peasants' fervor and led to intense conflict and violence.

Luther's early response to the peasants comes in the form of a reply to twelve articles that stated their beliefs and demands. The "Admonition to Peace" appears in early 1525 and first addresses the princes, then addresses the peasants, and finally takes up a point by point response to the peasants' twelve articles. Luther first admonishes the princes because he insists that they are to blame for the unrest in their cities and regions, having cheated and robbed the common people for years:

> We have no one on earth to thank for this disastrous rebellion, except you princes and lords, and especially you blind bishops and mad priests and monks, whose hearts are hardened, even to the present day.[30]

Luther insists that they must yield to the word of God and become just and fair rulers once again. He notes that God is punishing them for their errant ways, and is allowing the devil and false prophets to "stir up the

---

29. Charles M. Jacobs, "Introduction to the Admonition to Peace, A Reply to the Twelve Articles of the Peasants in Swabia" (1525), in *LW* 46:5.

30. Luther, "Admonition to Peace" (1525), in *LW* 46:19.

people against you."³¹ He refers to the demands of the peasants as just and right, and insists that the princes take them seriously and respond accordingly. The rulers are ultimately to blame for the situation that led to the present unrest.

Luther turns in the second section of his admonition to address the peasants, and while noting that their cause is just, and that they do have the right to economic justice as well as religious freedom, he states that they are committing two errors: listening to false prophets (Münzer and Hübmaier) and acting violently to advance their cause. The basis for this criticism is scripture. Luther describes his understanding of good order where, for example, all persons are subject to the governing authorities as stated in Paul's letter to the Romans, and that anyone who lives by the sword dies by the sword as Jesus says in Matthew's gospel. He explicitly says that even though the princes have been and are wrong, that the peasants' rebellion is even more wrong:

> The rulers unjustly take your property; that is the one side. On the other hand, you take from them their authority, in which their whole property and life and being consist. Therefore you are far greater robbers than they, and you intend to do worse things than they have done.³²

He alludes to the authority which is given to the princes and to rulers in the temporal realm in general. His concern stems from his belief that God is the one who grants authority to the temporal realm, and therefore rulers in it ought to be obeyed as agents of the authority of God. If they are not, then there is risk of the temporal realm collapsing, and all of God's creation being threatened with devastation.

Luther is careful to state repeatedly that their cause is just, but their methods are not. He says that it "is not my intention to justify or defend the rulers in the intolerable injustices which you suffer from them. They are unjust and commit heinous wrongs against you; that I admit."³³ But good order was being threatened and he insists that someone had to listen to him, to take instruction from the word of God, and stop the conflict before any more harm came to Germany. He insists that the peasants take seriously their self-identification as Christians, and that they be instructed

31. Ibid., 21.
32. Ibid., 26.
33. Ibid., 32.

by God's word and live by the gospel that they profess to embrace. One recommendation that he gives to them is that they leave cities where the gospel is being suppressed, and go where it is being affirmed. "It is not necessary, for the gospel's sake, for you to capture or occupy the city or place; on the contrary, let the ruler have his city; you follow the gospel."[34] The hardship of having to abandon their homes would accomplish two things, according to Luther: suffering and seeking the gospel. He believed that Christians had to suffer for the sake of the gospel, and that the gospel was God's way of delivering Christians from suffering. An exodus from cities under the rule of corrupt princes was a way to realize this because "the gospel needs no physical place or city in which to dwell; it will and must dwell in hearts."[35] This is why a violent social insurrection based on the gospel simply made no sense for Luther, and served as no more than a threat to the temporal order as established by God.

Later in 1525, Luther's tone becomes much more harsh, revealing how he grows increasingly frustrated when his initial recommendations are not followed. This time, he recommends actions to those rulers whose cities are being turned upside down by the peasants rebellion. In the brief treatise, "Against the Robbing and Murdering Hordes of Peasants," Luther insists that the peasants have committed terrible sins that merit "death in body and soul."[36] They have failed the word of God which requires them to submit to temporal rulers, they have become murderers and robbers, and they have called themselves Christians yet fail to live up to the name and compel others to violent action. Regarding their misuse of his idea that all Christians are free and equal in their baptism, he said that "baptism does not make men free in body and property, but in soul."[37] He insists that Christian freedom does *not* mean that one can do whatever one wishes and does not mean that the peasants can take the property of the princes and bishops, especially through violent action. Again Luther relies on Scripture to show how the peasants violate the word of God where Jesus instructs Christians to render to Caesar what is his (Luke 20:25), to be subject to governing authorities (Romans 13:1) and to be subject

---

34. Ibid., 36.

35. Ibid.

36. Luther, "Against the Robbing and Murdering Hordes of Peasants" (1525), in *LW* 46:49.

37. Ibid., 51.

to human ordinances (1 Peter 2:13). With yet another group of people, Luther loses his patience.

The instructions to the rulers are in several steps: A Christian ruler should first take the matter to God, pray for help against the devil, try to do the will of God, offer the peasants "an opportunity to come to terms, even though they are not worthy of it," and then finally, "swiftly take to the sword."[38] He goes on to say that anyone who dies in this effort will be seen as a martyr, and that death in service of the word and for the purpose of loving one's neighbor is the greatest possible action. "If anyone thinks this too harsh, let him remember that rebellion is intolerable and that the destruction of the world is to be expected every hour."[39] The revolt of the peasants was simply not acceptable on any level for Luther, and with the word of God as his guide, he advocated their suppression by any means necessary.

It seems that Luther has a keen sense that the peasants go too far for what he considers to be good order. When faced with a choice of whom to support in the end, it appears that Luther errs on the side of good order. He comes under later criticism for this position when critics charge him with being a "flatterer of princes."[40] Like his final position and recommendations for action toward the Jews, Luther's position with regard to the peasants rebellion can also be attributed to the social and cultural privileges that he continued to enjoy despite excommunication and threats against his life. Even if they were inspired by his explanations of Christian freedom and his calls to limit the tyranny of the church, the peasants went too far when they undertook action that threatened the social fabric of Germany.

This reveals a conservative self-protectiveness in Luther that may be lamentable. It may be lamentable because his own position on the matter of resisting temporal authority was complex and nuanced and had seemed to emphasize genuine freedom to resist corrupt princes: "What if a prince is in the wrong? Are his people bound to follow him then too? Answer: No, for it is no one's duty to do wrong; we must obey God (who desires the right) rather than men."[41] Applying these ideas, at least in the case of

38. Ibid., 52.

39. Ibid., 55.

40. Charles M. Jacobs, "Introduction to An Open Letter on the Harsh Book Against the Peasants" (1525), in *LW* 46:60.

41. Luther, "Temporal Authority: To What Extent it Should be Obeyed" (1523), in *LW* 45:125.

the peasants revolt, reveals a number of complications: Who determines that the princes or any temporal rulers are wrong? What if there is disagreement about whether they are wrong? What does it specifically mean to obey God in such a case? In this case, Luther actually seemed to agree with the peasants that the princes were wrong in their financial practices. He disagreed with what it meant to obey God, though, in how to resist that wrong. In this case, again like that of his writings on the Jews and against the papacy, he followed his pattern of attempting to first show the princes and the peasants how they were wrong based on scripture, using the word first and foremost. But, when that did not work, he falls into his tendency to side with the majority power and advocating the further suppression of the minority group. Therefore, Luther's interaction with the peasants in the rebellion of 1525 shows a limitation in his social ethic of resistance when political corruption is a reality and Christian freedom is taken seriously.

Notes on Abandonment

For Mary Daly, feminist women who remain within the church do not go far enough in their understanding of the problem or in their work for change. For Martin Luther, the peasants who wanted to stay in their homes and fight the corruption through radical rebellion went too far in their demands for change. This illustrates an interesting divergence in the two reformers at a certain point in their work. Social and cultural standing may again be the reason for this difference: Daly spoke as a feminist and as one who was leading the charge and the exodus, while Luther spoke to the peasants as one of the elites against whom they were revolting. In both cases, the reformer abandons the group who takes them seriously because the group does not come to all of the same conclusions as the reformer does. Some Christian women do think that the church and theology can and should change, and some German peasants believed they had no other recourse than to violently rebel against the princes who oppressed them. Both Daly and Luther have their own agendas, however, so they criticize the groups and continue pushing their own visions.

Feminism and Daly, Lutherans and Luther

Each of these two reformers planted the seeds for something that grew into something that they did not likely intend. What surrounds and comes after the individual work of Mary Daly and Martin Luther shapes their respective legacies. If feminism had not re-emerged in the 1970s as a powerful political and cultural force, then Daly's work would have been a curious blip in the history of Christianity. If Protestantism in general or Lutheranism in particular had not grown from Luther's reforming Christian theology, then his battles with the papacy would be relegated to the study of late medieval history. Perhaps neither thinker would have produced as much as they did had the resistance not been so great and had the effects been immediately realized.

What if, for example, the Roman Catholic Church had favorably received the work of these two reformers when initially offered? What if, upon reading Daly's first book, *The Church and the Second Sex*, the pope and clerical hierarchy in Rome realized the accuracy and coherence of her historical criticism and acknowledged that the church had in fact been complicit in the suppression of women, and that it was time to open the doors of the church and the priesthood to all whom the Spirit calls, including women? What if Boston College immediately celebrated that publication in 1968 and gave her immediate recognition and publicly affirmed her work as crucial for the future of theology? Daly may not have gone on to spin the worlds of characters and ideas that she did, and may not have relentlessly pursued a genuine critique of patriarchy. Women would perhaps be less aware of the true dangers of the systems of oppression if that were the case.

Imagine the pope reading Luther's "Ninety-Five Theses" and realizing that this Augustinian monk was right, that the papacy had indeed succumbed to some inappropriate practices, and that it was time to correct the course of the church and return to the fundamentals of the word of God. Luther would have "won" insofar as a real reform of the church would have taken place. But would we consider him as monumental a figure as we now do? He probably would not have produced the theological treatises and biblical exegetical work that he did subsequent to that moment, and the Christian tradition might be the less rich for it.

Of course, neither of those scenarios played out, and re-interpreting history with hypotheticals is little more than an amusing exercise. But it does suggest that the political resistance to and fallout from the work of Daly and Luther has been inextricably a part of their legacy. The movements or groups that follow their work, feminists and Lutherans, take the limitations of their reformer in stride, drawing out and securing their legacies, creating new traditions and new reforms in the process.

Daly on Feminists

The decades during which Daly's own work unfolded saw an increasing variety of feminisms and feminist theologies. While Daly clearly falls under the label of radical feminist, one who believes that gender is the prime category of oppression, and that male domination can and must be eradicated, other types of secular feminism emerge in the same era: liberal feminism focuses on women's rights and equality in society, romantic feminism celebrates women's superior feminine values and morals, and socialist feminism has a tandem focus on economic justice between women and men.[42] In the particular area of Christian theology, further varieties of theological feminisms emerge: revolutionary feminist theology advocates abandoning Christianity as an irredeemably patriarchal religion, while reformist feminist theology seeks change and accommodation for women within existing church structures, and reconstructionist feminist theology seeks to reinterpret the theological core of Christianity so that the institution remains but with a more liberating message for all.[43]

In both of these typologies, the explicitly theological feminisms and the secular feminisms, an "edge" is marked by the most radical option. The other varieties take their cues from that edge, altering their goals or practices according to other values that they hold, whether they be economic, cultural or religious. There will always be a most radical option that aids the less radical options to find their particular combination of change and stability. Because there is continuing debate and disagreement about just how liberated a woman can be while living within the structures of patriarchy, there will be options for expressing basic feminist ideals of the equality of women and men.

Mary Daly alludes to some of these other forms of "feminism" throughout her work. It is clear in many cases that anything short of the radical separatist feminism which she concocts is insufficient. Feminism in the 1980s, for example, comes under criticism for the ways in which it becomes popularized and media driven:

---

42. Types discussed more in-depth in Clifford, *Introducing Feminist Theology*, 21–25.
43. Detailed in ibid., 28–38.

> For now there is a recent tradition of feminist writing and activities—a feminist culture . . . this tradition is blunted by the plasticization of the feminist movement, its reification into a "thing" controlled by the media-men and other professionals.[44]

Daly argues that in contrast to the plastic or fixed feminism seen in the media, "true feminism is movement, just as true passions are movements."[45] Because of this criteria, anything that fails to produce real movement and real change is not truly feminism. Daly has a rather strict and limited understanding of what feminism is and ought to be, and this again is a limitation to her work. If the only way to be feminist is to toe the Mary Daly line, there will in fact be very few feminists.

Nevertheless, Daly goes to great lengths to establish a case for this position. She is reactionary, but she is not merely reactionary. It might be safe to say that no one is better educated and steeped in the history and traditions of patriarchy and Christianity than Mary Daly. She first describes how patriarchy seeks to dislocate female consciousness. Then,

> since this dislocation depends upon keeping women as the primordial other, the model for all other "others," the transformation must come from women who radically reject this otherness, and who move on to knowing our Selves as truly Other and acting accordingly. Feminism in this radical sense is Realizing reason, and it is Realizing Elemental potency.[46]

The only women, the only feminists, who can truly take on the work of dismantling patriarchy are those who are truly Other, who have rejected the ways of thinking and acting imposed by the "maledom." She goes on to say that "In this true and radical sense, feminism is a verb; it is female be-ing."[47] An important connection to earlier theological work can be made with her description of feminism as a verb, a movement that moves. While still considering and reworking the idea of God in *Beyond God the Father* in 1973, Daly asked "Why indeed must 'God' be a noun? Why not a verb—the most active and dynamic of all?"[48] She emphasizes the

---

44. Daly, *Pure Lust*, 202.
45. Ibid.
46. Ibid., 194.
47. Ibid.
48. Daly, *Beyond God the Father*, 33.

dynamic nature of God as essential to reclaiming the life-giving power that was supposed to be its essence. Further in that chapter, she concludes:

> When women take positive steps to move out of patriarchal space and time, there is a surge of new life. I would analyze this as participation in God the Verb . . . form-destroying, form-creating, transforming power that makes all things new.[49]

So feminism is a verb, and God is a verb. Is feminism God? Yes. The dynamism and power she initially tries very hard to ascribe to this word "god" she later ascribes to feminism. She reflects in *Outercourse* on her stubborn refusal to abandon the word God, and her eventual relinquishing of the term. As I see it, what she does is transfer the ideas about God as dynamic verb to her understanding of feminism. This makes complete sense because as Christianity maintains the basic claim that God is the agent of redemption and salvation, Daly establishes the claim that feminism is the agent of redemption and salvation for the whole world. In the previous chapter we saw how Daly explicitly sees women as agents of this redemption. To specify that even further, we can now see that radical feminism is the true agent of liberation from patriarchy:

> But if one understands feminism to mean the radical, ontological process of Realizing female Elemental potency, one does not move "beyond" it. One moves with it. *Feminism* is a Name for our moving/movement into Metabeing.[50]

Unlike God, which one must move beyond, feminism is for her that which takes you into the beyond. God is an irretrievably corrupted notion, forever a part of patriarchy. Feminism, on the other hand, is movement itself, transcending all structures and realms.

Evaluating Daly's position on feminists in general is very difficult because if limited to her own construction of radical feminism, then she holds them in high regard, as agents of world liberation. The fact that anything short of radical is not enough for her is perhaps a limitation to her understanding of feminism. However, a reconception of feminism ala Daly is important for understanding her work and its relationship to and impact on other women. Daly writes of her 1998 self, in a preface to the 2048 B.E. edition of *Quintessence*: "When standing onstage before her

---

49. Ibid., 43.
50. Daly, *Pure Lust*, 194.

audiences she had frequently yelled out her battle cry: 'Even if I were the only one, I would still be a Radical Feminist!'"[51] This image of Daly as a lone wolf or a raging prophet is one that she cultivates and relies on when all appears to be against her and against her radical feminist vision. She believes in radical feminism as a force, as coming from the Background and pushing through to the foreground in various times and places. It has an effect on women whether they know it or not. Anonyma, speaking with Daly again in 2048, refers to her mother Kate who taught her about the earlier patriarchal era:

> She often speaks about how important the works of Radical Feminists have been in moving women from apathy to action. I remember how she always was saying to me when I was a child: "We go on moving!"[52]

Radical feminism is a movement insofar as it is *the* principle of movement itself for Daly. It cannot be escaped and cannot be destroyed. Anywhere anyone is moving and dynamic and unfolding the power of Be-ing itself, then radical feminism is at work. Whenever women are moved "from apathy to action" then they have been inspired by radical feminism, no matter what they call themselves.

This reconception of what feminism is stands as a legacy of Daly's, but remains a limitation insofar as it takes careful and detailed analysis to fully appreciate how it can be inclusive rather than exclusive. Like the label Anti-male, the label Radical Feminist is easily misunderstood and used to dismiss the work of Mary Daly and others who profess to be radical feminists. Both ideas must be contextually examined to see how they are logical conclusions to thorough analysis of patriarchy and a true understanding of women's liberation. Both are reclaimed, redefined, and celebrated.

Luther on Lutherans

Most people know that Martin Luther's initial goal was not to establish a Lutheran church. His goal was to reform the Christian church. He did not spend a lot of time talking about what it meant to be "lutheran." Rather, he spent an extraordinary amount of time discussing what it meant to be

---

51. Daly, *Quintessence*, xi.
52. Ibid., 111.

"christian."⁵³ Following the Diet of Worms in 1521, he went into hiding at the Wartburg Castle, in fear for his life and safety amid the growing unrest in Germany. From here, he wrote to his followers to encourage measured action as they resisted the imposition of ecclesial and royal authority. At this relatively early stage in his reformation career, he revealed his reluctance to be the leader of a mass movement bearing his name. One statement he makes about being a Lutheran is often referred to, and I quote it at length here:

> In the first place, I ask that men make no reference to my name; let them call themselves Christians, not Lutherans. What is Luther? After all, the teaching is not mine [John 7:16]. Neither was I crucified for anyone. St. Paul, in 1 Corinthians 3, would not allow the Christians to call themselves Pauline or Petrine, but Christian. How then should I—poor stinking maggot-fodder that I am—come to have men call the children of Christ by my wretched name? Not so, my dear friends; let us abolish all party names and call ourselves Christians, after him whose teaching we hold.⁵⁴

The focus for Luther was not himself and his ideas. The focus was Christ and the gospel. The witness of scripture on the teaching, life, death, and resurrection of Christ was his single theological focus. He wanted it to be the single theological focus of the church and of the lives of all Christians.

In keeping with the emphasis on scripture, Luther uses Paul's words and work as a model for his instruction to those wanting to call themselves "lutheran." In a letter to the Corinthians, Paul counseled the new Christians to avoid identifying themselves based on their current human teacher:

> For when one says, 'I belong to Paul,' and another, 'I belong to Apollos,' are you not merely human? What then is Apollos? What is Paul? Servants through whom you came to believe, as the Lord assigned to each. I planted, Apollos watered, but God gave the growth. . . . For we are God's servants, working together; you are God's field, God's building. (1 Corinthians 3:4–6, 9).

---

53. A word search of the fifty-five volumes of the American Edition of Luther's Works and the Book of Concord on CD-ROM reveals that the world "lutheran" appears 541 times, while the word "christian" appears 10,488 times. Even without much detailed analysis of how the terms are used, the vast difference in numbers shows Luther's emphasis.

54. Luther, "A Sincere Admonition by Martin Luther" (1522), in *LW* 45:70.

Referring to those who followed him and those who followed Apollos, another teacher of Christians in first-century Corinth, Paul instructs his followers to avoid false human division and remember the unifying presence of God. He reminds them that it is not he, Paul, who is to be worshipped and whose name is to be honored; it is God. Luther does the same and asks that his followers understand that they are not following his, Martin's, teachings, rather they are following the teachings of Jesus the Christ. Luther views himself as Paul did, as a servant who merely brings the gospel to the people.

Luther's humility and idealism here may be authentic and it may be strategic. He truly believed that passion for Christ and for the gospel was the only thing that should matter to the church and to Christians. It was the central preoccupation of his life, especially in this early decade of his reforming work. However, at the time he wrote this, the year after his excommunication, he was in trouble with church authorities and was beginning to see the effect that his calls for freedom from tyranny were having among Christians and peasants in Germany. If they took to the streets chanting his name, he was obviously implicated in whatever action they took. He resisted and counseled others against the use of violent means to protest and overthrow tyrants of the church and the state.

However, Luther seems to resign himself to the fact that his followers begin identifying themselves with his name, witnessed by his letter to the clergy at the Diet of Augsburg in 1530. Charles, newly established German emperor, called the Christian clergy in Germany together to address the mounting divisions among Christians in the country, and to call for unity on religious matters. Luther was not free to attend the gathering, so sent his views in writing for consideration by all the clergy in attendance. In this "exhortation," he freely refers to the Lutherans as well as non-Lutherans. He allows this to occur perhaps because he wants to recognize who adheres to the truth of the gospel: "The Lutherans remain masters because Christ is with them and they remain with him, even though hell, the world, devil, princes, and all should go mad."[55] He even seems to embrace the reality of being a heretic in this context, because of this focus on communicating the truth of the gospel. "For I maintain that you will not very well be able to do without the Lutherans, the pious heretics, least of all their prayers, if

---

55. Luther, "Exhortation to All Clergy Assembled at Augsburg" (1530), in *LW* 34:52.

you want to achieve anything lasting."⁵⁶ To be a heretic against the corrupt Roman Catholic church was to be a pious defender of the gospel, which the Lutherans at Augsburg were in Luther's opinion.

So while Luther allows and himself uses the label of Lutheran after some time, his focus and his priority remained an emphasis on God's truth revealed in Christ. If it is the Lutherans who are fully identified with Christ, then he supports them, but only because of his and their focus on Christ. If anyone uses his name, it is acceptable only because he saw himself as merely a servant bringing the simple truth of God and Christ to the people. "I neither am nor want to be anyone's master. I hold, together with the universal church, the one universal teaching of Christ, who is our only master."⁵⁷ Lutherans, then, were authentic Christians who held to the universal teaching of Christ. There was nothing about Luther that made them unique, but their adherence to Christ made them right.

Notes on Followers

Most feminists who come after Mary Daly's groundbreaking work would not fall under her understanding of feminism as radical, but she might allow for the fact that they are motivated by radical feminism whether they recognize it or not. Lutherans who come after Luther's reforming work are first and foremost Christians in his understanding, but he allows them to use that name as long as they maintain an emphasis on Christ. This point of comparison shows an interesting contrast: Daly's preferred term is the more specific, radical feminist, while most who follow her use the more general term, feminist; Luther's preferred term is the more general, Christian, while most who follow him use the more specific term, Lutheran. This might be because women living and working within patriarchy often make accommodations, as Daly lamented, in order to protect themselves. At the same time, Christians who call themselves Lutheran are more concerned to identify what makes them different from many others who are also Christian. The different nature of the reforms that Daly and Luther sought and achieved are clearly a major factor here.

---

56. Ibid., 60.
57. Luther, "A Sincere Admonition by Martin Luther" (1522), in *LW* 45:70.

Parallels, Differences, and Inversions

Several comparative notes have already been made about the limitations and legacies of Mary Daly and Martin Luther. A few more must be noted with regard to their status as "heretics," their exclusion of groups of people, their social positions and their views on good social order. These illustrate once again that specific parallels, differences, and inversions emerge to indicate the political theological character of these two reformers.

Parallels: Happy Heretics and Limiting True Believers

Both Daly and Luther claim and agree with the heresy or blasphemy with which they are accused: Daly affirms being Anti-male as the only way to embody truth in a patriarchal context. To be a blasphemer as defined by patriarchy is to be on the side of Life. Luther speaks of the "pious heresy" of those identified as Lutheran, championing them because they were the ones allied with the truth of Christ. To be a heretic as defined by the Roman church is to be on the side of God. When both Daly and Luther claim the heresy with which they are charged, they take a definitive stance in a highly charged political situation. Both act strategically in order to further advance the vision of reform with which they began. If they claim a term or a position as their own, then it cannot be used against them. Yes, I am Anti-male, Daly says; Yes, Lutherans are pious heretics, Luther says. Both could add: So what?

In addition, both Daly and Luther have a keen sense of who actually understands their criticism and goals. For Daly, the only true feminists are those who are radical feminists. It is not because that is what she is, rather it is because the only way to be liberated from patriarchy is to live beyond its margins. She sees herself as the one who merely pointed out the way. For Luther, the only true Christians were those who called themselves Lutherans, not because they followed him or used his name, but because they did as he instructed, followed Christ. He sees himself as the one who merely pointed out the truth.

Difference: Social Position

When Daly affirms being Anti-male, she takes great risk in opposing the dominant culture because of her position within it, a woman in a male-dominated society. She makes herself vulnerable by isolating the dominant gender and deliberately working against them. When Luther emerges as anti-Semitic, he is affirmed by the dominant culture and has a position within it, a Christian in a majority Christian nation. He can afford to isolate and discriminate against a minority group and is blinded by his status and power to speak. Daly risks much personally because of the oppression of her gender in her context, while Luther ironically risks the gospel emphasis on justice when he advocates injustice in his context.

A case can also be made that the difference exists in the reverse based on historical context: Daly risks a job and in fact gains a lot of attention for her controversial academic work. It is academic work, and initially is that of a relatively young woman in a male-dominated profession, though, so its threat to society was perhaps not that great at the time. Luther risks his life and has to go into hiding for his controversial stand at Worms. His work cut to the heart of the papal system which was bound up with the political system in Germany at the time, and so its threat to society was fairly significant. In either case, Daly and Luther occupy very different positions in very different social hierarchies that affect the work they can do and the effect that their work has.

Inversion: Order and Disorder

Responding to groups of people who took them seriously, Christian feminists and the peasants respectively, Daly sides with disorder encouraging all women to leave the church and patriarchy and enter a new reality altogether, while Luther sides with restoring order, encouraging the princes to suppress the peasants for the sake of social control. Both end up "taking a side" when a choice must be made, but they end up on opposing sides of social conflict: Daly is basically in a new order altogether, newly imagined time and space, while Luther is in the old order, with the powers that be. In both cases, the political context and consequences of their different social locations and their theologies were definitive.

8

Two Reformers as Political Theologians

O worthless religion of this age of ours,
the most godless and thankless of all ages![1]

Under the conditions of patriarchy, women dis-cover our Original
Race through the release of deep ontological Fury.[2]

Martin Luther and Mary Daly emerge as political theologians who have a utopian vision that compels their political activism. How and why this is the case requires explanation because neither reformer has heretofore been analyzed thoroughly as a political theologian. Aspects of their political thought or political aspects of their careers have been dealt with by others, and those perspectives will be included here as part of fully examining the proposal to apply this label to them. Not only do characteristics of political theology apply to the work of Luther and Daly, but their work adds one further dimension to the analysis of political theology.

The parallels, differences, and inversions noted throughout this study of Luther and Daly provide introduction to how both of them exhibit three major characteristics of political theologians as identified in the introduction to this book. Ultimately, the utopian vision that compels their political activism will be fully examined to consider how it is in the nature of political theology to propose a vision of how things should be based on a critique of how things actually are.

Parallels

Though one would expect to find very little parallel between such apparently different figures as Martin Luther and Mary Daly, the following

1. Luther, "The Babylonian Captivity of the Church" (1520), in *LW* 36:43.
2. Daly, *Pure Lust*, 5.

list highlights key personal and substantive similarities between them that have emerged in the preceding chapters.

Both:
- Come from a peasant/working class family
- Have a Catholic childhood and education
- Pursue the heights of advanced education
- Work as professors at major universities
- Reject the Catholic Church and its hierarchy
- Become prolific authors
- Have a vision of the ideal human community
- Exclude a class of people from the utopia
- Challenge texts of the dominant authorities
- Harbor early positive hopes for change
- Equate the Word or words with the force of liberation
- Have an apocalyptic tendency
- Reach limitations of real change

The parallels begin with their backgrounds and family life, the things for which they were not responsible, rather were born into. Both Luther and Daly come from families who were not among the elite in their respective social contexts, whether it be Luther's farming and mining family or Daly's working-class parents. It is fairly evident that both had strong ties to their parents and were shaped by the religious environment in their home and town. Catholicism was part of the fabric of everyday life for both young reformers and it was reinforced in their educational experiences.

The personal details quickly become political for both as they each go through rigorous education in Catholic universities and communities. This element in their younger years affects their later scholarly work as Luther remains heavily influenced by Augustinian methods and ideas while Daly remains a Thomistic scholar and thinker influenced by her study of Aquinas long after leaving the work of Christian theology. Both reject the hierarchy of the Catholic tradition that formed them and begin to envision a renewed human community. Their methods of critique and creative application of language lead to both producing politically charged texts. Luther and Daly thus have parallel impulses as theologians, and parallel problems with the church hierarchy as they experienced it. In this way, they exhibit the first characteristic of political theologians named in the introduction: Theology and politics were integrated for the two reformers because as they began focused theological work, they were also doing significant political work. Neither sets out to "be" political and neither writes "about" politics. Rather, politics is simply integrated with their theology from beginning to end.

This integration is also reflected in the parallel early hopes and limited successes that each has: Thorough transformation of religious and cultural institutions is a long and complex process. Real change rarely happens completely within the life of any one person. Any activist with a grand vision for how things could be, a utopian vision of the world as it ought to be, will inevitably be somewhat frustrated because grand visions are rarely fully realized. This is where an apocalyptic theme emerges for both reformers: Luther spoke frequently of the Antichrist and of the wicked tyranny of the majority, while Daly envisioned a new world that takes shape after the destruction of the present world. In this way, a tinge of hopelessness and even apocalypticism is revealed in the work of both reformers, and the exclusion of a group of people in their utopias reveals their real allegiances in the end. Because theology and politics are so thoroughly integrated in their work, there are real political implications for their exclusive theological visions.

Differences

The differences between Luther and Daly are striking when put together. These things are a major reason why the pairing is a surprise to most at first. Such incredibly different figures would seem to have very little in common, but that has already been shown not to be the case. These differences speak to the second characteristic of political theologians seen in the introduction: They explicitly attend to the structures of human life in which they live. The contexts for Luther's and Daly's lives were in many ways very different. Consider some of the differences discussed so far:

Martin Luther	**Mary Daly**
Male	Female
Sixteenth century	Twentieth/Twenty-first century
Germany	United States
Heterosexual	Homosexual
Monk and pastor	Radical feminist philosopher
Christian	Rejects christianity
Heavy use of scripture	No use of scripture
Sin as personal	Sin as structural
Danger in captivity is spiritual	Danger in captivity is physical

These items contextualize Luther and Daly as individuals who inhabit specific times, places and structures that necessarily affect their theologies. Their differences are significant for the shape of the political theologies that they produce.

Gender and its meaning in these social contexts create one very basic difference: What it meant to be a man in Germany in the early sixteenth century was for Luther to have lived as monk, worked as a pastor, and eventually participated in social change by becoming a husband and father. What it meant to be a woman in the U.S. in the twentieth century, especially from the 1950s through the 1980s, was for Daly to have had traditional feminine expectations imposed early, and to eventually witness and participate in radical social change around women's rights and roles. Gender matters because it situates the two at different places on the social and political hierarchy in their respective eras. Luther was a man in a male-dominated world, Daly is a woman in a male-dominated world. This leads to different concerns and conclusions in their political theologies.

Because of historical shifts, these contexts are so radically different in terms of political structure and cultural ideology that two people inhabiting them simply have to be different creatures. These differences of context produce various substantive differences in their work. Luther's concept of sin as personal is deeply situated in medieval and early modern Christian theology, predating eighteenth century enlightenment discussions about human subjectivity, but expressing religious views with which he was raised and educated. Daly is able to conceive of sin as structural in part because of shifts in post-Enlightenment thinking. She was able to do criticism and analysis of systems using sociology and cultural anthropology which are modern scholarly disciplines.

Theological and religious differences between these two are also significant. Luther is convinced of the truth of God in Christ, and sees it as part of his vocation to spread the gospel and educate Christians. Daly specifically and strongly rejects christianity and all religion as an institution that serves the interests of patriarchy. These two reformers could not be at more wildly different places in relationship to Christianity. Luther's political and theological concern is to reform the whole church for the sake of the gospel, and the human organization to which he addresses his critiques and suggestions is the church. He remains firmly within the Christian religion. Daly's political and theological concern is to liberate women from tyranny and oppression, and once she determines that the human organization of Christianity is irredeemable and part of the problem, she moves beyond it. The human organization to which she addresses her critique is patriarchy.

All of these differences between Luther and Daly, whether concerning their personal identity, historical location, or religious commitments, shape their theological encounter with political realities and show how both pay explicit attention to the organization of human life which envelops them. These obvious differences, though, lead to some interesting inversions.

Inversions

This is the area where the parallels and differences noted above come together. In several ways, Luther and Daly have parallel theological and political impulses that take them in completely different directions. This is because of how the differences and parallels of their lives come together. These inversions exhibit the third characteristic of political theologians named in the introduction: Their theologies have significant political content and consequence. In each case, both reformers do the same thing with almost opposite consequence in their respective contexts:

Reject imposed marriage model	**Luther:** marries Katie **Daly:** is a lesbian
Resist imposed social status	**Luther:** rejects priestly rights **Daly:** demands women's rights
Overturn dominant model of human self	**Luther:** Christians to focus more on others **Daly:** women to focus more on selves
Include visual representations of extreme ideas	**Luther:** vulgar and negative cartoons **Daly:** amusing and positive cartoons
Exclude class of people from utopian vision	**Luther:** against a minority group **Daly:** against the majority group

In their personal lives, both Luther and Daly reject the model of the "appropriate" sex and marriage practices imposed on them. They have a parallel impulse. However, because of their differences and contexts, they go in opposite directions as they live it out. Luther is a heterosexual man and rejects the imposed celibate model of the Augustinian order to which he belongs. He is supposed to abstain from sex and not marry, according to church convention, but does not because of who he is and what he is committed to. Daly is a lesbian and rejects the imposed patriarchal model of dominant male-subordinate female marriage relations. She is supposed to marry a man, according to cultural convention, but does not because of who she is and what she is committed to. The inversion in their actions is because of the context in which the rejection of the dominant model takes place.

In addition, Luther and Daly occupy different places on the social hierarchy of the cultures in which they live. This affects several of the conclusions that they come to in their work. They have parallel impulses but come to different conclusions and take different actions on several issues based in part on their vested interest in the status quo. Consider these two parallel descriptions.

Luther is a man in a man's world, and as such is in the majority class in terms of power and status in the church and world. As a male priest, he is even more in the majority with regard to power and status in sixteenth-century German culture. His elite status is a political reality that is reinforced by theological justifications. This is precisely the experience that gives rise to his critical theological work. He is an insider, who is forced to become an outsider by excommunication, and eventually ends up as an insider again as the preeminent leader of the Protestant movement.

Daly is a woman in a male-dominated world, and as such is in the minority in terms of power and status in the church and in the secular world. As a female academic, she is even more in the minority, especially in the 1960s and 1970s. Her second-class status is a political reality that is reinforced by theological justifications. This is precisely the experience that gives rise to her critical theological and philosophical work. She is an outsider, who becomes an insider in many respects as a professor at a prestigious Catholic college, and eventually engineers her own outsider status once again, ideologically and logistically, as a retired professor and feminist philosopher.

The deliberately parallel construction of the two paragraphs above reinforces how Luther and Daly share much in terms of their basic commitments and rejections. They both reject the status imposed on the group with which they are identified: women and priests. This is at first a personal issue, and ultimately becomes public and very political showing how the content of their reforming work has significant consequence.

Other inversions between Luther and Daly emerge from the substance of their work: Where Luther focuses the self on the other, Daly encourages the self to focus on itself; Cartoons accompanying Luther's polemic work are vulgar and negative, showing excrement and related bodily functions, while cartoons accompanying Daly's most creative work are impish and constructive, showing happy animals and women cavorting freely; Luther's exclusion of and polemics against the Jews have much more of a negative impact and legacy than Daly's exclusion of men and reclamation of the label Anti-male.

Regarding their concept of the human person, difference of organizational focus again makes the parallel impulse take a unique shape. One problem that Luther confronted was the indulgence system wherein one was encouraged to buy one's salvation; his solution used the gospel to free the Christian self from works, and allow it to serve the other. One problem that Daly confronted was the patriarchal system wherein women were encouraged to deny their own needs; her solution used women's experience to free them from excessive focus on others, and allow them to name and attend to their own needs.

As political theologians, Luther and Daly are engaged in the same task in many respects, having parallel impulses and different contexts that lead to inverse ideas and practices. This begins to show how the two reformers embody three characteristics of political theologians; Focusing more explicitly on these characteristics and other aspects of Luther's and Daly's thought brings their work into even greater focus and leads to proposing a fourth characteristic of political theology that both reformers demonstrate.

Political Theologians

In many ways, Martin Luther and Mary Daly have been more politically and theologically influential than many who are already called political theologians. Few apart from specialists in Christian theology know the work of those mentioned in the introduction to this book: Johann Metz, Jürgen Moltmann, Dorothee Soelle, and Dietrich Bonhoeffer. In contrast, Martin Luther is a theologian about whom anyone with a passing acquaintance with Western history should know something, and the Protestant Reformation is unquestionably definitive for the history of Christianity. Mary Daly is a feminist whom anyone studying modern feminism and the women's movement will have heard about. The modern women's movement has had such a dramatic impact on culture, laws, and religious traditions that it is an integral part of any basic study of the twentieth century. Of course between the two, Luther is more widely known, having the benefit of five hundred years of history between our study and his work. Regardless of individual familiarity with them as reformers, the importance of Luther's and Daly's leading roles in definitive wider social and political movements is indisputed. As suggested, their work embodies the three characteristics of political theologians already named, each of which can now be more fully examined.

Integration of Theology and Politics

Politics and theology are thoroughly integrated in the life of the political theologian. One full length treatment of Luther's political thought is found in W. D. J. Cargill Thompson's posthumous book, *The Political Thought of Martin Luther*.[3] In this work, Cargill Thompson fully examines the political aspect of Luther's work, including lengthy treatments of his understanding of the two kingdoms of God and of the world and its implications for political theory. He makes a few brief references to the integration of theology and politics which concerns us here, including the note that "Luther's approach to political questions is always exclusively theological and moral."[4] In addition, Cargill Thompson suggests that several of Luther's ideas, including the belief that secular rulers received authority from God, his teaching of non-resistance to governing authority, and the sharp distinction between secular and church authorities, "amounted to a major revolution in political thinking."[5] Luther's rejection of ultimate papal authority and his claims of the spiritual freedom of Christians grows out of these ideas, and furthers what Cargill Thompson calls his political revolution.

---

3. The select bibliography in Cargill Thompson's text includes an extensive list of related texts and articles supplementing a study of Luther's political theory in the sixteenth century context.

4. Cargill Thompson, *The Political Thought of Martin Luther*, 5.

5. Ibid., 8.

Cargill Thompson has two passing references to Luther as a political theologian, including this one:

> Taken together, these ideas amount to a comprehensive theology of human society which provides an impressive theoretical substratum to his political ideas, giving them depth and substance and entitling him to be regarded as a political thinker, albeit a political theologian, of the first rank.[6]

The parenthetical "albeit" remark at the end here is interesting, as if Cargill Thompson is saying that Luther is a political thinker, even though he is "only" a theologian, or "only" concerned about theological matters. The other reference worth noting comes in the concluding remark of the book's introduction, when he refers to "the basic principles of his [Luther's] political theology."[7] Cargill Thompson goes on to treat Luther's political theory in depth and detail, but pays no further attention to what it might mean to specifically call Luther a political theologian.

AnaLouise Keating reads political theory and strategy out of Daly's work with language and myth. She says that Daly "employs metaphoric language performatively, to transform her readers."[8] Keating describes Daly's insistence "that words can have concrete, shape-shifting material effects."[9] In these cases, words are transformative, having the power to liberate as well as dominate. There is little distinction between words and action in Daly's thought, as one is always connected to the other: words are action, and action is always based on words. Integrating theory and practice, or theology and politics, is part of Daly's work from the beginning.

This integration comes in part from the field in which Daly works: feminist theology and philosophy are in essence political movements. Elizabeth Bounds states very clearly in the *Dictionary of Feminist Theologies* that "politics is at the heart of feminist theologies."[10] She further notes that theology for feminists is simultaneously "reflection and transformation of oppressive social structures."[11] Feminism broadly both criticizes all things that oppress women and constructs alternate visions of how reality might

---

6. Ibid., 9.
7. Ibid., 15.
8. Keating, "Back to the Mother?" 382.
9. Ibid., 367.
10. Bounds, "Politics," 212.
11. Ibid.

be constructed. Core principles of feminism named in one introduction to women's studies include a concern "for equality and justice for all women" which entails eliminating inequality and injustice, and intentional inclusion and affirmation of women.[12] That the personal is political reflects the integration that is at the heart of feminism and at the heart of Daly's political theological work.

For both Luther and Daly, therefore, politics and theology are thoroughly integrated throughout their lives and work. The political engagement comes because of their theological ideas, and their theological engagement is inevitably political. One is hard pressed to separate the political and theological in the work of these two reformers.

Explicit Attention to the Polis

Political theology takes explicit account of the social and cultural reality in which it emerges. Luther attends to the *polis* that surrounds him not only in terms of his criticism of the church hierarchy but also in terms of his writing on the temporal or worldly authorities. Several of his major writings are in fact directed toward the secular rulers, including "To the Christian Nobility of the German Nation" in 1520 and his comments and instruction to the princes and rulers involved in the peasants war in 1525. In fact at several points throughout his public career he offers advice to the secular rulers on how they might rule better and how they might be guided by Christian principles.

Andrew Bradstock discusses the entire period of the Reformation for a section of *The Blackwell Companion to Political Theology*, and begins by discussing Martin Luther. Bradstock notes that any discussion of Luther's theological "rediscovery" of the doctrine of justification "will be at best partial if it takes no account of its political and ecclesiological repercussions."[13] These repercussions included instability for the church and disruption of the status quo. Bradstock's discussion of Luther in this section is relatively brief, but he suggests that "Luther's political theology is pragmatic" and that the "weaknesses of Luther's political theology have been remarked upon often enough."[14] The weaknesses include Luther's

---

12. Shaw and Lee, *Women's Voices, Feminist Visions*, 9.
13. Bradstock, "The Reformation," 62.
14. Ibid., 65, 66.

"insistence that rulers be obeyed almost at all costs"[15] and this attitude later brought him blame for encouraging Christian quietism and failure to act in the fact of state tyranny. Coupled with his own tirades against the Jews and the peasants, this insistence on good order often mitigated the political reforming power of Luther's work. Nevertheless, it is clear that he continuously paid attention to the social and cultural reality in which he was enmeshed.

María Lugones shows how Mary Daly's *Wickedary* itself contains layers of explicit commentary on allocations of power and authority in patriarchy, and webs of explicit construction of alternate realities. This is one example of the type of work that pervades Daly's body of work. Lugones describes Daly's *Wickedary* as:

> A linguistic political contemporary document of resistant lesbian relating, an explicitly and deeply interactive linguistic adventure that both theorizes and disrupts its own relation to patriarchal domination.[16]

Lugones offers an intricate analysis of the *Wickedary* as a document that both theorizes about and practices its challenge to patriarchy. She argues that it "challenges a system of domination through conceptual maneuvering" and "stakes its 'domain' in the 'background,' dissociating from domination"[17] Daly's entire body of work does this because of her explicit attention to the *polis*, to the ways that human communities have and continue to organize themselves: Male domination expressed in patriarchy is the problem that shapes all of her thought and that compels all of her creative work.

Both Luther and Daly pay explicit attention to the ways that human life is organized in their time and place. This attention to the *polis* irrevocably affects their theologies and in turn affects the *polis* itself. This leads directly into the third characteristic of political theologians.

Political Content and Consequence

Political theology is theology with significant political content and consequence. Jean Bethke Elshtain refers to Cargill Thompson's labeling of

---

15. Ibid., 65.
16. Lugones, "Wicked Caló," 253.
17. Lugones, "Wicked Caló," 262.

Martin Luther as political theologian as she discusses some of the paradoxes of Luther's political legacy in a 1986 article, "Luther *Sic*—Luther *Non*." Her goal is to make the complexities of Luther's legacy apparent, ensuring that a facile reading of Luther as sixteen century freedom-fighter does not dominate the study of his ideas on freedom. She acknowledges that "Luther emerges as radical in his views, penning a political theology that bears both liberating—with our notion of freedom in mind—and baneful implications."[18] The "baneful" implications that concern Elshtain in this article seem to center around Luther's fear of disorder, also noted by Bradstock, which feeds his insistence on submitting to temporal authority. It is this view, which she paraphrases as "it is better that all the peasants be killed rather than sovereign authority destroyed," that Elshtain laments.[19] Her use of the phrase, "political theology," in relation to Luther is noted here, though she also does not focus at length on what it might mean to call Luther a political theologian.

Much of the political content and consequence of Luther's thought has already been discussed, and Bradstock further notes that occasionally Luther does pay attention to the political implications of this theology at times: "In places he is clearly working out the political consequences of his religious discovery, elsewhere he would seem to be drawing upon other sources for his ideas."[20] This might be accounted for because Luther is first and foremost a theologian, but is inevitably drawn into the political arena because of the implications of his ideas and criticisms. Despite some of the negative consequences or weaknesses of Luther's political theology, it was a major factor in the shift from the medieval to the modern era challenging the church and shifting society dramatically.

A section of the Blackwell volume on political theology discusses North American feminist theology at length in terms of its content and consequence. Elaine Graham defines how feminist theology is political theology, and it becomes clear how Daly's work is part of this:

> Feminist theology may therefore be characterized as political theology in multiple ways: first, in its protest at women's subordination

---

18. Elshtain, "Luther *Sic*—Luther *Non*," 155–68.
19. Ibid., 164.
20. Bradstock, "The Reformation," 64.

within church and society and second—. . . in its vision of a renewed ecclesial and social order.[21]

Though Daly abandons the label and structure of "theology," she continues to protest women's subordination and to construct her vision of a new order. This is the content of her work, and its consequences are wide-ranging. Despite Daly's abandonment of various causes of Christian feminist women, their activism brings about the inclusion of women in the leadership of most mainline Protestant denominations, and ongoing agitation for change in the Roman Catholic church in the U.S. A growing and diversifying body of feminist theological work continues to emerge as a consequence of feminist pioneers in the second wave, and new models of human communities including women-church organizations have emerged as real alternatives to patriarchal traditions.

This third characteristic of political theology reflects the other two as the integration of theology and politics along with explicit attention to the *polis* forms the political content and consequence for both reformers. A final characteristic of their political theologies remains to be explored, however, and looking at it suggests that it is a characteristic of political theology heretofore unexamined.

Expressing Political Theology: Utopian Activism

Luther and Daly have dramatic utopian visions that are simultaneously political and theological. They are visions that compel their activism. Each has a sense of how the world, the church, and human beings should be. In Luther's Christian utopia he takes basic theological ideas to their logical end, describing a community where all people freely serve each other and glorify God in Christ. In proposing this as ideal, he suggests that lack of authenticity in Christians and Christianity is the central problem in the world as it currently is. Daly's feminist utopia articulates the vision of a female-centered and female-identified reality. In concocting this as ideal, she insists that male-centeredness and male-identified reality is the central problem with the world.

Ironically, the utopian visions that compel so much of their creative work become a final problem for both theologians. Because they exclude groups of people from their utopias and separate so radically from existing

---

21. Graham, "Feminist Theology, Northern," 210.

social and ecclesial structures, Luther and Daly cannot finally succeed in reforming the institutions they initially challenge. The real reforms that do occur in the church and the world come about perhaps despite their exclusivism and because of the communities of believers and scholars who are instructed and inspired by them. This is because both Luther and Daly are political activists driven by their utopian visions.

Whether it be Luther burning the papal bull excommunicating him in 1521 or Daly leading an exodus out of Harvard Memorial Church in 1971, both theologians take public and concrete steps to enact their theology and their politics. Each of these actions, while concrete in themselves, eventually serve as symbols for those who adhered to these reforming theologies. That the words of the pope might be nothing more than ashes was a profound insight for emerging Protestants. That women might have the courage and support to leave the church and inhabit new spiritual and physical space was a profound statement of second wave feminism.

Despite this concrete activism, it is in the nature of utopias to not be fully realized or realizable. Definitions of utopia contemporary to both Luther and Daly help clarify each of their concepts as well as suggest their limitations. The root of the word coined by Sir Thomas More in 1516 is the Greek *ou* (not) and *topos* (place).[22] A utopia is no place, or *eu-topos*, good place. This describes Luther's vision of a Christian community very well. It is a good place in that all freely serve each other and God, and it is no place because it does not actually exist completely. Sally Miller Gearhart, in her study of eleven feminist novels, provides a relevant four-part definition of a feminist utopia that applies to Daly:

> A feminist utopian novel is one which *a.* contrasts the present with an envisioned idealized society (separated from the present by time or space), *b.* offers a comprehensive critique of present values/conditions, *c.* sees male institutions as a major cause of present social ills, and *d.* presents women not only as at least the equals of men but also as the sole arbiters of their reproductive functions.[23]

Daly's work fits each one of these characteristics nicely: She creates an alternate space-time reality, constructs sustained criticism of the present,

---

22. Thomas More was a contemporary of Martin Luther's and a vociferous defender of the Catholic faith. Whether a reading of his classic *Utopia* can be seen as a mocking satire of everything that Luther advocated is a provocative question for another study.

23. Gearhart, "Future Visions: Today's Politics," 296.

understands patriarchy as the root cause of all injustice, and pushes for women to have complete control of every aspect of their own lives.

With a few alterations, the definition of feminist utopias might even be applied to Luther: He also understands another space-time reality known as eternal life that is contrasted with the present; he certainly has a detailed critique of his present circumstances; while he clearly does not see male institutions as the cause of present injustice *because* they are male, he does insist that the (all-male) institution of the papacy is the root of evil; finally, if we substitute Christian for women in Gearhart's definition, we can see how he does insist that Christian be the "sole arbiters" not of their reproductive function but of their relationship with God. At the same time, More's basic definition and the etymology of the word clearly applies to Daly: her Otherworld is in another space-time continuum, it is no place; from her various visits to the Otherworld, we can see that it is a very good place for women. Using these definitions, we can see that Luther and Daly are engaged in the same task in terms of their construction of utopias though again, they take different specific forms.

Luther's idea of the Christian community wherein all are freed from works for salvation, and therefore gladly serve one another as Christ served them, informs every step of his theological work. This leads him into direct political conflict with church and secular authorities insofar as he limits their authority and eliminates their role in the salvation event. Where others focus on Luther as a political thinker more broadly, and his particular writings on specifically political issues like the authority of temporal rulers and the merits and perils of resistance, I think that the focus on him as a political theologian allows a better understanding of how his theology and politics were always bound up together. Nowhere is this better seen than in his utopian Christian community. It is a distinct theological proposition to envision life among true Christians, modeling themselves after Christ and living in communion with God. Theological utopian ideas can be seen throughout the Christian tradition in everything from the Garden of Eden story to the new heaven and new earth envisioned by the author of Revelation. These ideas have had remarkable political consequence, both positive and negative, throughout history. Luther's vision too has had consequences both positive and negative: his reform of the Christian tradition is looked upon favorably by many historians and theologians, while his wretched anti-Semitism is lamented by nearly everyone. Luther's sharp criticism of the papacy as the prime block between the ideal and the present world is based on his vision of that ideal world. The pope and his hierarchy were the ones that Luther blamed for this utopia not being realized. They got in the way between Christians and God.

Just as Luther's Christian utopia fits with a tradition of nonexistent peaceable kingdoms envisioning human life with God, Daly's feminist utopia is one in a long line of imaginary communities centered on women and/or inhabited by all women. From Charlotte Perkins Gilman's 1915 novel *Herland* to Marge Piercy's 1976 book *Woman on the Edge of Time* women writers and feminist activists have a tradition of creating imaginary worlds where women are the only inhabitants or are the class of people who rule. These are *ou-topos*, no place, and *eu-topos*, good place. Daly's Background and her imagined time and place of Biophilic reality provide just this sort of vision. H. Lee Gershuny describes Daly's book *Gyn/Ecology* as "revelatory and utopian literature that unites passion and thought in nonlinear metaphors of space and time."[24] These metaphors dominate Daly's work to a greater degree over the decades of her work.

A key characteristic of utopias is that they are *ou-topos*, no place. They do not exist, and perhaps cannot exist. This is certainly the case with Luther's vision. It is not realistic or even pragmatic to envision a world wherein all inhabitants are Christians. The actual world is a religiously diverse place, and was so long before Christianity even existed. Luther's vision fails to account for this. This is precisely where he finds himself on the wrong side of history. By excluding everyone but Christians from his utopia, Luther fails to live up an ideal perhaps found in Jesus' new interpretation of the law, as described by the author of the gospel of Matthew:

> You have heard that it was said, "You shall love your neighbor and hate your enemy." But I say to you, Love your enemies and pray for those who persecute you, so that you may be children of your Father in heaven; for he makes his sun rise on the evil and on the good, and sends rain on the righteous and on the unrighteous. For if you love those who love you, what reward do you have? Do not even the tax collectors do the same? And if you greet only your brothers and sisters, what more are you doing than others? Do not even the Gentiles do the same? Be perfect, therefore, as your heavenly Father is perfect. (Matthew 5:43–48).

---

24. Gershuny, "The Linguistic Transformation of Womanhood," 197.

Matthew's account of Jesus' sermon on the mount includes this passage where followers are encouraged to look beyond their divisions, as God does, and to love beyond the boundaries of sameness or even likeability. If you only love those who love you, then you have really done nothing remarkable. If your community is only those people who are like you, then you do not understand the command. Christians in the world are directed here to look beyond themselves. The command to "be perfect" and to be like God can be read as a command to include even outsiders in Christian love. Luther's ideal Christian community excludes or at best ignores non-Christians. He may say that everyone in fact can become Christian, so it is open to all. This may be theoretically true, but history has shown how an insistence on religious homogeneity leads to violent conflict and imperialistic judgment of others. We have already seen how that happens in Luther's own writings against the Jews.

This homogeneity of utopias is also a factor that emerges to limit their appeal and practicability. This is true in Luther's vision and it is also true in Daly's vision. Gearhart analyzes several aspects of feminist utopian novels, including the aspect of lesbian separatism we find in Daly, and one aspect particularly relevant here: racism. Gearhart concludes that most feminist utopias she has examined "fail to be anti-racist and in this failure end up supporting a stereotype of the dominant culture."[25] As we have seen in Daly, the central preoccupation of feminist utopian authors is gender equality. This leads most authors, including Daly, to mostly ignore race, class and other significant inequalities. Gearhart describes this as "an almost nonexistent awareness of the issues of race and class."[26] This flaw in Daly's utopia first identified publicly by Audre Lorde seems to be a flaw of feminist utopian visions generally speaking.

The utopias that compel the political theological work of Luther and Daly might also be found in the work of other political theologians, though such an angle has not been widely studied previously. John Cobb makes comments in this direction in his proposal to think of process theology as a political theology: "For all political theologians, theory is in the service of practice. This practice is not, of course, blind activism. It is activity informed by thought. . . . Political theologians seek the salvation of

---

25. Gearhart, "Future Visions: Today's Politics," 306.
26. Ibid., 309.

all humanity."²⁷ The salvation that Cobb speaks of here is salvation in the broad global sense of liberation from domination and oppression wherever and in whatever form it occurs. This is clearly the goal of Luther's and Daly's reforming work: the salvation of all humanity. In addition, their activism is fully guided by their thoughts about utopia—the good place that is no place.

Do other political theologians have utopian ideals about how the world ought to be? An in-depth study of even a few representatives presents a possibility for future work. We know that Dorothee Soelle was a dedicated peace activist and engaged in theology and politics throughout her life. Dietrich Bonhoeffer wrote extensively about Christian community life and risked his life for a vision of truth. These two already recognized political theologians did seem to be guided by a keen vision of the world as it ought to be. Soelle and friends enacted this in their communal Political Evensong, and Bonhoeffer instructed his students and fellow pastors how to endure the present evil age with the hope for a better sustainable community in the future. The suggestion that they too had utopian visions is credible.

For this study, however, it is the case that the paramount expression of Luther's and Daly's political theologies is their exclusive utopian communities. The idea of it drives their criticism of the existing world and compels their vision for constructing the future and anOtherworld. Each presents a powerful vision consistent with the body of their work that ultimately limits their success and threatens their legacies. The communities that come after them must deal with these limits in various ways: Lutherans have to answer tough questions about Luther's anti-Semitism particularly after the Holocaust of World War Two; Feminists have to fend off "charges" of being man-haters to the present day. That Luther and Daly are in their own ways intolerant calls their visions into serious question. Nevertheless, these utopias are critical parts of the entire political theological systems devised by Luther and Daly. We are left with one final question . . . given these problems and issues, was it all worth it for Luther and Daly?

---

27. Cobb, Jr., *Process Theology as Political Theology*, 14.

9

Conclusion: Was It All Worth It?

*The animals, grasses, trees, and women are swaying and dancing.
And, once again, we have overcome!*[1]

We are beggars. That is true.[2]

Concluding this study of Mary Daly and Martin Luther is somewhat problematic because Daly is still alive and working at the time of this writing. She has not yet written or uttered her last words. Luther of course has. The above lines are the final words of Daly's latest book to date, and the final words that Luther wrote the day before his death. They reveal something quite fascinating about each reformer: Daly expresses in this statement a tremendous optimism about a future based in another reality, while Luther communicates a stark realism about what it means to be human. How is it that the final truth issued from Luther's pen is that humans are beggars? And does Daly really think that women have overcome?

A closer look at the above sentiments suggests that both Daly and Luther have abandoned the world as they know it in part because it is irretrievably flawed. Daly's statement comes at the end of a description of her arrival at the "Lost and Found Continent" with Matilda Joslyn Gage. She is in the Otherworld now. Luther's statement follows his remark that no one has really understood scripture because God and his word completely transcends this world. In both cases, they fully and finally realize that there are problems in the world as they know it and true liberation only comes with escape. This is why each concocted a utopia, a good place that was no place. It was the only place where they knew that real freedom, truth, and peace could exist.

1. Daly, *Amazon Grace*, 231.
2. Luther, "Luther's Last Observation Left in a Note" (1546), in *LW* 54:476.

These utopias end up functioning as coping mechanisms for two reformers intensely critical of reality. Daly's ideas about the Otherworld, whether it be the Background or the Lost and Found Continent, flourished because of her intense dissatisfaction with this patriarchal world. Luther's ideas about God, whether expressed through a vision of eternal life or the kingdom of God, grew because of intense awareness of the corruption in the papist dominated church of his day. In this way, despite the fact that both reformers failed to bring about the grand changes they initially sought, it was all worth it for both Mary Daly and Martin Luther.

"It" here refers to the struggle, the dangers, the threats, the frustration, and the criticism that each endured throughout her/his life. It was worth it insofar as each reformer's legacy provides something with which subsequent followers and scholars can address their own limitations. Daly's rigorous and logical work with words and their subjectivity, her practice of theology as "philosophy in another realm," and her reclamation of the direct relationship between women and Reality empower others to follow her consistent theological argument, understand patriarchy and feminism in depth, and use their own agency to construct the most plausible method for surviving in the world as they know it. Luther's careful attention to scripture both in original languages and in the vernacular, his theological method of calling things by their right names, and his reclamation of the direct relationship between Christians and God empower others to use careful text study, responsible theological analysis, and personal insight to shed new light on Luther's own problematic attitudes toward the Jews and the peasants.

Given this, we can take from Daly an understanding of radical feminism as a necessary principle motivating all activism toward justice and equality in the world, whether or not that activism goes in the direction she does. Likewise, Luther teaches us that detailed attention to biblical texts using all available scholarly tools is a necessary approach for all religious reflection. There is not enough of either—activism and textual analysis— in many corners of the world. Further, Daly's gendered essentialism is instructive and the truths that it contains must be sorted out from the problems. Luther's misplaced racism and cultural imperialism are instructive in what not to do. Both reformers articulate their ideas boldly and with a great deal of certainty. And at one level, both are right in their claims: I know from experience and from that of colleagues' experience teaching undergraduate gender and women's studies courses that the presence of men in those classrooms can still seriously distort the classroom dynamic and redirect the women's energy toward education and justification of truths that they already know. This is because patriarchy is still reality. I also know that by using scripture and Luther's own methods, his religious prejudice against the Jews can be upheld, while his misplaced racial prejudice cannot, suggesting a deep seated flaw in Christianity that all must acknowledge and confront. This is because the human tendency to subjugate others deemed less valuable is also still a reality.

For those of us who come after Daly and Luther, who take them seriously and attempt to discern their relevance in the world and in the Christian theological tradition, we can learn from the flaws and failures that they exhibit. More importantly, we must learn from their remarkably comprehensive visions of the world as it is and as it ought to be. Human beings in almost every culture and almost every religion articulate some version of the familiar story: there is some truer more authentic human nature that is presently corrupted or unreachable because of some flaw or barrier. Daly and Luther give very specific names and details of this state of human freedom, captivity and longing for community. The also give very specific criticism about the flaw and the barrier standing between us and that truer more authentic human self and world community. These names, details and critiques bring them into conflict with cultural and religious forces around them. Nevertheless, they do all of this political theological work with rhetorical flourish, unique style, and no shortage of controversy, making them irresistible subjects for scrutiny.

An Unlikely Encounter

"Can you believe this?" Mary waves a copy of the book, *Two Reformers*, as she stomps into the clearing, muttering to herself.

"What's that?" Martin looks up from his Bible, startled at the sight of this woman in pants, boots, and a cotton t-shirt emblazoned with a labrys. "W-w-h-h-o are you?" he asks as he sits up straight against the oak tree giving him shade for reading.

Mary stops, looks around bewildered. "Where the hell am I? Where's Matilda? Where're Annie and the others?" She looks disgustedly at the little man in the black robe shrinking up against the tree. "And who the hell are you?"

Martin puts his bible down, brushes off his robe and stands up straight. "I am Martin, child of God. May I ask what book that is that you seem to be so upset about?"

"O.K. Seriously. Where the hell am I?" She looks back in the direction from which she came and sees only the trees and tall grasses blowing in the breeze. "I was just sitting back there talking to Matilda and Annie when this book dropped into my lap. It had my name on the cover so I had to take a look. I got up to try to figure out where it came from . . ." Mary peers at Martin, her eyes growing wide. "What did you say your name was?"

"I am Martin. Doctor Luther to some." He is growing irritated with this woman who will not give him a direct answer. "Who are you?"

Mary looks incredulously at the book in her hand again. "Martin *Luther*? Oh, hell, you've got to be kidding." She holds up the book for him to see the cover.

Martin sees his name on the cover too, and he starts to chuckle. "I presume you are this Mary Daly person also named on the cover. What sort of book would that be, that would have both of *our* names on the cover? I mean no disrespect, but look at you." He gives her short hair, faded jeans and industrial wristwatch the once over. "And look at me." He gestures to his simple haircut, flowing black robe, and prominent cross necklace.

"Well," Mary says, looking at the book in her hand again, "I have no idea what is going on here or where we are, but it seems to have started with this damn book." She opens it and starts to howl with laughter. "Get this, Marty, the author says that you and I are actually doing the same thing in our theologies. Well, there's your first clue that this girl is cracked up. I haven't done theology since 1975. Wait . . . she quotes me here, saying something about Aquinas and how theology is philosophy in another realm. Shit. She's got a point there."

Martin grabs the book from Mary. "You? Doing theology? Surely you are joking. And anyway, what could the two of us have in common anyway?" He flips some pages. "Hey, look at that. I think that you might have hated the Roman Catholic church as much as I did. Did you really say that women lost their heads giving head to the holy host? Goodness, woman! That's almost as bad as my talk about the bishop of hermaphrodites!"

Mary starts laughing. "Well, I did say at one point that the holy spirit was a drag queen and that the christian trinity was the perfect all-male marriage."

Martin stops and looks up at Mary sternly. "You will not blaspheme God in my presence."

"Oh give it up." She looks at his cross and the Bible he left on the ground. "It's pretty obvious that we don't agree on a number of things. Still, it is odd, isn't it, how we do have some of those things in common?"

"Yes. Odd is one way to put it." Martin closes the book and looks at the front once again. "Political theologians? The author thinks we are political theologians? What in the world does that mean?"

"Well," Mary replies, "I don't know what she means by that, and I've never been called that before, but I do know that my philosophy—or, theology as she calls it—did bring me smack dab into some pretty intense political conflicts for most of my adult life. I know that politics in my lifetime changed the world pretty remarkably, though the world was not changed nearly enough for my taste."

"Oh let me tell you about intense political conflict, Mary. Did you have to go into hiding for fear of your life? Were you excommunicated from the church to which you devoted your life? Did you get punished for pointing out basic and obvious truths?" Martin implores his conversation partner.

"Yes, I was punished in a whole bunch of ways, you crazy monk. It didn't matter to me, though, after I figured out it was better just to depart from this ridiculous world and inhabit true Reality." Mary's eyes begin to sparkle. "That's where I was when this crazy encounter began."

Martin looks around the clearing again. They've still not figured out where they are and how they both happen to be there together. "It's just that we're so opposite. But then again," he turns to pick up his bible, "it is said that there are none of these false human divisions when all are united." He flips the book open for her to see. "See, Saint Paul says in his letter to the Galatians that 'there is no longer Jew or Greek, slave or free, there is no longer male and female; for all of you are one in Christ Jesus." (Galatians 3:28).

"I have nothing to say about your guy Jesus and don't get me started on Paul. However, I did once say in my *Wickedary* that there could be a 'Sin-thesis,' sort of like what you might call a synthesis, that is 'the transcendence of patriarchal false opposites by Crone-logical Naming of Truth.'"[3] She thinks about these two statements for a minute. Then asks, "Could it be that this author, whatever her name is, sees some Truth that transcends both of us, that transcends the obvious opposites in our lives to uncover something that neither of us saw?"

"Well, I guess that is possible." Martin closes his Bible. "Shall we look around here and see what else we can find out about this place?"

---

3. Daly, *Wickedary*, 164.

Bibliography

Adams, Nicholas. "Jürgen Moltmann." In *BCPT*, 227–40.
Altmann, Walter. *Luther and Liberation: A Latin American Perspective*. Translated by Mary M. Solberg. Minneapolis: Fortress, 1992.
Anti-Defamation League. "101 Ways to Combat Prejudice." http://www.adl.org/prejudice/prejudice_terms.asp (2003).
Ashley, J. Matthew. "Johann Baptist Metz." In *BCPT*, 241–55.
Augustine. *The City of God (De Civitate Dei)*. London: Dent, 1947.
Bainton, Roland. *Here I Stand: A Life of Martin Luther*. Nashville: Abingdon, 1978.
———. "Psychiatry and History: An Examination of Erikson's *Young Man Luther*." In *Psychohistory and Religion: The Case of Young Man Luther*, edited by Roger Johnson, 19–56. Philadelphia: Fortress, 1977.
Barufaldi, Linda L. "Letters from the Exodus Community." *Religious Education* 67 (1972) 333–35.
Bell, Daniel M., Jr. "State and Civil Society." In *BCPT*, 423–37.
Berger, Peter. *The Sacred Canopy: Elements of a Sociological Theory of Religion*. New York: Random, 1967.
Bertens, Hans. *The Idea of the Postmodern: A History*. London: Routledge, 1995.
Borgstadt, Charles H. "Celebrating the Small Catechism." http://www.elca.org/christianeducation/programs/smallcat.html.
Boston College Office of Public Affairs. "Mary Daly Ends Suit, Agrees to Retire." http://www.bc%5Forg/rvp/pubaf/chronicle/v9/f15/daly.html (February 15, 2001).
Bounds, Elizabeth M. "Politics." In *Dictionary of Feminist Theologies*, edited by Letty M. Russell and J. Shannon Clarkson, 212–13. Louisville: Westminster John Knox, 1996.
Bradstock, Andrew. "The Reformation." In *BCPT*, 62–75.
Cargill Thompson, W. D. J. *The Political Thought of Martin Luther*. Sussex: Harvester, 1984.
Clifford, Anne M. *Introducing Feminist Theology*. Maryknoll, NY: Orbis, 2001.
Cobb, John B, Jr. *Process Theology as Political Theology*. Louisville: Westminster John Knox, 1982.
Daly, Mary. *Amazon Grace: Re-Calling the Courage to Sin Big*. New York: Palgrave Macmillan, 2006.
———. *Beyond God the Father: Toward a Philosophy of Women's Liberation*. Boston: Beacon, 1973.
———. *The Church and the Second Sex: With the Feminist Postchristian Introduction and New Archaic Afterwords by the Author*. Boston: Beacon, 1985.
———. *Gyn/Ecology: The Metaethics of Radical Feminism*. Boston: Beacon, 1978.
———. *Outercourse: The Be-Dazzling Voyage*. San Francisco: HarperSanFrancisco, 1992.
———. *Pure Lust: Elemental Feminist Philosophy*. Boston: Beacon, 1984.

———. *Quintessence . . . Realizing the Archaic Future: A Radical Elemental Feminist Manifesto.* Boston: Beacon, 1998.

———. "Sin Big." *The New Yorker* (February 26 & March 4, 1996) 76–84.

———. *Websters' First New Intergalactic Wickedary of the English Language.* Boston: Beacon, 1987.

———. "The Women's Movement: An Exodus Community," *Religious Education* 67 (1972) 327–33.

deBeauvoir, Simone. *The Second Sex.* Translated and edited by H. M. Parshley. New York: Vintage, 1989. Original French edition, 1949.

Durkheim, Emile. *The Elementary Forms of the Religious Life: A Study in Religious Sociology.* Translated by Joseph Ward Swain. New York: Macmillan, 1915.

Edwards, Mark U., Jr. *Luther's Last Battles: Politics and Polemics 1531–1546.* Ithaca: Cornell University Press, 1983. Reprinted, Minneapolis: Fortress, 2004.

Eliade, Mircea. *The Sacred and the Profane: The Nature of Religion.* Translated by Willard R. Trask. New York: Harcourt Brace, 1959.

Elshtain, Jean Bethke. "Luther *Sic*—Luther *Non.*" *Theology Today* 43 (1986) 155–68

———. "Augustine." In *BCPT*, 35–47.

Erikson, Erik H. *Young Man Luther: A Study in Psychoanalysis and History.* New York: Norton, 1958.

Gearhart, Sally Miller. "Future Visions: Today's Politics: Feminist Utopias in Review." In *Women in Search of Utopia: Mavericks and Mythmakers,* edited by Ruby Rohrlich and Elaine Hoffman Baruch, 296–309. New York: Schocken, 1984.

Gershuny, H. Lee. "The Linguistic Transformation of Womanhood." In *Women in Search of Utopia: Mavericks and Mythmakers,* edited by Ruby Rohrlich and Elaine Hoffman Baruch, 189–99. New York: Schocken, 1984.

Graham, Elaine. "Feminist Theology, Northern," In *BCPT,* 210–26.

Gray, Frances. "Elemental Philosophy: Language and Ontology in Mary Daly's Texts." In *Feminist Interpretations of Mary Daly,* edited by Sarah Lucia Hoagland and Marilyn Frye, 222–45. University Park: Pennsylvania State University Press, 2000.

Gritsch, Eric W. *Martin—God's Court Jester: Luther in Retrospect.* Philadelphia: Fortress, 1983.

Hauerwas, Stanley. "Dietrich Bonhoeffer." In *BCPT,* 136–49.

Johnson, Roger, editor. *Psychohistory and Religion: The Case of Young Man Luther.* Philadelphia: Fortress, 1977.

Keating, AnaLouise. "Back to the Mother? Feminist Mythmaking with a Difference." In *Feminist Interpretations of Mary Daly,* edited by Sarah Lucia Hoagland and Marilyn Frye, 349–88. University Park: Pennsylvania State University Press, 2000.

Lewis, Bernard. "Anti-Semites." In *The Holocaust: A Reader,* edited by Simone Gigliotti and Berel Lang, 17–41. Oxford: Blackwell, 2005.

Lohse, Bernhard. *Martin Luther: An Introduction to His Life and Work.* Translated by Robert C. Schultz. Philadelphia: Fortress, 1986.

Lorde, Audre. "An Open Letter to Mary Daly." In *Sister Outsider: Essays and Speeches,* 66–71. Freedom, CA: Crossing, 1984.

Lugones, María. "Wicked Caló: A Matter of the Authority of Improper Words." In *Feminist Interpretations of Mary Daly* edited by Sarah Lucia Hoagland and Marilyn Frye, 246–65. University Park: Pennsylvania State University Press, 2000.

Lull, Timothy F., and William R. Russell, editors. *Martin Luther's Basic Theological Writings.* 2d ed. Minneapolis: Fortress, 2005.

Luther, Martin. *Luther's Works, American Edition.* 55 vols. Edited by Jaroslav Pelikan and Helmut T. Lehmann. Philadelphia: Fortress [Muhlenberg]; St. Louis: Concordia, 1955–1986.

———. *Luther's Works on CD-ROM: 55 Volume American Edition.* Edited by Jaroslav Pelikan and Helmut T. Lehmann. Minneapolis: Fortress and Concordia, 2002.

———. *Martin Luther: Gesammelte Werke. Digitale Bibliothek Band 63.* Directmedia: Berlin, 2002. Page numbers cited are *Digitale Bibliothek* page numbers.

———. *D. Martin Luther's Werke. Kristische Gesamtausgabe.* 58 vols. Weimar: 1883–1928.

———. *The Bondage of the Will.* Translated by James I. Packer and O. R. Johnston. Tarrytown, NY: Revell, 1957. German original, 1525.

Marius, Richard. *Martin Luther: The Christian Between God and Death.* Cambridge: Harvard University Press, 1999.

McGrath, Alister. *Luther's Theology of the Cross: Martin Luther's Theological Breakthrough.* Grand Rapids: Baker, 1990.

University of Notre Dame. "About Notre Dame." http://newsinfo.nd.edu/content.cfm?topicid=56

Radicalesbians. "The Woman Identified Woman." In *The Second Wave: A Reader in Feminist Theory,* edited by Linda Nicholson, 153–57. New York: Routledge, 1997.

Riswold, Caryn D. "From a Babylonian Captivity to the Otherworld: Martin Luther and Mary Daly." *Currents in Theology and Mission* 24 (1997) 50–58.

———. "Two Reformers: Martin Luther and Mary Daly as Political Theologians." *Political Theology* 7 (2006) 491–506.

Schreiter, Robert J. "The Impact of Vatican II." In *The Twentieth Century: A Theological Overview,* edited by Gregory Baum, 158–72. Maryknoll, NY: Orbis, 1999.

Shaw, Susan M., and Janet Lee, editors. *Women's Voices, Feminist Visions: Classic and Contemporary Readings.* 2d ed. New York: McGraw Hill, 2004.

Soelle, Dorothee. *Against the Wind: Memoirs of a Radical Christian.* Minneapolis: Fortress, 1999.

———. *Political Theology.* Translated by John Shelley. Philadelphia: Fortress, 1974.

Spitz, Lewis W. *Luther and German Humanism.* Brookfield, VT: Ashgate, 1996.

Walker, Alice. *In Search of Our Mother's Gardens.* San Diego: Harcourt Brace Jovanovich, 1983.

www.ingramcontent.com/pod-product-compliance
Lightning Source LLC
Chambersburg PA
CBHW021726220426
43662CB00008B/727